Mathematical Model Building in Economics and Industry

Second Series

GRIFFIN'S STATISTICAL MONOGRAPHS AND COURSES

*Now published independently of the Series.

Descriptive brochure on statistical and mathematical books
available on request from the Publishers

Mathematical Model Building in Economics and Industry

Second Series

Being the collected papers of conferences organized by Scientific Control Systems Ltd and held in London in June 1968 & June 1969 and Montreal in October 1969.

Griffin 18 20 London

CHARLES GRIFFIN & COMPANY LIMITED
42 DRURY LANE, LONDON, WC2B 5RX

First published 1970
ISBN: 0 85264 200 8

9 x 6 in., viii + 277 pages

Set by E.W.C. Wilkins & Associates Ltd., London N.12
Printed in Great Britain by Compton Printing Ltd., Aylesbury

PREFACE

The articles in this volume include papers given at Scicon Model-Building Conferences held in London in June 1968 & June 1969 and Montreal in October 1969. As for the first volume of papers, our object was to organize the presentation of material by persons who had actual experience of constructing models in economics and industry, and hence would be able to discuss not only the theoretical but the practical problems involved and the experience which they had gained.

We are greatly indebted to the many distinguished authors who contributed to this collection. A mere glance through the papers will show the enormous amount of work which has gone into them. A more detailed study will, we hope, give a very good idea of the scope and nature of model building and, in default of a systematic exposition of the subject (which is hardly possible at the present stage of development) will help the many workers in economics and industry who are engaged in model building.

Our thanks are due to Mrs. Agnes Whitfield and Miss Jane Powell for the work which they have done in preparing this material for final publication.

M. G. Kendall
Chairman, Scientific
Control Systems Ltd.

London, April 1970.

CONTENTS

◆

1. ECONOMETRIC FORECASTING

R. J. BALL

Measurement in economics

Economics as an intellectual discipline means many things to many
people — including economists themselves. In part this arises, as in other
disciplines, due to the wide scope of the subject and so to the different
specialised economic problems that people focus on. Historically, economics
in the United Kingdom grew out of what became known as political
economy which, by and large, was directed to a study quasi political and
quasi historical, of how the economy worked. Economics in this sense
was explanatory. In his classic, 'Wealth of Nations', Adam Smith ranged
over problems such as how the value of commodities was determined, how
population growth affected the accumulation of wealth, the significance of
trade for economic strength and the proper relation of Government to
the economic environment. The late Sir Denis Robertson defined the
older political economy as a 'body of maxims for statesmen'. This is a
good reflection of the fact that political economy in the classical sense
was not so much concerned with problems of the individual firm but
with problems of the economic state. And in this context, of course,
the economist runs into difficulties, which may be illustrated by the
considerable criticisms to which economists have been subjected in recent
years. At the level of managing the modern economic state it becomes,
as always, very difficult to separate economic and political questions. Thus
it may be said that economists have failed to solve the problem of controlling the rate of inflation or of how the balance of payments may
be improved. But, of course, in one sense this is not true. There are
several ways of doing both, but the key problem is that many of the
solutions are not politically or socially acceptable. Thus inflation might be
prevented if we were prepared to deflate the economy and exercise the
strictest monetary control. But this would almost certainly involve the
creation of a level of unemployment that would not be acceptable. It
is possible to improve the balance of payments by imposing import
controls, but this becomes a political matter in dealing with our international trading friends. In this context economics is only one discipline
within the much broader range of the social sciences which deal with

the many aspects of what might be described as social engineering. One reason why economists *qua* economists have not, in my view, been visibly successful in contributing to the generation of a higher growth rate in the United Kingdom, is that the problem of faster growth is not simply an economic problem. As amateur psychologists or amateur sociologists economists have no special competence that is not available to anyone outside the specialised subjects.

Of course, these things have become increasingly apparent to economists over the last twenty years or more. The result has been to both narrow and broaden the subject at the same time. The subject has been narrowed by the increasing reluctance of professional economists to intervene in discussions of economic welfare. There has grown an awareness of the lack of a scientific approach to analysing economic phenomena and of a need to reconsider and reshape the methodology of economics as a research based discipline. On the other hand, the subject has be broadened by the awareness of the need in many traditional subject areas of economics to introduce the results and concepts of other disciplines, such as those of the behavioural sciences. Thus a view has developed that the firm as an economic decision making unit cannot be divorced from the firm as a social organisation with complex goals.

Methodologically the major development in economics has been the increased use and development of quantitative techniques. The importance of measurement and quantification has entered into applied economics on many fronts. In the field of resource allocation this has lead to the wide use of programming techniques and the development of forms of cost benefit analysis. Here economic has begun to increasingly overlap with the work carried out by accountants and operational research workers. The use of statistical techniques and the analysis of statistical information are becoming an increasing part of the stock in trade of the professional economist. The formulation and testing of economic hypotheses by more rigorous methods has increasingly characterised the pages of the learned journals. Mathematics as a tool and as a language is becoming an essential part of the economist's equipment.

Econometrics is concerned with the problems of measurement in economics. Strictly speaking there is no need for such a separate name, since econometrics is no more than a particular form of applied economics which concentrates on the development of statistical techniques which are of use to the economist and their application in formulating and testing economic hypotheses. By the same token, what have come to be known as econometric models are no more than statistical relationships, singly or in systems which are manifestations of economic hypotheses.

This increase in rigour has probably had as much value in a negative as in a positive sense. It has not unlocked the door to a roomful of new knowledge ready to be taken from the shelves at the drop of a technique. Unlike the physical scientist the social scientist has no well fitted laboratory in which he can conduct his experiments. It is hard for him to design the rigorous controlled experiment of the laboratory kind. The world as he sees it is for the most part his laboratory, chaotic and uncontrolled, from which he must attempt to squeeze knowledge about the underlying laws of economic behaviour. And here he faces further problems in that the laws of economics are not like the laws of the physical sciences. They are at worst tendencies and at best statistical laws hidden in the noise of the information which we collect as manifestation of the economic world. Thus positive progress is hard and slow. Negatively, however, this increase in rigour has brought great gain. It has taught us that in many areas of economic operation we are ignorant, and that much economic mythology which passes for stock in trade knowledge is based on very shaky foundations. And, as emphasised by Socrates, the ability to define our areas of ignorance is a major stepping stone en route for greater knowledge.

These remarks are not intended to reflect a pessimistic attitude to the development of measurement in economics. The formulation and testing of economic propositions in quantitative form will increasingly characterise the development of the subject. But, for the reasons given, it is not easy. There will be no revolution but a positive and painful addition to both our knowledge and our ignorance as we proceed.

Economic measurement in the firm

Historically the best documented exercises in econometric or quantitative economic model building by economists have been those that have dealt with the behaviour of the economy as a whole. The reasons for this are probably twofold. The first is that, as already mentioned, the traditional orientation of economics as derived from political economy has been toward the economic system as a whole both in terms of the domestic and international economies. Even the traditional economic development of the theory of the firm has been directed primarily toward the theory of markets and implications of such theories for general economic welfare. Thus the traditional theory of the firm seems to lead to public policy conclusions about monopoly and restrictive practices rather than the economic problems of the individual firm. A second and major contributory cause, however, arises from the nature of information available for research. Macro information, or information relating to the economy as a whole or broad aggregative sectors has been by comparison with data for the individual firm more readily abundant for obvious reasons. If an economic researcher wants information to study or on which to try out particular quantitative techniques, it is much easier to study the relationship between union wage demands and the level of unemployment than the impact of advertising expenditures on sales of brand X. For what are regarded as good competitive reasons firms are often reluctant to release such information for a study. Thus the erstwhile student of economics is able to obtain much detailed information about the macro economy and very little about the costs and expenditures of individual firms.

The majority of what may be described as sophisticated information systems in firms are built around the principle of budgetary control. Of course, information is collected and used by specialised departments in large companies for particular ad hoc purposes but the budgetary framework is a common link between most good firms. By and large the immediate purpose of a budgetary control system is, as the name suggests, for purposes of control and for locating trouble. Budgets provide standards against which to measure performance and so practise management by exception in some form. This control aspect has tended to emphasise the cost information that has gone into such budgets, the emphasis being further reinforced by the fact that such systems are almost invariably installed by accountants. The result is that compared with the effort that goes into the preparation of costing methods, the analysis of revenue or sales data has been neglected.

On the cost side the economist has a great deal to say in a conceptual sense. Unlike the accountant with his standard costs, however, the economist thinks in terms of cost functions which emphasise the predictive character of relationships between volumes and costs. However, the role of the economist in firms where economists have been employed as such has usually been little concerned with the analysis of cost data which has been left to the accountant. On the other hand, the economist has played some role in firms in relating the firm to the external economic environment and has certainly been involved in the budgeting process on the sales or revenue side. Probably the most common occupation of economists in large firms is with some aspect of forecasting related to the economic environment. The most usual point at which the quantitative economist is coming into contact with the firm is in the application of quantitative methods to problems of market analysis. While there are other problems relating to business decisions for which econometric analysis of some kind may be helpful, the remainder of this paper is devoted to a discussion of some problems of an econometric approach to forecasting and market analysis.

Economic forecasting

The nature of forecasting is often misunderstood since the process of preparing and assessing forecasts is by and large divorced from the process of decision making. This point is worth some further discussion.

It is clear that all forecasts by definition are intended to say something about the future. However, it is clear that there are differences in viewpoint between people about what can be said about the future and how it should be said. At one end of the scale one has the decision maker and forecaster who may be conceived of as trying to determine exactly what will happen. Thus a decision maker may ask the forecaster what will be the level of sales of product X in 1968. The demand is single valued and the response may also be single valued. That is to say, there corresponds to each possible forecast value a specific action. The decision is a simple function of the forecast value. Thus for example the decision might relate to the purchase of raw materials, where the quantity of materials purchased is a direct function of the forecast value of sales. On this basis the forecaster and his method of obtaining the forecast is likely to be judged on a simple accuracy criterion of the extent to which he was right or wrong, or by some direct function of the discrepancy between the outcome and the forecast value.

Evidently some forecasting procedures and some situations may stand up to this sort of criterion better than others and it is indeed generally a criterion that is of importance to us. But in general this kind of criterion imposes restrictions that are for the most part in practice onerous and moreover, depending on how the forecast is prepared, will throw away a great deal of information.

At the other end of the scale one may look at the forecasting process in probability terms which is in line with the approach of the econometrician to the specification of economic relationships. The first step in the forecasting process from this point of view is to consider the possible range of future outcomes and the second is to consider the probabilities that may be attached to the possible alternatives. This approach does not seek solely to determine what actually will happen in the future but accepts as a datum that the future is inherently uncertain. The best one can do about the future is to try and quantify the uncertainty that surrounds the list of possible outcomes. At one extreme the future is like a black box which generates outcomes according to some probability distribution. The task of the econometrician is in part to throw light on the nature of that distribution which is likely to be affected by variables that can be identified from past experience and experiments where they are possible. Thus if sales budgeting is taking place at a time when the price of a product has just been cut, the sort of question one is trying to answer is, what is the probability that sales will rise one per cent of five per cent or not at all, etc., conditional on the new price set?

The need to consider forecasts in these terms is related to the theory of rational decision making. In dealing with uncertainty, the decision maker has either explicitly or implicitly to equip himself with a strategy. To illustrate the point let us consider a naive example of an executive who is deciding whether or not to build a plant to produce product X, with a given capacity. Let us suppose that over the next five years there is some average rate of sales that will just justify building the plant allowing for the opportunity use of capital resources. Thus if the decision maker knew with certainty that the volume of sales would be above that level, he would build the plant and, if below it, he would not. Suppose then that to fix his mind he asks the appropriate staff man to prepare a forecast, which is then served up to him in the form of a particular level of sales. One strategy or decision rule would be to build the plant if the forecast came above the level required to break even, and not to build it if it fell below. But suppose that we knew (unrealistically) that sales could take on only any one of four values $a_1, a_2 \ldots a_4$ and that we can assign probabilities to these events. Corresponding to each event there are two possible costs (benefits) — the cost incurred for example if a_1 occurs and the plant is built, and the cost incurred if a_1 occurs but the plant was not built. Clearly, if all the a's exceed the critical value of sales there is no problem, so we assume that some lie below and some above. Given this information we can now consider a whole set of possible decision rules. One is to ignore the probabilities and simply to undertake that action that gives the smallest maximum loss. This is the minimax principle. Thus given the data in Table 1, where the $1_1, 1_1^1$ are the losses (or forgone benefits) one would

TABLE 1

	Go	No-Go
a_1	1_1	$1_1^!$
a_2	1_2	$1_2^!$
a_3	1_3	$1_3^!$
a_4	1_4	$1_4^!$

select the action, go or no-go in whose column one found the smallest maximum (or foregone benefits). However, this ignores some valuable information, since by assumption the outcomes a_1 are not all equally likely and we have information on the likelihood of each of them. A second rule would be to calculate the expected gain or loss from each decision and choose the decision with the largest expected gain or smallest expected loss. However this makes use only of the mean of the supposedly known probability distribution, and ignores the variance. So one may go on to develop more complex rules for decisions.

The essential point here is that it is the probabilities, or at least rough estimates of them, plus the alternative outcomes as defined that are the basic ingredients in the forecasting process. Of course, the forecaster is likely to be wrong in sticking his neck out for a single figure. In presenting his forecast he may use the most probable outcome as a forecast. But this is not in general sufficient information on which to develop a rational decision. The forecaster cannot foresee the future and should not pretend to. He has, however, an important role to play in ordering and using information to throw light on the odds and possible outcomes that will qualify the uncertainty about the future and try to bring it under managerial control in the decision making process.

An illustrative model

The model building process can best be discussed with the help of an example. The example is drawn from the recent work of a group of first year students at the London Business School, as a part of a term project investigating the future of the U.K. car industry to 1975. Here we specifically consider the simple model used to project UK output of cars, and cars on the road to 1975. The object of the exercise might be thought of in terms of information related to decision to expand capacity by motor manufacturers and suppliers up to 1975. This exercise has been carried out by the National Institute of Social and Economic Reasearch* in some detail and their calculations are compared with those discussed here. It is important to emphasise that this was a learning exercise carried out in very limited time—it is not intended to be a professional project. However, the structure enables the problem of model building to be discussed.**

---

* NIESR *Economic Review*

** For the work, information and calculations I am indebted to Messrs. Adcock, Dequae, Edelshain, French, Marshall, Matthewman and O'Connor R, graduate students at the London Business School.

In formulating the demand for cars as related to economic factors is is customary to consider the demand for cars as a stock. This is because strictly the demand for a car, like the demand for any durable good, is in essence a demand for a service. In principle the stock should be measured as stored up services and it is usually assumed that it is this that is related in a more systematic way to say, the level of consumers' income. For more detailed discussion of this issue see NIESR [2], O'Herlihy [3], and Chow [1]. This stock concept, however, raises many measurement problems that in a more sophisticated study would have to be taken into account. Thus for example, the number of cars on the road (or what is known as the 'car park') is not in principle at least a measure of the car stock in the sense defined, for a given number of cars (units) will vary according to the size and age structure of vehicles. Depreciation and size of car should enter into the calculation of the car stock. However, it was not possible in the study referred to, to devote the required time to such an activity and so use was made of the simple numbers of cars on the road — the car park.

The variables we seek to explain are the total output of cars per year and the number of cars on the road. Total output includes sales to both home and export markets, so one must give some attention to the international trading environment and the exports of cars. On the home front we need to determine the demand for cars as a whole and then the proportion of total home demand that is to be satisfied for home production and how much from imports. Since these variables are related by identities (e.g. new registrations = home sales in the UK + imported sales) we may choose which variables to explain and which to obtain as a residual. In the event it was decided to attempt to explain the car park (stock), new registrations, the level of exports, the level of imports, and the scrapping rate of cars.

We first note that

(1) $$C(t) = C(t-1) + R(t) - S(t)$$

where C = car park, R = new registrations, $S(t)$ number of cars scrapped in year t. Thus to explain the change in the number of cars on the road we need to explain the rate of new registrations and the number of cars scrapped. We adopt a simple theory of scrapping, namely that the number of cars scrapped depends on the total car stock, the rate at which the stock has been changing and a time trend. The rate of change is to provide a rough index of age structure, i.e. faster growth should mean younger age. The time trend is put in to take into account any trend towards shortening vehical life over time. Thus we may write

(2) $$S(t) = a_0 + a_1 C(t) + a_2 [C(t-1) - C(t-2)] + a_3 t + u(t)$$

where t is a time trend and $u(t)$ a random disturbance. Combining this with (1) we may conveniently reduce this to a relationship between new registrations and the car stock, i.e.

(3) $$C(t) = \frac{-a_0}{1 + a_1} + \frac{1 - a_2}{1 + a_1} C(t-1) + \frac{a_2}{1 + a_1} C(t-2) + \frac{R(t)}{1 + a_1} - \frac{u(t)}{1 + a_1}$$

The rate of new registrations may be related to specific factors affecting the car market and some general index of consumers purchasing power. The latter is usually taken as related to consumers and business income (since many cars are purchased on business account), but for the rough purposes of this exercise use was made of the Gross Domestic Product as an activity variable. Some attempt was made also to include a measure of hire purchase stringency in the form of the minimum down payment on H.P. contracts as fixed by the authorities, and a variable relating prices of cars to other prices. Thus we may write

(4) $$R(t) = \beta_0 + \beta_1 Y(t) + \beta_2 \left[Y(t) - Y(t-1) \right] + \beta_3 \frac{P_c(t)}{P(t)} + \beta_4 d + \epsilon(t)$$

where Y = GDP in 1958 Constant Prices, P_c = car price index, p = index of other prices, d = minimum down payment, It is also possible to include an additional time trend in this equation.

In explaining exports the approach was to examine first the relationship between the level of world trade and the level of world production. So we have

(5) $$X_w(t) = \gamma_0 + \gamma_1 P(t) + w(t)$$

where X_w = world trade in cars, P = world production, w = random disturbance. Secondly we consider the relation between UK exports, X_1 and world trade given by

(6) $$X(t) = \sigma_0 + \sigma_1 X_w(t) + \sigma_2 t + \sigma_3 D + q(t)$$

where D is a dummy variable taking zero-one values which allows for the introduction of the compact car in the United States, and q is a random disturbance. Finally UK imports of cars are related to the volume of UK imports in total and a time trend, so

(7) $$M_c(t) = \lambda_0 + \lambda_1 M(t) + \lambda_2 t + s(t)$$

M_c = imports of cars, M = volume of imports, s = random disturbance, and total imports are made to depend on the level of GDP and the rate of unemployment, so

(8) $$M(t) = \mu_0 + \mu_1 Y(t) + \mu_2 U(t) + r(t)$$

U = % of the labour force unemployed, r = random disturbance.

A simple flow chart representation of the basic model is given in Figure 1. This emphasises firstly the dependence of the calculated outputs of the model on the initial input assumptions with respect to world production and the UK Gross Domestic Product. Most statistical models are open ended in this sense. It also serves to illustrate that a model is a set of interrelationships between information flows, and so from one point of view, a model is a systematic way of processing information to back up a decision. It is not intended to be descriptive *per se*, but to provide a conceptual framework within which to bring together information.

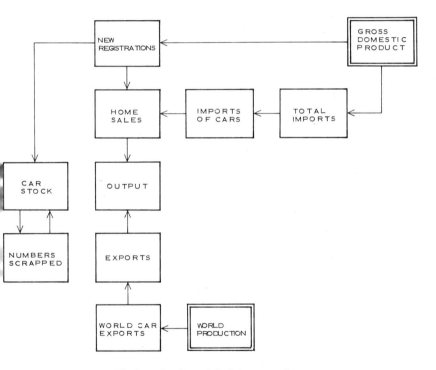

Fig 1. A simple model of the car market

In Table 2 there is given a collection of statistical results of estimation of some of the equations suggested and variants of them. All the data used were annual data. The coefficients of the equations were estimated by classical least squares. In practice it is doubtful whether any alternative method of estimation would have led to significantly different results for the purpose of this exercise, and in any case, it was not practical to adopt any other method. The sample period used covers the years 1955 — 1966.

TABLE 2

Statistical Results

1. $C(t) = 78 \cdot 419 + 1 \cdot 084\, R(t) + 0 \cdot 939\, C(t-1) - 7912 \cdot 0\, t$
   $\quad (193 \cdot 623)\ (0 \cdot 278)\quad (0 \cdot 073)\qquad\qquad (52187 \cdot 0)$
   $\bar{R}^2 = 0 \cdot 99$

2. $R(t) = -1727750 \cdot 0 + 112 \cdot 46\, Y(t)$
   $\quad\quad (282668)\qquad (12 \cdot 39)$
   $\bar{R}^2 = 0 \cdot 89$

3. $R(t) = 204142 \cdot 0 + 169 \cdot 19\, \Delta Y(t) + 73118 \cdot 0\, t$
   $\quad\quad (46671)\qquad (51 \cdot 18)\qquad\quad (6298)$
   $\bar{R}^2 = 0 \cdot 95$

4. $R(t) = -3013920 \cdot 0 + 113 \cdot 54\, Y(t) + 12105 \cdot 5\, P_c/P\,(t)$
   $\quad\quad (1453010)\quad\ (12 \cdot 58)\qquad (13409 \cdot 0)$
   $\bar{R}^2 = 0 \cdot 88$

5. $R(t) = -1572530 \cdot 0 + 111 \cdot 14\, Y(t) - 6788 \cdot 3\, d(t) + 8498 \cdot 0\, U(t)$
   $\quad\quad (288813 \cdot 0)\ (12 \cdot 26)\qquad (3352 \cdot 3)\qquad (66743 \cdot 0)$
   $\bar{R}^2 = 0 \cdot 89$

6. $M(t) = 2184 \cdot 0 + 0 \cdot 2772\, Y(t) - 394 \cdot 3\, U(t)$
   $\quad\quad (487 \cdot 8)\ (0 \cdot 0178)\qquad (131 \cdot 4)$
   $\bar{R}^2 = 0 \cdot 964$

7. $M_c(t) = -75 \cdot 800 + 12 \cdot 39\, \Delta Y(t) + 23 \cdot 35\, M_G$
   $\quad\quad (10 \cdot 970)\quad (5 \cdot 273)\qquad (2 \cdot 698)$
   $\bar{R}^2 = 0 \cdot 92$

8. $X(t) = 3250100 \cdot 0 + 0 \cdot 376\, X_w(t) - 39435 \cdot 0\, t + 4123 \cdot 9\, D(t)$
   $\quad\quad (1788900)\quad (0 \cdot 157)\qquad (35471 \cdot 0)\ (59848 \cdot 0)$
   $\bar{R}^2 = 0 \cdot 88$

9. $X_w(t) = 10828000 \cdot 0 + 749 \cdot 77\, P(t) + 215460 \cdot 0\, t$
   $\quad\quad (2697500 \cdot 0)\ (1107 \cdot 50)\qquad (63158 \cdot 0)$
   $\bar{R}^2 = 0 \cdot 95$

It may be seen from the results that collinearity distorts a number of the calculations, as is common in this kind of work. Thus in explaining the car stock as a function of new registrations and its lagged values, the lagged values are, of course, themselves highly collinear. However, as would be expected, the year to year calculated values of the stock (car park) are very close to each other, as may be seen in Figure 2. Collinearity also appears in the equations for new registrations, where the rate of change of *GDP*, and the hire purchase down payment rates are all related to some extent. In part, the failure of the the hire purchase variable to appear significant may also be due to the weighting of the quarterly values. The apparent insignificance of the hire purchase effect that appears here is not consistent with other findings based on quarterly data. It may also be noted that the prices variable plays no role. Actual and calculated values for equation (3) are given in Figure 3.

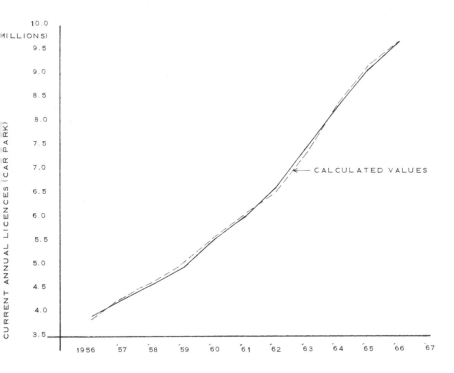

Fig 2. Current annual car park licences as a function of new car registrations and current licences lagged one year. Calculated and actual values plotted over the sample period.

Actual and calculated values of exports and imports are given in Figures 4 and 5. In dealing with exports and imports, no account was taken of dock strikes and the Suez crisis, with the result that the 1967 figures are not well estimated. However, the point of the exercise was to get some feel for the underlying determinants of trend and to quantify the effect of these, so, short run errors and aberrations were largely ignored, with the exception of the introduction of the compact car in the United States and its subsequent effect on United Kingdom exports. The associations between the relevant variables are not as high as one would have liked them to be, however, they provided a starting point for this exercise. It was, of course, necessary in the time to ignore detailed attempts to quantify tariff changes and explicit price effects, although in projecting to 1975 some rough adjustment was made for the effect of devaluation.

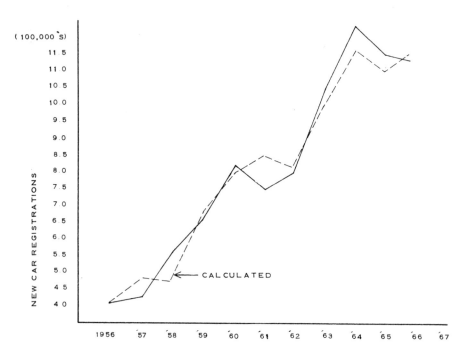

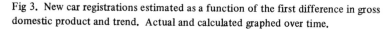

Fig 3. New car registrations estimated as a function of the first difference in gross domestic product and trend. Actual and calculated graphed over time.

For the purposes of projection to 1975, the model was reduced to equations (1) (3) (6) (7) (8) (9) and the appropriate identities. The actual and projected values of new registrations, car stock, output, exports and imports are given in Table 3. In order to make these projections it is necessary to make some assumption about the rate of growth of *GDP* and world production. In one sense the model may be seen as a system for translating estimates of these two variables into their implications for the growth of the car market. In practice estimates of these variables may be obtained from groups engaged in deeper study of the long run outlook for the economy as a whole. Projection systems employed by large United States corporations invariably start from the level of economic activity as a whole, which is then translated into implications for particular markets. Here estimates of the rate of growth of world production were related to past growth and it was thought that a rate of growth of about 5% p.a. to 1975 was plausible. With regard to *GDP*, it was estimated that 3–3½% constituted the minimum range for United Kingdom growth to 1975 — with the hope that it would be higher.

TABLE 3

New registrations

Actual

1955	522,000
56	416,000
57	444,000
58	577,000
59	672,000
60	835,000
61	770,000
62	812,000
63	1,042,000
64	1,229,000
65	1,160,000
66	1,102,000
67	1,119,000

Projections

	(a)	(b)	(c)	(d)	(e)
68	1,403,912	1,426,712	1,342,000	1,362,000	
69	1,512,030	1,536,230	1,437,000	1,472,000	
70	1,589,268	1,614,548	1,537,000	1,590,000	1,612,000
71	1,666,666	1,693,666	1,637,000	1,702,000	
72	1,742,584	1,772,884	1,737,000	1,812,000	
73	1,821,802	1,852,402	1,837,000	1,942,000	
74	1,899,520	1,931,720	1,942,000	2,072,000	
75	1,976,638	2,011,638	2,062,000	2,202,000	2,458,000

(a) Projected from equation (3) with 3% rate of growth of *GDP*.

(b) Projected from equation (3) with 3½% rate of growth of *GDP*.

(c) Projected from equation (2) with 3% rate of growth of *GDP*.

(d) Projected from equation (2) with 3½% rate of growth of *GDP*.

(e) NIESR most optimistic assumptions.

TABLE 4

Cars on the road (car park)

Actual

1955	3,609,000
56	3,981,000
57	4,283,000
58	4,651,000
59	5,081,000
60	5,651,000
61	6,114,000
62	6,706,000
63	7,541,000
64	8,436,000
65	9,131,000
66	9,747,000
67	10,309,000

Projections

	(a)	(b)
68	11,250,000	11,305,000
69	12,175,500	12,318,500
70	13,186,500	13,361,400
71	14,239,000	14,434,400
72	15,372,400	15,527,400
73	16,240,200	16,675,400
74	17,383,400	17,795,000
75	18,521,400	18,953,400

(a) and (b) projections are consistent with (a) and (b) in Table 3.

It is interesting to compare the different projection of new registrations from the simple equations. Using equation (3), it is estimated that new registrations in 1970 would run at about 1·6 m. vehicles, this result being virtually independent of the *GDP* growth rate, due to the dominant character of the trend variable alone in that equation. By 1975 the rate is about 2·0 m. However, if we project from equation (2), which makes *GDP* alone relevant, then the figures are 1·5 m. and 1·6 m. for 1970 (for 3% and 3·5% growth in *GDP*) rising to 2·0 m. and 2·2 m. in 1975. Thus, if *GDP* is used, the difference in projected level in 1975 is about 10%, and this equation is clearly more sensitive to differences in assumptions about *GDP*. We cannot make a direct comparison with the National Institute forecasts, because for one reason they make assump-

TABLE 5

	Car exports	Car imports
1955	390,703	11,581
56	337,052	7,003
57	424,320	8,908
58	484,034	8,008
59	568,971	19,512
60	569,916	51,584
61	370,744	24,431
62	544,792	28,093
63	616,016	47,125
64	679,383	63,725
65	627,567	55,697
66	556,044	67,340
67	511,560	92,000

Projections

	(a)	(b)	(c)	(d)
68	687,897		76,200	84,300
69	711,122		82,200	91,350
70	747,648	785,000	88,200	99,350
71	812,978		94,200	107,750
72	871,498		101,700	118,850
73	945,623		108,200	128,900
74	1,019,749		115,700	136,800
75	1,049,262		122,200	143,600

(a) Export forecast adjusted for devaluation - plus 8% in 1968 and plus 10% thereafter.

(b) NIESR forecast.

(c) Imports based on 3% growth in *GDP*.

(d) Imports based on 3½% growth in *GDP*.

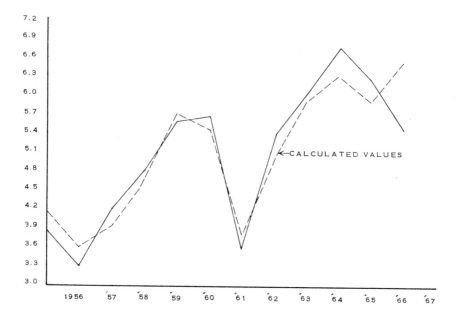

Fig 4. United Kingdom exports of cars. Calculated and actual values plotted over time.

tions about disposable income and not *GDP*, which they assume on a real per capita basis to vary between 2½% and 3½% growth. Given these and other assumptions, they project a figure for 1970 ranging from 1·5 m. to 1·6m., and for 1975 2·1 m. to 2·4 m. Bearing in mind the starting figure of 1·1m. in 1966, the estimates ᵃgree closely up to the early 1970s but by 1975 the Institute estir ... .e s ᵇstantially higher. However, as a broad conclusion, it may be said that both sets of estimates based on the range of assumptions, suggest that the rate of new registrations should about double between 1966 and 1975.

Comment

The model discussed briefly in the previous section is not intended, as already explained, to serve as a sophisticated application of econometric technique. It · is intended solely to give the flavour of the nature of quantitative economic relationships that may play a role in a business information system. As explained, an economic statistical model of this kind serves as formal framework within which to pull together in a systematic way economic information that is related to economic variables that affect a particular market. It turns out that, as shown, even a model as crude as that presented here yields conclusions based on comparable assumptions that are not that far different as these things go from the results of a much more sophisticated study carried out by the National Institute of Social and Economic Research.

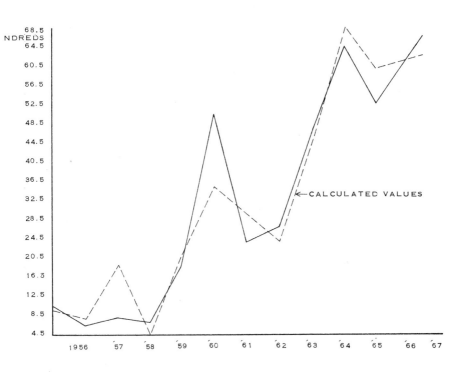

Fig 5. Imports of cars. Actual and calculated values plotted over time.

The advantages of a more formal approach are several. At one level such an approach requires complete honesty insofar as what assumptions and adjustments are made are explicit and not fudged over under the heading of intuition. Secondly, models of this kind provide formal frameworks for testing out the impact of different assumptions on the forecasts. In this particular case the two crucial assumptions made in the forecasting procedure related to world trade and the rate of growth of United Kingdom *GDP*. Insofar as these variables are crucial to a forecast of the rate of growth of the car market, one needs to have some mechanism for measuring the impact of different assumptions on the final outcome. Thirdly, even with this simple model it is possible in principle to develop more refined forecasts in the sense that probability limits may be computed from the data to assess the risk involved in accepting any of the forecasts or projections. Finally, such an explicit model provides a vehicle for learning in the sense that in models of this type one has a better chance in principle of identifying why a particular forecast was wrong, or at worst eliminating some assumptions and some variables as the cause or causes of the poor projections.

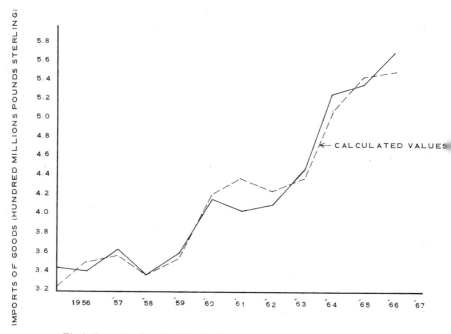

Fig 6. Imports of goods. Calculated and actual values plotted over time.

The extent to which exercises of this kind can be successfully and usefully carried out varies from situation to situation. A great deal depends, for example, on the information available. All reasonable forecasting and projection systems depend on the information from the past. One way of looking at forecasting is to say that it is concerned with distilling the information of the past into a format that enables one to narrow the uncertainty or quantify the uncertainty about the future. But here one is heavily dependent on information about the past, and in particular on the information content of what material is available. The information content of data will depend on the richness of experience covered by the data and the behaviour of the particular explanatory factors that one is trying to use and whose influence one may be attempting to isolate. Thus, sample information may reflect only trend movements in a particular variable and so provide little information for inferring what might happen during a servere cyclical fluctuation. Or the sample information might be such that excessive collinearity between explanatory factors completely obscured the causal elements in the problem. All this is a matter of what is contained in the information actually available.

The example briefly presented in this paper has dealt with an analysis at total market level. Here it is important to distinguish between the problem of prediction at the market level suitably defined and the problem of prediction at the level of the individual product. The point is that by and large with some exceptions the market may by defined in its totality in terms of variables that largely, from a decision making point of view, are beyond the control of the individual firm. Thus, the demand for a particular product may depend in the long run on the growth in consumer purchasing power, and in the short run on fluctuations in the general level of economic activity. These factors may be said to constitute the economic environment external to the firm. But when one comes to forecasting the actual share of the market gained by a particular firm one must now take into account the specific competitive factors that enter into the market share. This, of course, raises questions of marketing strategy that are beyond the immediate province of the economic forecaster. Nevertheless econometric analysis at the overall market level can provide important data for the development of such strategy.

REFERENCES

1.   CHOW, "Statistical Demand Functions for Automobiles" in *Demand for Durable Goods*, (ed. A.C. Harberger).

2.   *National Institute Review*, May 1967.

3.   O'HERLIHY, "Demand for Cars in Great Britain", *Applied Statistics*, 1965.

2. MODEL BUILDING FOR AIRLINE PLANNING AND CONTROL SYSTEMS

R. W. LINDER

CONTENTS

GENERAL INTRODUCTION

The nature of airline planning and control systems

A major task of top management in any organization is to formulate and promulgate sound corporate policy. Such policy will define the objectives to be pursued in the long-term, and will set limits within which the organization must conduct its operations.

Given such a policy it becomes both feasible and desirable to develop sensible strategic plans for attaining the long-term objectives of the organization. Such plans must consider the nature and magnitude of future demand for the products or services supplied by the organization, and the most profitable means of satisfying this demand. For practical purposes, strategic planning and long-range planning may be considered to be synonymous. In the context of the commercial aviation industry strategic planning decisions relate to such major issues as the selection and procurement of equipment and facilities such as jet aircraft, airport terminal facilities and automatic reservations systems. These decisions are also concerned with the broad questions of deployment of such resources to both new and existing routes and services in the longer term. The elapsed time between making a decision on such matters and the actual implementation of results may well be several years. Consequently before any strategic plans can be prepared and evaluated, traffic forecasts must be developed for periods up to ten years or more into the future.

Having developed an acceptable long-range plan of activities for the organization as a whole, management must consider the details of its implementation in the light of current and immediate future conditions. It is at this point that tactical or short-range planning takes over the dominant role. In constructing a short-range plan the organization will be constrained by the many limitations of existing circumstances (i.e. those created by previous planning decisions). Thus the range of opportunities in tactical planning is much more restricted than in the longer-term planning process. In a commercial airline most tactical plans relate to the detailed utilization of available equipment and personnel during the immediate year or two ahead. The elapsed time between any tactical planning decision and the actual deployment and assignment of resources is therefore relatively short compared with the corresponding interval for strategic planning. However, the results will be in the form of very detailed flight schedules and resource assignments, and therefore much more detailed traffic forecasts must be prepared for this shorter time horizon before any plans can be developed and evaluated.

As the organization will generally be in a continuous state of operational activity, management must be able to monitor actual progress against the short-term goals established by the tactical planning processes. Feedback of information in the form of control decisions can then be used to adjust the existing tactical plan in order to adapt the operations to perceived changes in circumstances. Operational control decisions therefore have almost immediate effect, but only over a limited time-span. In an airline such as Air Canada most operating decisions are implemented within minutes or hours, and have an immediate but very short-term effect on the organization whose time-span can usually be measured in hours, days or weeks. The particular point here is that such decisions are usually based on analysis of existing conditions, rather than on forecasts of the situation which may exist in some future time period. This fact underlines a fundamental difference between planning and control systems, since in both strategic and tactical planning processes the decisions are based primarily on forecasts of future traffic volumes. Existing conditions are only useful for planning purposes to the extent that they indicate the direction of future events.

It is essential in practice that the processes of strategic planning, tactical planning and operational control should interact with one another to a considerable extent. The flow of information, in the form of goals and objectives, from strategic planning through tactical planning to the procedures for operational control is a logical one already implied by the above descriptions of each stage in the process. The reverse flow or feedback of information on actual performance compared to plan is a less clear, but equally important aspect of such interaction. Such feedback can be used to check the validity of various models used in the planning processes, and it can also be used to revise and up-date the forecasts of future traffic volumes which form the basis of strategic and tactical planning decisions.

It is clear that the relationships between the various levels of planning and operational decision-making in an airline such as Air Canada are very complex in practice. Most airline planning and control models, like those in other spheres of business and industry, attempt to relate some appropriate measure of effectiveness (profit, revenues, costs, etc.) to the set of controllable and uncontrollable factors which are believed to affect the situation. A typical planning or operating decision will specify a particular configuration of the controllable variables (price, frequency of service, type of aircraft, cruise speed and altitude of a flight, etc.) in order to optimize the appropriate measure of effectiveness. Various forecasting models provide predictions for the uncontrollable variables (demand volumes, degree and nature of competition, socio-economic conditions, etc.), and ideally these predictions should be independent of any particular configuration of the controllable or policy variables. Unfortunately this is not always the case, and least of all with airline traffic forecasts. Consequently forecasting and planning processes in a typical airline tend to form an iterative cycle of events. In such a system, modifications are introduced at each stage until the process converges to an acceptable and consistent set of results. Such a situation imposes a number of limitations and constraints on the whole procedure, and this important aspect of airline planning models will be discussed at greater length later on in this paper.

The classification of planning and control models in Air Canada

The preceding discussion serves as a general background to the development and use of planning and control models in Air Canada. It also presents a useful classification scheme for such models which will now be adopted in this paper.

1. *Strategic planning models*

a. Forecasting models. Into this category fall the models for forecasting passenger and cargo traffic flows on an annual basis by major routes and groups of routes up to about ten years ahead. These models are econometric in nature and relate socio-economic, competitive and policy variables to the corresponding volumes of air traffic.

b. Long-range planning models. Here the models generate broad plans for the procurement of aircraft, and for their efficient utilization on the existing and planned network of routes. They also evaluate these plans im terms of their ability to adequately serve future traffic volumes and provide an acceptable financial return to the airline. While the plans specify the levels of service and types of equipment to be operated on each route, they do not go into the fine detail of time-of-day scheduling of individual flights.

2. *Tactical planning models*

a. Forecasting Models. At this level of planning the forecasting models produce detailed passenger and cargo traffic projections by month between every pair of cities in the Air Canada network, and up to about two years ahead. These models either employ very simple relationships with a single explanatory variable, or they are purely descriptive models which merely extrapolate past experience into the short-term future.

    b. Schedule evaluation models. Into this category fall a number of models for evaluating a detailed flight schedule plan. Air Canada does not at present have a model which will generate a time-of-day flight schedule for any Summer or Winter planning period. However it does have a series of sophisticated models for testing the ability of any such plan to adequately serve the expected passenger and cargo markets, and to produce an acceptable financial return to the Company. In addition a complex simulation model enables management to explore the operating performance characteristics of any proposed flight schedule before it is finally implemented.

    c. Manpower and facilities budgeting models. Having produced detailed flight schedule plans for the immediate future, a variety of models are then used to develop manpower and facilities budgets for each of the major operating functions within the Company. These models produce detailed plans and staff schedules for reservations offices, airport functions and flying operations.

3. *Operational control models*

    Here a wide variety of models is in continuous use assisting operation management in the control of day-to-day activities of the airline. The list includes models for controlling passenger booking levels in the automatic reservations system, establishing daily load plans for cargo traffic, generating efficient flight plans for individual flights, controlling the levels of inventory of spare parts and materials for the aircraft maintenance functions, and monitoring the quality of customer services offered both on the ground and in the air.

    Comprehensive sets of models in each of the above categories are either already in use, or presently under development in Air Canada. However the limitations of this present paper do not permit a detailed and exhaustive description of each and every one of them. Instead the remainder of this paper will review, in some detail, the models developed for tactical planning in particular. The planning systems of which they form an important part are therefore concerned with the future operations of the airline up to about two years ahead. This time span coincides roughly with the delivery lead-time for the major resource of the Company—namely the modern commercial jet aircraft. References in the text are to published papers which describe the individual models in more detail.

REVIEW OF MODELS FOR TACTICAL PLANNING

A. Forecasting models
Very-short-range forecasting

    Very-short-range forecasts of passenger traffic volumes are regularly required in Air Canada for periods up to three or four months ahead. They are used to assist management in short-term financial planning, flight schedules adjustments, sales promotional spending and manpower planning.

Simple relationships between advance booking levels on each major set of international routes and corresponding monthly traffic volumes are used to predict future traffic flows for each of the next four months ahead.

The relationships are remarkably stable, and a set of books and charts display historical values of the ratios of actual traffic to corresponding advance booking levels on each major group of routes. Each book is divided into twelve parts, each one referring to the booking situation at the end of a specific calendar month. The information is displayed in both tabular and graphical form to give an immediate and straightforward visual indication of trends over the years and a general picture of the stability of these relationships.

Advance booking levels are entered in the books at the end of each month, and ratio values are chosen based on the historical data and on a knowledge of any changing circumstances. Forecasts are then obtained by simple multiplication of the booking levels by their appropriate ratios.

Additional information can be entered in the books to indicate variations due to moveable feasts and unusual incidents, and records of seating capacity offered can pinpoint the effects of historical capacity constraints (i.e. an insufficient supply of passenger seats in some past period).

This model has been in continuous use for the past three years, and although a few minor innovations and extensions have been made, the basic procedure has remained unchanged. It has proved to be simple, straightforward and very effective. The results are easy to understand and interpret, and the complete model is a compact, easily accessible set of books which contain all the necessary data in a simple, readable format. When used with common sense and good judgement, it produces accurate short-range forecasts for the various applications already mentioned.

Medium-range forecasting [1]

Medium-range forecasts (up to two years ahead) are required for both passenger and cargo traffic at least twice a year in Air Canada. They are used as basic inputs in the development of detailed flight schedules for future Summer and Winter seasons. Forecasting errors in this area can therefore have serious consequences in terms of poor scheduling of future operations and potential loss of revenue and customer good-will. The achievement of precise medium-range traffic forecasts is therefore worth a good deal of effort, falling into two distinct categories:

1. The forward projection of historical traffic volumes.

2. The evaluation and modification of these projections in the light of current and expected future levels of competition, socio-economic conditions, etc.

These forecasts are required by month for traffic between every pair of points in the Air Canada network (more than 3,000 in all). Not all pairs of points are worth a detailed study, however. As might be expected, some 200 combinations provide 85 to 90 per cent of the Company's passenger traffic.

The forward projection of historical data consists of a large amount of tedious, mechanical work, and the present medium-range forecasting model has succeeded in transferring these particular operations to an electronic computer. In this way the human analysts in the system are able to devote most of their time and effort to the essential, but more subjective tasks of evaluating and modifying the results.

The technique of exponential smoothing is used in this particular forecasting model, and a typical series of monthly traffic volumes is assumed to be made up of four components: an average level in any month, a trend or growth component from month to month, a seasonal pattern which repeats itself every twelve months, and a random or irregular component.

The exact formulation of the mathematical model depends on whether the trend and seasonal components are assumed to be additive or multiplicative in character. Extensive tests on a wide variety of traffic series have confirmed that the fully multiplicative model is most representative of Air Canada's data. The trend component is therefore measured as a percentage change from month to month, and the seasonal pattern is measured as a series of ratios of actual traffic volumes to their corresponding average levels in each month of the year.

The model consists of three exponential smoothing equations which are used to estimate the current average traffic level, the current trend factor, and the current monthly seasonal factor. The corresponding smoothing constants are called alpha, beta and gamma respectively. A fourth equation multiplies these current estimates together in a logical manner to produce the required monthly projections of future traffic volumes.

Based upon many initial experiments, and also on several years of experience with these models, all the smoothing constants are held at a nominal value of 0.10 as long as external conditions remain unchanged, and the forecasting system remains "under control". In this sense the forecasting model is like a black box or processor into which are fed historical data, and out of which are produced traffic projections. As long as conditions do not change, the magnitude of the forecasting error is determined by the amount of unexplained random variation in the data. If the process does go out of control, its response to changing conditions can be altered by changing the values of alpha, beta and gamma.

Extensive analyses of forecasting errors for a one-month lead-time have shown that the random component is also multiplicative for most Air Canada traffic series. It is therefore measured by the ratio of actual to forecast traffic, and is approximately normally distributed with a mean of unity (when the forecasting process is unbiased and under control), but with a variability which depends on the particular traffic series.

A straightforward control procedure compares the ratio error each month to appropriate control limits, and prints out warning signals on an exception basis. If a real cause can be found for the out-of-control condition, immediate action is taken by altering the smoothing constants according to a set of simple rules. If no cause can be identified, two successive warning signals must appear before any action is taken. The emphasis is on caution, and on the importance of retaining at least some of the past history contained in the current estimates of the trend and seasonal components.

This forecasting model has been in regular use since the beginning of 1963, and it adequately performs the task it was designed for. It is straightforward, economical on storage space and processing time in the computer, and fairly easy to adjust and control when changes have occurred or are expected. Its simplicity imposes a number of limitations on the results, but once these are clearly understood and accepted, the projections serve as an invaluable base from which to build up the final detailed forecasts required for schedules planning.

B. Schedule evaluation models

The passenger allocation model [2]

A detailed flight schedule defines a network of paths over which passengers will flow from one point to another. Any point can usually be reached from any other by several different paths. The passenger preference for any alternative is influenced by the types of aircraft used, the number of en-route stops and connections, the frequency of service and the times of departure and arrival of the different flights.

In practice, any prospective passenger may be unable to travel on his preferred flight because it is already fully booked. He will then either choose some alternative flight, or some other means of transportation (e.g. a competing airline). The load-factors on our flights, and the schedules of competing carriers are therefore important influencing factors in this process.

Given a proposed flight schedule it therefore becomes important to evaluate it in terms of its ability to service the prospective passenger market in the most acceptable manner. The Passenger Allocation Model is a computer-based model which simulates the real-life processes by which passengers are allocated to Air Canada flights. In doing so it takes into account the above-mentioned factors in assigning the passenger traffic to the various flights available.

The primary inputs to this model are the complete set of point-to-point passenger forecasts obtained from the medium-range forecasting model already described, and a coded version of the proposed flight schedule. The main outputs from the model are detailed and summary listings of expected passenger flows and resulting load-factors on all flights in the schedule. Three types of report are produced. The first summarizes the flow of passengers classified by their origin and destination points. It shows how each set of passengers distribute themselves among the alternative flights available. The second type of report concentrates on each flight throughout its entire routing, and shows the overall loads to be expected on each leg of the flight without regard to the mix of passengers. The final type of report examines the total flows of passengers over all flights operating between every pair of points in the network. These total leg flows as they are called, indicate the "importance" of each connecting arc in the whole system.

The model itself breaks down conveniently into three sub-processes as follows:
1. The Attractive Path Generator which applies a series of decision rules to distinguish between the attractive and non-attractive paths between each pair of points in the network. The procedure selects, from all possible flight paths, a particular sub-set of paths which dominate all other possible paths (based primarily on their speed advantage). Each attractive flight defines a corresponding period of attraction about its departure time. These periods of attraction are mutually exclusive, and completely cover the effective travelling day.

2. The Traffic Distribution Estimator which breaks down the monthly passenger forecasts for every pair of points into traffic distributions by time-of-day, and by day-of-week. These detailed passenger breakdowns are accomplished using passenger behaviour information which is partly based on historical data and partly on the judgements of experienced airline personnel. Quite obviously historical data alone is highly influenced by past schedules, and cannot be too heavily relied upon to predict the desired departure times of prospective passengers.

3. The Passenger Allocation Process which applies a further series of sequential decision rules to allocate passengers to particular flights. These rules take into account the times prior to flight departure at which passengers request space between the different pairs of points in the network. They also allow capacity constraints to come into play by removing fully-loaded attractive flights and introducing additional flights which were previously unattractive. Whenever this occurs, there is feed-back to the first sub-process to re-determine the new periods of attraction of available flights. The allocation process terminates when all the traffic has been allocated between every pair of points in the system.

This model is presently being integrated into the tactical planning system in Air Canada. It will prove invaluable in identifying unforeseen bottlenecks in the flight schedule, and any under-utilized areas of capacity. It represents a powerful evaluation tool for the planning personnel in the Company.

The cargo allocation model [3]

With the rapid expansion of the air cargo market Air Canada has become increasingly concerned with schedule planning and profitability in the field of freight traffic. A major problem in tactical planning therefore is the determination and evaluation of the actual usable cargo space provided by any proposed flight schedule. A second problem, more closely associated with the marketing function, is concerned with the kinds of delivery standards which can realistically be advertised to the air freight shippers.

The core of the cargo allocation model is a continuous linear programme which can be formulated either to minimize the cost of achieving a desired set of delivery standards, or to maximize these standards for a given flight schedule. The various constraints are related to the available cargo capacities of the aircraft, the limitations on cargo loading imposed by the scheduled ground times at individual stations, and the availability of freight which results from the time of day of receipt at any originating point.

In addition to examining delivery performance, the model can be used to identify bottlenecks in the proposed schedule. Those stations which have inconvenient flight departure times as far as cargo traffic is concerned, can be quickly identified, and flight legs which have serious deficiencies in cargo capacity can be inspected and improvements made wherever feasible.

To cover a typical week of operations for a given flight schedule, the model includes a cycling feature which enables the linear programme to carry forward the unsatisfied demand from one day to the next. The size of the model to cover an entire week of cargo operations approaches 2,000 rows. An important derivative of this same model is to be utilized as part of a more general operational control system to provide daily cargo load plans for the entire airline system.

This particular allocation model is presently being implemented in the overall tactical planning system, and promises to be a very useful additional tool in evaluating any proposed flight schedule.

The operations schedule simulation model [4]

In developing a detailed flight schedule for some future period, the planners not only have to consider its ability to adequately serve the needs of the passenger and cargo markets. They must also ensure that it satisfies various Company standards of operating performance, and that it does so as efficiently as possible.

In practice the operating performance of flights on a given schedule is affected by such factors as adverse winds and weather conditions, airport congestion problems during landing and take-off, unpredictable aircraft maintenance requirements, station delays due to ground and passenger handling difficulties, and a multitude of other random effects. To accommodate these situations, spare time is built into the flight schedule, and spare (or stand-by) aircraft are located at strategic points in the system. The development of a flight schedule is therefore a delicate balancing act between achieving an acceptable level of operating regularity and punctuality, and incurring a minimum opportunity cost in terms of built-in slack time and spare aircraft capacity.

The Operations Schedule Simulation Model in Air Canada has been developed to evaluate a proposed flight schedule in order to determine whether or not a reasonable balance has been achieved, and if not, to identify where adjustments can be made to improve the situation.

The model simulates the movement of aircraft under a given schedule by a series of decision rules which are programmed for an electronic computer. These rules specify how a particular aircraft will be selected to operate a given flight, and what unpredictable situations might occur during the particular operation. Whenever a random occurrence (such as adverse winds, or airport congestion) has to be considered, an appropriate probability distribution is inspected to determine the outcome in each case. In this way some flights will be subjected to this particular condition while others will not, and the relative frequency of occurrence will be approximately the same as in the real-life situation.

The probabilities of occurrence of different random effects are estimated directly from past experience in the airline and involve an enormous amount of data collection. This chore must be repeated at regular intervals to ensure that the inputs to the model adequately reflect existing circumstances. A large and compre hensive automated data collection system has in fact been developed for this purpose.

The decision rules are partly based on existing operating practices in the airline but several of them are unique to the simulation itself. In particular a very sophisticated network search procedure is used to set up an efficient sequence of paths for routing any aircraft into the maintenance base whenever it is approaching the time for a scheduled check or major overhaul.

The practical utility of the simulation model lies in its ability to experiment with a schedule without affecting the real-life situation. For example, the effect upon the departure performance of originating flights, of introducing an additiona stand-by aircraft at some strategic location, can be predicted by running the mode in a manner which could never be contemplated in reality.

There are problems, of course, in using a simulation of this type. Extensive experimental runs must be performed against historically known situations and results in order to calibrate and "tune-in" the model and its decision rules. Fortunately the Air Canada model (after some adjustment) has proven to be free of any consistent bias, and the random variability of the results (caused by the probabilistic elements in the model) has been estimated for various levels of summary results by replicating simulation runs using the same inputs except for variations in the mechanisms which generate the probabilistic factors. As a result, the model is able to reproduce reality with acceptable accuracy, and is proving to be of considerable assistance to the schedule planners in their evaluation of the operational characteristics of any flight schedule.

The financial evaluation model [5]

Having developed a detailed set of flight schedules, and evaluated them in term of their ability to satisfy the projected passenger and cargo markets and also to meet acceptable standards of operating performance, the final step is to examine their overall profitability and return on investment.

Air Canada's route patterns, stage length variations and traffic density and frequency differences lead to widely differing degrees of profitability on different services. The situation is perhaps not too different from any other organization with a large variety of product lines, and it requires a much more detailed and comprehensive financial evaluation than the traditional corporate Income Statement and Balance Sheet.

The financial evaluation model has been developed to satisfy these needs. It acknowledges the wide differences in profitability over the various route patterns and services in the total network, and it shows how the different parts of the airline will respond to alternative scheduling policies. It is also consistent with the Company's method of recording route profitability for regulatory purposes.

Air Canada's routes fall into three major geographical categories: North American, Atlantic, (United Kingdom, Ireland and Western Europe) and Southern (Florida, Bahamas and the Caribbean). The Atlantic and Southern routes are typified by long average journeys, seasonal traffic and relatively low unit operating costs. The North American routes fall into three sub-categories: Transcontinental, High Density and Other North American.

The primary financial evaluation is broken down into the above five categories of routes, and in addition the charter services. A more detailed analysis examines individual groups of routes within each of the five major breakdowns. The inputs to the model are the flight schedules for a complete calendar year, forecasts of passenger-miles and corresponding expected revenue yields per passenger-mile, forecasts of cargo revenues, operating costs, forecasts of non-operating revenues and expenses, the magnitude of current investment, and various other supporting data. The major outputs are the financial forecasts of revenues, expenses, net income and return on investment, together with a variety of related summary statistics broken down by major route category, and further divided by individual groups of routes within each category.

The primary processing functions in the model itself are concerned with the allocation of revenues, expenses and investment to the major and secondary classifications of routes. These apportionments are made in relation to the relative magnitudes of various operating statistics inherent in the flight schedules. Consequently the initial task of the model is to generate these operating statistics by groups of routes from the flight schedule inputs. The statistics produced include flight frequencies by aircraft type, available seat-miles, available ton-miles and flying hours by aircraft type.

The allocation procedures are fairly simple and straightforward. Direct flying costs are allocated in proportion to flying hours by aircraft type. Direct ground costs have been found to be linearly related to passengers boarded with no significant fixed component (simple regression analysis was most helpful here).

Unit costs per passenger boarded are therefore used to allocate this item of expenditure. Flight equipment depreciation is allocated in proportion to flying hours by aircraft type. Other indirect expenses including maintenance burden, promotion and sales and general and administrative costs are allocated in a straightforward manner to arrive at total expenses by groups of routes. Total investment by aircraft type is allocated among the groups in proportion to the number of flying hours operated by each type of aircraft on these routes. There are of course, several shortcomings in this overall allocation process, and the difficulties here are not unlike those encountered in the financial evaluation of many other business organizations.

The financial evaluation model provides a detailed picture of profitability on all the major groups of routes in the network for a particular calendar year. It is obviously a vital tool to management in identifying weaknesses and problem areas in any set of tactical plans. Its value is increased even further because it is a fully automated model which can be quickly run on an electronic computer. This provides tremendous flexibility in financial evaluation through systematic modifi-cation of plans and re-runs of the model to quickly examine the effects of alternatives.

C. Manpower and facilities budgeting models

Reservations office manpower and facilities planning model [6,7]

Once tactical plans, in the form of detailed flight schedules, have been developed, evaluated and accepted in principle by senior management, all operating line functions have the task of finalizing their own individual resource budgets prior to the completion of a corporate budgeting exercise and profit test.

In a typical reservations office, telephone sales agents man a number of reserva tions lines and deal with customer requests for seats, flight arrival information, and a wide variety of special enquiries. Certain minimum standards of service mu be maintained to retain the goodwill of the travelling public, and to foster the growth of new business. Two of these standards relate to the busy signals and delays which customers may encounter when placing their calls. The Reservation Office budgeting model relates these standards to the numbers of agents and tele-phone lines required to handle the expected volume of telephone workload. The model therefore enables any office manager to estimate, using forecasts of future telephone workload, the minimum numbers of lines and agents required in any hour to meet the prescribed standards. It also provides the manager with a comprehensive method for estimating his total manpower establishments through a process of shift-scheduling and rostering which allows explicitly for meal-breaks vacations and sickness.

The model began as a probabilistic computer simulation of a typical reservatio office. The construction, development and testing of this comprehensive simulati model was undertaken because the congestion and queuing processes of the real-life situation were too complex to be modelled by any mathematical equation. The original simulation model was used to build extensive tables showing the call rejection and waiting time performances to be expected for many combinations of agents and lines and for many levels of telephone workload.

After several setbacks and misunderstandings in the use of these tables, some very simple linear decision rules were developed from the extensive tabulated results. These decision rules were, and still are used to directly calculate the minimum numbers of agents and lines required in any hour to meet the prescribed standards of service at a given level of telephone workload. In addition, a general method of shift-scheduling and rostering has been developed and implemented to enable any office manager to quickly determine his overall manpower requirements.

More recently the original tabulations of the simulation results have been used to develop alternative decision rules under newly proposed standards of service to the public. These new decision rules were quickly developed and used to determine the effects on total manpower and facilities costs of changing the standards of service. As revised standards are proposed or considered new decision rules are derived to analyse their relationship to direct labour and facility cost. This process has been repeated several times during the last three years, and on each occasion the results have been invaluable guides to the policy decision-makers.

Meanwhile the basic budgeting model itself has been completely automated. More attention is now being given to the problem of forecasting future telephone workload since this has proved to be a sensitive input to the whole model. Basically these forecasts are obtained from a very simple relationship with corresponding forecasts of boarding passengers (produced by the medium-range forecasting model and the passenger allocation model). The average number of calls per boarding passenger is determined from historical data and then multiplied by the forecast of boarding passengers to obtain the estimated number of telephone calls to be expected in a given month. The monthly call volumes are broken down into daily and hourly figures to feed into the decision rules for determining hourly agent and lines requirements. The average number of calls per boarding passenger is unfortunately changing over time for a variety of reasons, and work is currently planned to develop more sophisticated relationships for producing telephone traffic forecasts. Nevertheless the model and its surrounding automated system has come to be well-accepted by senior management. Individual office managers throughout Air Canada have been using the method for the past two years, and presenting its results in detailed support of their regular manpower and facilities budgets.

Airport manpower and facilities planning model

Just as the reservations functions in an airline are affected by variations in passenger traffic volumes, so obviously are the passenger handling operations at airports. These operations include selling tickets, checking-in passengers and baggage, issuing boarding passes and checking boarding loads at flight departure gates or lounges, and a variety of miscellaneous functions which include escorting V.I.P.'s, invalids and women with infants, etc., etc.

Most of these airport functions are also directly affected by the nature and timing of scheduled flight arrivals and departures. In fact every time the flight schedule changes, manpower and facilities requirements have to be re-evaluated.

As in the case of reservations offices, the Company has laid down standards of service for handling passengers at airports, and the Airport Manpower Planning Model has been developed as the core of a computer-based system to determine the minimum staff levels required to maintain service at the prescribed levels.

This model, however, is not a simulation model, but is based directly on analytical results from mathematical queuing theory. Historical patterns of passenger arrivals are combined with passenger boarding forecasts by flight (obtained directly from the Passenger Allocation Model described earlier) to estimate the number of arrivals in five minute intervals throughout each day of the week. The elementary queuing results are then used to convert these arrival volumes into the corresponding numbers of agents and counter positions required in each interval to guarantee an acceptable level of service (measured in terms of the waiting times of passengers).

The schedule of flight arrivals and departures is used directly to estimate staff requirements at departure gates, and the additional staff required for other miscellaneous activities. The individual requirements are combined to obtain the total airport requirement by time of day and day of week, and hence the total manpower establishment. Once again shift scheduling and rostering techniques are utilized, making allowance for meal breaks, sickness and vacations.

Aircrew scheduling model [8]

The manpower required to operate the flights specified by the detailed schedule or tactical plan must also be budgeted for and re-assessed whenever the schedule changes. This is a very important problem, and not the least because aircrews represent a very expensive resource. Not only are their basic salaries very high because of the tremendous responsibilities they undertake, but also the union agreements include a number of penalty clauses which can cost the airline a good deal of additional expense if the crews themselves are not scheduled or assigned to flights as efficiently as possible.

The crew scheduling model in Air Canada has been developed to solve the problem of crew allocation in such a way as to minimize the total variable or penalty costs incurred. It is recognized that some crew or other must fly every flight in the schedule on every day of operation, and therefore the basic crew costs are regarded as fixed (once the flight schedule is determined).

The first problem is to link up the individual flights in the schedule to form what are known as "pairings". A pairing is a sequence of flights of a particular aircraft type which will take a crew out of its home base in a circuit of paths which eventually return to that base. Many thousands of such pairings can be generated from a given flight schedule, but only a certain sub-set of these will be legal in the sense that they satisfy various regulatory and union constraints. Once the sub-set of legal pairings has been generated, they are arranged in a two-way table or matrix which identifies the particular flight-legs contained in each of the pairings. Each pairing also carries a certain cost which represents the magnitude of the penalty costs which would be incurred if that pairing were actually flown by an aircrew.

The second problem is to select a certain number of pairings from the table in such a way that each flight-leg is flown once and only once on each day, and the total variable cost of the complete schedule of pairings selected is minimized. This is a particular type of problem amenable to the techniques of linear programming. However, the solution must allocate integral or whole numbers of crews to the various pairings, and the particular methods of integer linear programming must be used in this situation. In fact only one crew may be assigned to a chosen pairing, so that the problem specializes to the particular case known as "zero-one" linear programming. Sophisticated algorithms have been developed for this particular case, but their reliability and efficiency leave a good deal to be desired.

The Air Canada crew scheduling model in fact adopts a more straightforward approach to the problem based on the idea of a guided trial and error or search technique. However, rather than enumerating all possible combinations of pairings, it takes advantage of any results already obtained to reduce the amount of searching at every stage. This implicit enumeration technique is popularly known as "branch and bound" because it branches out and searches through the set of pairings, but bounds the amount of searching that actually has to be performed. Even so the amount of computation is very great and the volume of data to be stored for any practical problem is enormous. Consequently the procedure has been programmed for a large computer in the Company, and the inputs and outputs which make up the total system have also been completely automated.

Very good and useful results have recently been obtained with this model, and it is presently being implemented as a regular manpower planning tool for both flight crews and cabin attendants.

FURTHER DEVELOPMENTS AND GENERAL CONCLUSIONS

Time-lags in short-range planning

It is a fact that the short-range plan or flight schedule that is eventually accepted will be based on traffic forecasts that, by the time implementation starts, will be out of date. It is obviously impossible to wait until the plan has been finalized, and then up-date the forecasts and re-evaluate the plan. But even if this were possible, the re-evaluation would generate further time-lags which would again make the forecasts out-of-date.

The practical solution to this apparently never-ending cycle of events has been to develop automated models which can rapidly evaluate all the consequences of any proposal. With a comprehensive set of such models it is now becoming possible in Air Canada to reduce the time required for evaluation, making it feasible to consider more alternatives and modifications to any original proposal, and also being able to explicitly consider the effects of any significant changes in the expected levels of future traffic flows.

The iterative nature of short-range planning

Earlier in this paper it was mentioned that the traffic forecasting models do not produce results which are independent of any proposed plan of action. This results in an iterative process of tactical planning, where successive modifications are introduced to both plans and forecasts until the final result is both internally consistent and acceptable to senior management.

In practice, of course, this kind of iterative planning procedure could only be carried out to a very minimal extent until the advent of a comprehensive set of evaluation models. The point has already been made that, if it takes too long to evaluate any proposal, there may well be little or no time left to modify either the forecasts or the plans themselves.

Part of the solution to this problem has already been described, in that the automated models described in this paper can provide the time which is essential in order to make the iterative planning procedure as efficient and productive as possible.

In the longer term, however, there is a real need to develop forecasting models to predict future demand or potential market levels which themselves are independent of any proposed plan or flight schedule. If such forecasting models can be built, the evaluation models will also have to be extended in such a way that their outputs are the very same expected future traffic volumes which now form the inputs to the existing set of models.

Before such models can be developed, a working definition of demand must be agreed upon. Almost certainly such a quantity could not be directly measured, but would have to be indirectly estimated from historical traffic data and the characteristics of past flight schedules, fare levels, etc., etc. Relationships between these historical demand estimates and corresponding socio-economic variables could lead to a suitable demand forecasting model whose outputs would feed into a demand allocation process similar in principle to the existing passenger allocation model.

Research in this area is currently being carried out for Air Canada[9] and some promising results have already been obtained. However, it is too early to say just how far this approach can be taken in replacing the existing iterative planning procedures.

A schedule generation model

Another problem which imposes time constraints on the tactical planning process is the difficult and time-consuming manual task of preparing a detailed flight schedule in the first place. At the present time this task is performed in several stages starting with the point-to-point traffic forecasts. Dividing these forecasts by the seating capacities of the different aircraft types leads to a plan of flight frequencies between the different pairs of points in the network. These frequencies are then linked together to form flight routings for the available aircraft. Finally, times of departure and arrival must be assigned to every flight leg to arrive at a complete flight schedule.

In practice this process is both complex and very subjective, and up to now it has not been amenable (except in part) to a mathematical model-building approach. However, developments are under way in Air Canada, and in a number of other airlines, which show some promise of bearing fruitful results. The long-term objective is to develop an automated model which can generate a variety of flight schedules subject to obvious constraints on available resources. These schedules could then be rapidly evaluated by the kinds of models already described in this paper.

It does not seem possible, at this point in time to generate an optimal flight schedule by one pass through a very comprehensive, but closed-form mathematical model. The rapid evaluation of many alternatives currently seems to be the only feasible line of development.

The use of manpower budgeting models

The financial evaluation model is a most important element in tactical planning in Air Canada. However, its methods of estimating operating expenses are both elementary, and subject to certain shortcomings. At the same time there are now available in Air Canada a number of relatively sophisticated and automated models for producing detailed manpower and facilities budgets for the short-term future.

These budgeting models use as inputs many of the same traffic forecasts and operating statistics as are fed into the financial model. The outputs from these budgeting models could easily be converted into major elements of direct operating costs (both in-flight and on the ground). As yet the Company has not taken advantage of these more sophisticated cost models to improve the estimates of expenditure used in the financial evaluation.

An important and useful development in the future will therefore be to integrate these budgeting models more directly with the financial evaluation processes of tactical planning.

THE INTEGRATION OF INDIVIDUAL PLANNING MODELS

Once a number of individual planning models had been developed in Air Canad
it became clear that, not only could they be linked together through manual processes and procedures, but they could be integrated into several fully-automated
systems. In such integrated systems the outputs from one model flow directly as
inputs into the next model in sequence.

For example, the medium-range forecasting model, the passenger allocation
model and the reservations office manpower budgeting model now form a fully-
automated and integrated planning system. As well as producing detailed manpower budgets for individual offices, this system can now be used to rapidly
evaluate a proposed schedule in terms of direct labour costs in reservations offices
across the system. By varying the quality of service standards it can also determin
the effects of proposed policy changes in the area of customer service.

In this particular example point-to-point traffic forecasts are fed directly from
the forecasting model into the passenger allocation model along with the coded
version of the flight schedule. The allocation model in turn feeds predicted levels
of boarding passengers by station into the budgeting model which converts these
into telephone workload and produces both physical and financial manpower and
facilities budgets.

A similar integrated planning system links the forecasting and allocation model
to the airport manpower and facilities budgeting model and can be used in essentially the same variety of ways.

Yet a third example of such an integrated set of models will be developed in the
future if the concepts of demand estimation and allocation can be sufficiently
well developed. Such a system would directly link the demand estimation, forecasting and allocation models in order to proceed rapidly and automatically from
historical traffic and schedule data to forecasts of future traffic volumes by point-
to-point and by flight and leg flow.

Conclusions

It has not been possible in the space available to review in any detail all of the
models which have been developed in Air Canada to assist decision-makers at all
levels in the Company. The paper has therefore concentrated almost exclusively
on the area of tactical or short-range planning.

It would be remiss of the author, however, not to mention the existence of a
wide variety of other models which are currently in use in the airline. Brief reference has already been made to the types of models used in strategic planning and
in the areas of operational control. In addition a number of more specialized
models have been developed over the years to examine and evaluate various
aspects of corporate policy. Questions of reservations policy, insurance policy, ai

freight and air express policies, sales promotional policies, and fuel policies and procedures have all, at one time or another been studied by means of mathematical models.

In summary a great deal has already been accomplished throughout the Company using the scientific principles of model-building, but as the final part of this paper indicates the problems in the future will be even more challenging than those of the past.

REFERENCES

1. H.J.G. Whitton & R.W. Linder (1962). "Computer Forecasting of Passenger Flows". *Proceedings of 2nd AGIFORS Symposium*, Rome, 1962.

2. J.G. Gagnon (1967). "A Model for Flowing Passengers over Airline Networks". *Proceedings of 7th AGIFORS Symposium*, Noordwijk, 1967.

3. A.T. Batey & J.C. Tennant (1968). "Schedule Evaluation for Air Cargo". Paper presented at the *8th AGIFORS Symposium*, Princeton, 1968.

4. A.M. Lee & J. Fearnley (1963). "Two Problems in Pre-Testing Proposed Flight Schedules by Means of Simulation". *Proceedings of 3rd AGIFORS Symposium*, Montreal, 1963.

5. F.T. Coyle & J.C. Maloney (1966). "Flight Profitability Forecasting". Paper presented at 18th Meeting of IATA Data Processing Sub-Committee, Dublin, March, 1966.

6. H.J.G. Whitton (1961). "A Study of an Airline's Telephone Reservations Offices". *Proceedings of 1st AGIFORS Symposium*, New York, 1961.

7. R.W. Linder (1966). "The Further Development of Manpower and Facilities Planning Methods for Telephone Reservations Offices". *Proceedings of 6th AGIFORS Symposium*, Killarney, 1966.

8. J. Fearnley (1966). "Crew Scheduling Development in Air Canada". *Proceedings of 6th AGIFORS Symposium*, Killarney, 1966.

9. G.C. Shaw (1968). "The Schedule—Its Effect on Passenger Volumes". Paper presented at the *8th AGIFORS Symposium*, Princeton, 1968.

3. SEQUENTIAL ECONOMIC PROGRAMMING

MARSHALL K. WOOD

Background

Sequential economic programming is a name we have adopted to denote a family of models being developed at the National Planning Association. I use the term "family of models" advisedly, since it refers not to one model, but rather to a philosophy of model building, together with a language and a set of associated algorithms for model construction. Within this broad framework, many widely different models can be constructed.

This family of models is the culmination of more than 25 years of development, starting with the formal organization of the Air Staff for hand computation of Air Force training and procurement programs in World War II; continuing through the formal development of triangular models and linear programming procedures in the first post-war decade in the Air Force Planning Research Division Project SCOOP [1]*; the associated development of detailed national input-output models [2]; and the development at the National Planning Association of the PARM System of emergency planning models during the last decade [3 & 4].

Although sharing many of the features of its progenitors, the new family of models differs in one major respect. The previous models were primarily purposive; designed to determine the present actions necessary to accomplish stipulated future objectives subject to specified constraints. As such the direction of causality was from the desired future objectives back toward the present actions needed to accomplish them.

The new family of sequential economic programming models is to a much greater extent behavioristic: designed to project the future consequences of present actions (though purposive behavior, insofar as it is judged to exist, is incorporated at a lower level in the model structure). Thus the new models project from the present toward the future, by incremental stages, in a sequential fashion.

---

*Numbers in brackets refer to numbered references in the bibliography at the end of this paper.

The shift from a purposive to a behavioristic orientation reflects a major chang in the intended use of the models. The earlier models were designed as tools for planning and management of activities which were subject to a relatively large amount of purposive central direction. The new sequential programming system is designed for application to national and regional economies comprising large numbers of independent decentralized decision-making units, and in which only a minor fraction of economic decisions are subject to direct purposive central control.

The purpose of the sequential programming system is to appraise the consequences to the economy under study, both as a whole and with respect to particular functional and/or geographic components, of stipulated changes in government policies and programs, or in external environmental or economic constraints.

In trying to serve this purpose, we have rejected the use of mathematical programming techniques as the primary tool primarily because of the difficulty of establishing meaningful objective functions. The attempt to find a precise mathematical optimum for a problem whose objectives are very ill defined has not seemed particularly useful.

The pluralistic character of our society precludes the establishment of national goals with clearly defined quantitative weights. Still less is this possible in considering the disparate effects of proposed policies and programs on different regions of the nation. Even after political decisions have been made, it would be difficult, if not impossible, to infer the weights used in making the decision; the decision making process in a pluralistic, decentralized society is never wholly rational. To define a meaningful objective function before the fact seems quite impossible.

It does, however, seem possible and useful to develop tools for introducing a somewhat greater degree of rationality into at least the public decision-making process, through analysis *before* the fact of the likely consequences of public policies and programs under consideration for adoption, while taking due accoun of their interaction with decentralized private decisions, and of the behavioristic relationships involved therein. This is the purpose of the proposed system. Within this general framework, it will be feasible and probably useful to introduc mathematical programming techniques for performing some functions within particular sectors.

In order to allow maximum flexibility in studying the consequences of differe kinds of stipulated changes, the basic system is formulated as a nearly closed model, which projects forward in successive steps from stipulated initial conditions. Provision is then made for replacing endogenous relationships by stipulating changes in the particular policies, programs, or resource constraints whose consequences are to be evaluated. It follows that if no changes are stipulated, it should be possible to use the model for projection purposes, although this it not the primary interest. In most applications of the system, it is expected that at least some and possibly all of the endogenous relationships which provide an approximate behavioristic characterization of government activities will be replaced by exogenous stipulation.

Major emphasis in the design of the model structure is placed on direct causal relationships among activities. Major reliance is placed on accounting identities of the resource balance, perpetual inventory type. For each type of resource, the activities which create, transform, import, export, consume, or destroy the resource are identified and represented explicitly in the model. Constraints are established to insure that the quantity of a given resource in existence at the beginning of a time period, plus the gains and losses during the period, are equal to the quantity of the resource in existence at the end of the period. A second class of resource balance relationship establishes an inequality constraint between the quantity of a resource in existence and the amount required in use for the performance of some function or activity. This second type of constraint is characteristic of productive capacity and working inventories.

The variables in the system will have widely diversified characteristics. Some may be policy variables, such as tax rates, transfer payment eligibility criteria, or school class size criteria. Others may be programmatic assumptions or stipulations about the composition and magnitude of government programs, such as defense, space, public works, housing, etc. Still others may be demographic, such as number of individuals in particular age, sex, race, and marital status strata. The largest single class probably will be economic production activities, defining input-output relationships within the economy.

To make the system most useful for its intended purposes, it is essential that the model contain in considerable explicit detail the instrumental variables through which policies and programs are effected. This is being done to the maximum feasible extent. As in all serious model building efforts, it has of course been necessary to adapt the activity classification and the model structure to the data which are or can be made available. This has inevitably entailed compromises with the ideal model structure, which we hope can be alleviated in subsequent model revisions.

In order to facilitate the resource balance accounting, both with respect to products and with respect to productive capacity, economic production activities will be defined on a product, rather than on an establishment basis. Secondary product transfers will be eliminated by a system of statistical adjustments of the establishment-based input-output table.* Although no secondary product transfers remain in the input-output table, by-products will be permitted; these are treated in the formal model as negative input coefficients. The output of an activity is always measured by its production of its primary product. In manufacturing we are working with activities defined at close to the 4-digit level of the

---

*These procedures have been programmed and applied to the 1958 U.S. input-output tables at the 80-sector level; analogous techniques will be applied to the 400-sector input-output tables for the U.S. now under development.

U.S. Standard Industrial Classification. In other sectors, activities are generally defined at close to the 2-digit level, though many important departures from the SIC basis of classification result from the replacement of the establishment by the activity basis of definition. In agriculture, for instance, activities are defined almost entirely on a crop or product basis.

System structure

Before describing the component parts of the system, it may be useful to give a concise characterization of the system as a whole. Decision makers are grouped into classes, called activities, such that the collective behavior of the decision-makers in each class can be observed and measured, and/or inferred from *a priori* reasoning. The response of each such class of decision-makers to relevant external stimuli and constraints is then expressed in some appropriate algebraic form.

The consequences of such decisions, with respect to the production and con-sumption of all the distinct types of resources affected thereby are also estimated and expressed in some appropriate algebraic form, usually incorporating lags in time after the decisions from which they result. The resource flows which result from such decisions are generally subject to accounting identities and constraints of a perpetual inventory type, which interrelate all the transactions affecting each resource. Such resource balance constraints are also applicable to individual regions, but are linked by a network of interregional flow relationships.

It is postulated that each class of decision-maker may also be influenced by (generally incomplete) knowledge of decisions made by other classes of decision-makers, and by the resource constraints resulting therefrom. Each class of decision-maker may also be influenced by its expectations about future decisions of other classes of decision-makers; but such expectations can be based only on information available prior to the time of decision. The decision criteria for each class of decision-maker are contained in a separate sub-model for each activity. The complete model of the economy may contain thousands of such sub-models.

The macro-structure of the economic programming system is designed to organize and interrelate these sub-models in such a way that the separate sub-models can be solved sequentially. This system macro-structure thus defines the sequence of sub-models, and provides for information storage and retrieval, in a way which insures that the relevant information about the rest of the economy is available to each class of decision-maker as it is considered in turn.

The sequential structure permits great freedom in defining the structure of the sub-models for individual activities. Any appropriate algebraic form may be used within these sub-models. The model-builder need not restrict himself to linear forms, as is generally necessary (to insure computational feasibility) when work-ing with the conventional types of large models, in which simultaneous multi-variate relationships are used. An important corollary is that in the sequential programming framework it is relatively easy to change the structure of individual sub-program modules, without doing violence to the system macro-structure. This is an essential feature of a large system model, which can only be created gradually, on an incremental basis, and which must be continually modified, in evolutionary fashion, if it is to be useful.

The primary structure of the system—the outer recursion loop—is time recursive. Decision processes, and the consequent physical transformations and transfers of goods and services, are simulated sequentially for successive periods, starting with the earliest.

Time periods of any desired length may be used—in fact the length of the time period could be varied within a single projection, to provide greater detail and greater possible precision in the period of principal interest. Models presently under construction will use annual periods.

Within each time period, activities are considered sequentially, so arranged that the primary determinants for each activity either precede it in the computational sequence in the current period, or else precede it temporally—in the preceding period or periods. It is not *a priori* obvious that such an arrangement exists, but it will be shown presently that it is, in fact, possible.

Historical time series and initial status data at the beginning of the first time period are supplied exogenously. (Time series are used, as explained later, in applying lagged factors and in developing future expectations). Based on these data, and on other exogenous policy and program stipulations for the first period, the decisions and economic activities of the first period are simulated. The simulation for the first period also constructs new initial status data for the second period, and updates the historical time series to provide a quasi-historical time series up to the beginning of the second period. This process is then repeated for each period in turn. There is no limit to the number of successive periods which can be projected (although the projections obviously will be of progressively lower reliability for more distant future periods).

Demographic model

The process starts with the demographic model for the first period (Chart 1). Procedurally, this model brings in all the exogenous data on initial status and historical trends, and updates them during the computations for each successive period. Substantively, it performs transformations in the status of variables which are affected by the passage of time. These are principally demographic transformations, which project changes in the initial status of the population strata by age, sex, and color, as a result of births, deaths, and migration. Age-, sex-, and race-specific birth, death, and out-migration rates are applied to the initial status data for each stratum as in a concentrated cohort-survival model to obtain the terminal status for each year (ignoring in-migration).

This assumes that out-migration, like other demographic transformations, can be projected by use of age-, sex-, and color-specific coefficients with time as the

Chart 1

SEQUENTIAL ECONOMIC PROGRAMMING

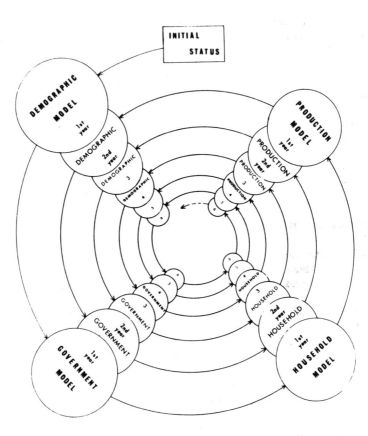

only independent variable. This is consistent with Lowry's findings [5]. In-migration will be based on lagged economic opportunity measures for the destination region. Probable increase in employment over several previous yea will be the dominant measure of economic opportunity. The lag appears to be greater for non-white than for white. Out-migrants from all regions, stratified by initial status, will be aggregated at the national level, allocated to regions as a function of relative economic opportunity, aged, and added into the initial status of the respective destination regions for the next time period.

Census data will be used to derive "headship rates" by age, sex, and color. These rates will be applied to the demographic data, derived as outlined above, to obtain an estimate of families, by age of household head and family size.

Government model

Government activities, at the national, state, and local levels, will be defined in programmatic and functional terms. Rates of operation for each government activity will be derived from application of current (or stipulated alternative) policies and criteria to data on production activity and income distribution of the preceding period, and to data on demographic characteristics for the current period. Transfer payments will be estimated by application of relevant criteria to demographic data of the current period and gross income distribution of the preceding period. Tax rates will be applied to gross income and expenditure data to derive government revenues. Government expenditures for specific goods and services are derived by the application of factors to the activity levels for each government function.

Some local government activities, such as sanitary services, electric power, and local transportation systems, may be treated as endogenous, and driven by consumer demand. Postal services might be similarly treated. Other local government services may be partly endogenous, and partly exogenous. The demand for elementary education, for instance, would be generated by the demographic model in terms of student attendance, but the quality of the service provided, in terms of classroom size, teacher-student ratios, and other factors, would generally be stipulated as (exogenous) policy variables.

Other government programs can be projected by extrapolation of past trends endogenously; or, more commonly, stipulated as exogenous policy and program variables. In most applications, it will be the stipulation of alternative government policies and programs which will be the primary driving force for the model. Such stipulations will include policy criteria, such as eligibility for transfer payment programs, as well as programmatic data, such as defense and public works programs.

Household model

The household model starts with a series of activities representing households as consumers, stratified by family size and disposable income class. Gross income is derived from production activity levels of the preceding period, including salary and wage payments, dividends, and interest. These income payments will be linked to family composition primarily by Census data on family income by age of household head. Some use may also be made of data on occupational composition patterns and associated wage rates, and of data from individual income tax returns on dividend and interest payments. Data on transfer payments and taxes from the government model will be used to modify gross income data from the previous period to derive disposable income data by demographic stratum for the current period. The use of gross income data from the previous period reflects a lag in adjusting expenditures to changes in income, consistent with Milton Friedman's "permanent income" hypothesis. Savings and capital expenditures will be estimated first from a combination of time series and cross-section data, and subtracted from disposable income. The remainder will then be distributed among commodities and services in accordance with factors derived from cross-section data.

Cross-section data from the BLS 1960–61 Consumer Expenditure Survey will be used to develop consumption expenditure, tax, and savings coefficients for each household stratum. These coefficients will be tested, reconciled, and adjusted to insure consistency at the national level with aggregate time-series data.* Many of these coefficients will be regionally invariant, but some regional differentiation is expected and will be retained in the model, especially in the food and apparel areas.

Investment in housing and perhaps expenditures for consumer durables will be generated endogenously, when desired, based on multivariate relationships involving demographic data (especially new family formation), income distribution, and the size and age distribution of the existing stock of consumer durables. This stock will be aged and depleted in a cohort survival model, and augmented by new investment as it occurs. For many applications, of course, one may wish to stipulate consumer durable investment exogenously.

Production model

The production model follows the basic Leontief input-output structure, using the personal consumption and government final demand estimates developed earlier. Investment and foreign trade components of final demand are developed endogenously within the input-output portion of the economic activity model. Also incorporated into the input-output model are value-added computations. Depreciation allowances are based on a perpetual inventory balance of capital stock. Compensation of employees is derived from base-period factors, adjusted for productivity and wage differentials in space and time. Taxes are based on the rates defined in the government model. Profits are derived as a residual.

This completes the cycle for one time period, and we return to the demographic model for the next period. The demographic model then uses the data from the other three models to extend the historical time series and to construct a new initial status for the next period. The entire process may then be repeated for as many time periods as desired. Changes in exogenous stipulations may be made after the computations for each period, as a result of the analysis of the computation for the period. Alternatively, all stipulations may be made at the outset, and the projections for any specified number of periods may be made as a continuous machine run.

---

*Such adjustments will correct reporting biases, as in alcohol and tobacco consumption, adjust for definitional inconsistencies, and introduce appropriate additional secular trend variables.

Production model

It may now be useful to examine in somewhat greater detail the internal structure of the production model. It was noted earlier that the logical structure of the system depends heavily on sequential, rather than simultaneous, algebraic relationships. We have already suggested the general character of these sequential relationships among the major components of the system. We will now examine the nature of the sequential relationships within the production model.

If the input-output relationships in the production model are expressed in matrix form, as in a conventional input-output transactions table, we are at liberty to make any arbitrary permutation of the sequence of rows and columns, without changing the basic relationships, provided that the row and column permutations are identical. In order to achieve a sequential relationship, we must make such permutations as would result in concentrating the transactions on or below the principal diagonal, so that the cells above the diagonal would be either zeros or relatively very small. We have developed a computer algorithm which will accomplish this.*

The effect of this procedure is to order the activities so that the principal consumers of each commodity or service precede the producer in the computation sequence. Application of this algorithm to the 82 production sectors of the U.S. input-output table for 1958 gives more than 95% determination within the lower triangle for 22 sectors, 90%–95% determination for 14 sectors, and 85%–90% determination for 33 sectors, and 80–84% determination for the remaining 13 sectors. This includes all capital account transactions in the table, and not in final demand. With more disaggregated tables, an even more completely triangular arrangement is possible.

Use of this triangular sequence permits a computational procedure which solves the system sequentially for each variable in turn, with only one unknown variable in each equation. The procedure is analogous to the back-solution of the Gauss-Seidel system for solving simultaneous linear equation systems. The computational simplicity of this procedure permits extensive use in the system of inequalities, multivariate relationships, and other non-linear forms, and makes it possible to work with systems including hundreds or even thousands of variables.

---

*Working with an output coefficient matrix, the algorithm assigns the first ordinal number to the activity selling the largest proportion of its output to final demand and to itself. The next ordinal number is assigned to the activity selling the largest proportion of its output to final demand, to the first activity, and to itself. Continuing, the next ordinal number is assigned in turn to the activity, not yet assigned an ordinal number, which sells the largest proportion of its output to final demand, to activities previously assigned ordinal numbers, and to itself. This criterion has the effect of maximizing (among all possible permutations) the minimum (among activities) of the percent determination of each activity by final demand and preceding activities. However, because of the high proportion of zeros in the matrix, further reassignments are generally possible which are equally consistent with the primary criterion. Therefore, a secondary criterion is introduced which makes further permutations whenever by so doing it is possible to increase the percent determination of any activity without reducing the percent determination of any other.

As each production activity is considered in turn, a series of sequential operations is performed, leading to the simulation of the relevant production and investment decisions for the period. These are summarized in Chart 2, and will be discussed in turn below.

Chart 2

Sequential Economic Programming
Single Activity Processing

Demand Estimation
Stipulated Demand
Household Expenditures
Government Expenditures
Industry Inputs
   Old/New Technology
   Lower/Upper Triangular
   Regional Differentiation
Investment Expenditures
Inventory Change
Foreign Trade
Total Demand (Current and Projected)

Investment Decisions
Long Run Expectations
   (Stipulated/Extrapolated/
   Market Analysis)
Return on Investment
Near Term Factors
   (Capacity Utilization;
   Profits, etc.)
Expansion/Modernization

Interregional Relationships

Demand estimation

The first step is the estimation of demand for the output of the activity under consideration. Demand is estimated by interrogating data, stored in randomly accessible computer memory, which defines the activity levels of the current activity's customers. The identity of these customers, and the parameters of the input functions defining their demand for the output of the current activity, are given in factor records. These factor records are read sequentially and the resulting demands computed. Usually the input factors are Leontief type input coefficients, but more elaborate functional forms may be used whenever appropriate.

Input functions for many activities are subject to change over time, as a result of adoption of new technology. Each activity may have two (or more) different sets of input functions. The first will represent the mix of technology present in the most recent base period for which an input-output table is available. A second set of input functions, representing the "best current practice", or "state-of-the-art" technology, may also be used. These advanced technology input functions may be derived from engineering estimates, by time-series analysis, or by any other feasible and appropriate method, depending on the empirical data available. The model assumes that all plants constructed or modernized after the base period will incorporate the advanced technology. Accordingly, the mix of technology present in any period is assumed to be a weighted combination of the base period technology and the advanced technology. The weights used will be:

the base period gross capital stock reduced by retirements since the base period; and the cumulative new investment since the base period. These weights are computed and stored for each activity in each period, and used as a basis for applying the two sets of input functions.

Some of the input functions may involve leadtimes; that is, the inputs may be required substantially earlier than the outputs. Where this leadtime is small relative to the unit time period of the model, it may be ignored. This will probably be appropriate for most inputs on current account in a model using annual periods. Most investment inputs, on the other hand, will have associated lag times; that is, the inputs will lag the decision to invest. (Viewed from the time of completion of an investment project, of course, these would be leadtimes rather than lag times.)

A projection procedure is used to allow for leadtimes. Simulated decisions are always made on the basis of information available at the time the decision is made. To the extent that a decision depends on information or conjectures about the future (and every decision does, to a greater or lesser extent) the future is projected in the system, but always on the basis of information available at that point in simulated time.

A spectrum of alternative procedures for projecting future demand for production activities will be provided. These alternative procedures may be grouped into two broad classes: extrapolation procedures, and simulated market analysis procedures. Extrapolation procedures depend on the maintenance of historical and quasi-historical data (either explicitly as time series or in the form of product moments). Several alternative procedures have been formulated for storing and updating such historical and quasi-historical data. Given the quasi-historical data, a variety of extrapolation functions may be used, ranging from a level projection of the current rate, through linear, quadratic, or higher-order polynomial projections, exponential projections reflecting a constant growth rate, or logistic projections. A choice among these may be made, separately for each activity, reflecting a judgment (based on analysis of past behavior) about the degree of sophistication and sensitivity to current trends which best characterize the decision-makers in each industry.

The second class of projection procedures involves the summarization and analysis (via the input-output structure of the model) of the simulated production decisions made by principal customers of the activity. These decisions will have been recorded for the customer in its earlier position in the triangular sequence. This second procedure closely simulates that which might actually be performed by sophisticated market analysts.

A judgment may be made for each activity, and entered as an exogenous system parameter, as to whether this simulated market analysis procedure will be used for any application of the system; whether one of the alternative extrapolation procedures will be used; or whether some weighted combination will be used. Exclusive use of the market analysis procedure for all activities is substantially equivalent to assuming complete central programming and control, or perfect market analysis coupled with perfect dissemination of information.

A third alternative is of course to stipulate the projection of demand for any particular activity or activities, based on exogenous information or assumptions.

The procedures just outlined provide for the estimation of demand from the principal customers of the current activity: those which precede it in the triangular computation sequence, and whose demands are expressed in lower triangular factor records. But we must also make some allowance for the upper triangular demands even though they are relatively small. For this purpose we make the projection techniques described above do double duty: we use the projection to the current period which was made during the computation for the preceding period, to obtain estimates of the activity levels of activities which follow the current activity in the computation sequence. The input factors are then applied to these activity levels in the usual way.

In general, the same input functions will be assumed to apply to all the regions under consideration in the model. In order to minimize regional differences resulting from differences in product mix among regions, a relatively detailed activity and product classification will be used. Despite this, there will clearly be significant regional differences in input functions for fuels, energy, and factor payments. Data are available, in general, to estimate such differences, and will be incorporated in the factor file wherever appropriate and feasible.

Demand arising from investment expenditures by or on behalf of other activities will be estimated in the same way as for current account demands, except that the relevant activity level is the investment rather than the production level of the consuming industry. A complete set of input functions for investment by each production activity is included in the factor file.

Demand (positive or negative) for inventory change will be estimated in the aggregate for each product at the time its total demand is being estimated, based on current inventory levels and projected future demand.

Demand (positive or negative) arising from foreign trade (exports and imports) will be estimated from historical and quasi-historical data, modified by current and projected domestic demand and supply for the product, and (when appropriate) by stipulated changes in tariff rates, prices, quotas, or other relevant factors.

Investment decisions

Investment decisions will be based on a combination of long-run expectations and near-term factors. Long range projections of demand will be derived from one or more of the alternative projection techniques described earlier. As noted earlier a choice among these alternatives, or some weighted combination of them, may be elected by the user of the model, based on his judgment about the techniques which are used or are likely to be used by decision-makers in each industry. The tentative long-run investment decisions might depend on comparison of the long-run demand projection with present capacity to produce, as measured by the capital stock. Alternatively, a "return-on-investment" analysis could be simulated, although it is not clear that the data on regional differences in cost structure would be good enough to justify such a procedure.

The long-run expectations are in any event likely to be tempered by near-term factors. Chief among these will be measures of current capacity utilization, and availability of funds for investment from retained earnings. At some point it may be feasible and desirable to try to project (or stipulate) interest rates, and to use them as a variable in the simulated investment decision.

Within the framework of total investment, a breakdown will be made between investment for expansion of capacity, either by new plant construction or by enlargement of existing facilities, and investment in modernization of existing plants. (It is recognized that enlargement and modernization are often combined in the same project, but it seems important to maintain the conceptual distinction.) These three types of investment have significantly different capital : output ratios, as well as significantly different input patterns. Also, the first is geographically footloose, while the latter two are tied to existing locations.

In investment, as elsewhere in the model, the option is retained to override the endogenous decision functions by exogenous stipulation. It is likely that this option will be used more often for investment than for other types of decisions.

Inter-regional relationships

In general, geographic interrelationships are represented within each of the individual activities of the model, though some activities may exist only at the national level. This level of the system is in general logically parallel or simultaneous, not recursive.

The system is adaptable to the use of any arbitrary set of mutually exclusive and exhaustive regions which are appropriate to the class of problems under consideration. (For many purposes, of course, a single national region may suffice.) However, the system structure contains certain implicit assumptions which need to be observed in defining regions, if the model results are to be realistic. The basic criterion is that there is a high degree of intra-regional mobility of resources, and a much lower degree of inter-regional mobility of resources. A corollary of this is that regions should generally be centered around major transportation centers. A second criterion is that it is desirable to make regions conform as closely as possible to existing administrative and political boundaries, both to facilitate compilation of basic data and to facilitate the use of model results.

Because of the widely differing degrees of mobility of the different kinds of
resources under consideration, it appears necessary to establish a two-level
hierarchical classification of regions. At the lowest level we may have Functional
Economic Areas, as defined by Karl Fox [6]. These are essentially labor market
or commuting areas, but will also generally approximate the local service areas for
utilities, retail trade, building materials, and service industries. Resource balances
and capacity constraints for these activities will be maintained at the FEA level.
FEA's will correspond roughly to Standard Metropolitan Statistical Areas,
enlarged to include contiguous suburban and rural counties within commuting
distance. In order to create a mutually exclusive and exhaustive classification
system on this basis, it is also necessary to establish some functional economic
areas in the more sparsely settled parts of the country which are centered around
smaller cities, not classified as Standard Metropolitan Statistical Areas. A first
attempt to define such a set of functional economic areas has recently been completed by B. J. L. Berry of the University of Chicago, under a contract from the
Census Bureau, supervised by the Social Science Research Council [7]. There
might be approximately 400 of these Functional Economic Areas in the U.S.

These functional economic areas will be aggregated into perhaps a dozen
broader regions, probably representing a slight disaggregation of the Census
Bureau's geographic divisions. These regions will represent major wholesale trade
areas, centered around major transportation centers. They will approximate the
regions within which there is relatively high intra-regional (as contrasted with
inter-regional) mobility of all resources other than those mentioned above in the
discussion of functional economic areas. Resource balances for the activities producing these resources will be maintained in the model at the regional level.

Final demands will be generated or stipulated at the area or regional level,
based on correspondingly disaggregated data in the demographic model and initial
status file.

Inter-industry demands will be generated by the application of input factors to
activity levels, separately for each region or area. In general, the same input factor
will be applied to levels of basic activities at all regions or areas producing a given
primary product. However, input factors may be differentiated by regions and
areas, with separate factors for each, with respect to those particular inputs which
are believed to vary among regions, and for which regionally differentiated data
are available.

A regional demand allocation procedure will be used to distribute demand
from consuming regions to producing regions in a way which is consistent with
the production capacity associated with each region, while allocating relatively
more demand to those producing regions which are closer to consuming regions.
The relative weight given to this location preference will of course vary widely
among commodities, and is subject to empirical evaluation. Regional demand
allocation will be the first step in processing each activity, in turn, within the
(triangular) computation sequence.

A variety of different algorithms will be used to distribute demand from the consuming region to the producing region. Different algorithms may be employed for different products. Among these will be a modified gravity model, with the exponent (defining the inverse relationship to distance) varying by activity; an LP transportation cost minimizing model; and procedures for allocating demand in proportion to base period or other fixed patterns. The choice among these, for any particular commodity, will depend upon empirical analysis. *A priori*, the gravity model seems likely to be the most generally useful.

Production of those commodities which move in interregional trade will be performed by activities which are defined at the regional level. Computation of inputs to support such regional production activities will be performed separately for each region. Input commodities which are produced by residentiary activities (manpower, plant capacity services, local utilities, etc.) are transferred from the region to the associated residentiary activities in areas by means of an intra-regional procedure. These residentiary inputs to regional production activities will generally be represented in the aggregate by a single input coefficient which we may call "industry services."

A set of "industry service" activities may be defined at the area level, to provide residentiary services for a group of related commodity production activities, defined at the regional level. The assumption is that the mix of these residentiary inputs needed is less sensitive to variations in output product mix than is the input mix for production of commodities that move in inter-regional trade. The group of related commodity production activities which is supported by a single kind of industry service activity will be those which are judged to have a similar mix of residentiary inputs, and to be producible in the same kind of plants with a similar mix of generalized production equipment. Specialized production equipment (and the associated production capacity) is assigned to the commodity production activities at the regional level.

System adaptation

It will, I am sure, be obvious to everyone that the system framework which I have sketched implies a heavy investment in new empirical research, especially if the model is disaggregated to several hundred production sectors and several hundred areas, as I have proposed. I believe that ultimately at least this level of detail will be necessary to account satisfactorily for interregional flows and regional investment decisions. However, the system structure is quite flexible in this respect.

As a matter of research strategy, we propose to design the system for initial implementation at a relatively more aggregative level of activity, regional and temporal classification. This will greatly facilitate the problems of initial implementation, both with respect to empirical data and with respect to computer programming. A relatively aggregative model will be able to incorporate the results of work done by many other research groups, will be much easier to test and validate, and will still be of considerable interest for many current economic analysis problems. In terms of the formal logical structure of the system, there may be little difference between the aggregative and the detailed models. But even in terms of the computer system, the more aggregative version will be simple to implement, because it will avoid many of the troublesome and onerous problem of input-output control and use of auxiliary storage which would be encountered with more detailed models.

The model is structured in terms of major components and can be implemented in much the same way as a pre-fabricated house is built. Specifically it allows for each component to be empirically developed in greater or less detail as data, policy objectives, and research funds permit. We believe that this will facilitate the evolutionary development of the model. Second, when the model is used to evaluate policy actions, selective parts of the overall structure can be implemented. The value of this is not so much that machine time can be saved in running the overall model as that "side" calculations can be more effectively interpolated into the model runs.

New York State model

This may be illustrated by sketching briefly the ways in which we propose to simplify the model in a sequential economic programming system which we are developing for the State of New York. This system will be designed to give guidance to the Executive Department of the State in its policy planning functions. In particular, it will aim at measuring economic and social impacts of various possible alternative economic policies, whether originating at the national, state, or local level.

We propose to work with annual time periods, since any shorter period would create major empirical problems in developing appropriate seasonal patterns. This implies that we are abstracting from short-run seasonal and cyclical problems, and focusing primarily on long-term trends. The classification of production sectors will include about 280 in New York State itself; this contains substantially all the detail which is relevant to New York State out of a 400-sector input-output model of the U.S. These 280 will be aggregated to approximately 100 in representing New York's trade with other regions. Only these 100 will be represented explicit in the inter-regional trade model.

The regional structure will initially represent New York State as a single region but may later be expanded to 12 or more functional economic areas within New York State. New York will be embedded in a U.S. national model, but the other regions will mostly be more aggregative, with respect to both geographic and sector classification. Tentatively, the other regions will be: (1) New England; (2) Pennsylvania; (3) New Jersey; (4) South Atlantic; (5) the South Central; (6) the East North Central; (7) the West North Central; (8) the rest of the (western) U.S.; (9) the rest of the world.

The sectoral classification of the other regions will contain about 100 sectors, consistent with the 100-sector aggregation of the New York classification which is used in the model of interregional trade.

In initial applications of the system the final demand and output levels for the regions outside New York will be stipulated, based on judgment projections derived from the regular NPA national and regional economic projections series. Later, as time and research resources permit, part of final demand and output levels for other regions may also be generated endogenously in the model.

Korean adaptation

Another major application of the sequential economic programming approach is now being made by the National Planning Association for the Republic of Korea. A dynamic input-output model with 43 sectors was developed by the Korean government and the AID staff two years ago and used for preparation of the Second Five Year Plan. A year ago the Korean Economic Planning Board instituted annual revisions of the plan, in the form of Overall Resources Budgets. The dynamic input-output model is the primary tool used for testing alternative development paths and for maintaining consistency among the annual investment programs prepared by the various ministries. Each ORB deals with investment and foreign trade decisions for the coming year, in the context of a seven-year projection of the development path of the economy as a whole.

Recently the Korean planning model has been expanded to 109 production sectors, and reformulated as a sequential economic programming model. Preliminary work has been initiated on formulation and data development to expand the model into an interregional model, subdividing the country into 16 functional areas within four major regions. It is hoped that this interregional model will provide a better framework for rational decisions on the location of new investment, especially of investment in social overhead and infrastructure.

At a later date, it is expected that this model will be expanded further to about 300 production sectors. Input-output tables with 270 sectors were prepared for 1960 and 1963, and a 300-sector table for 1966 was completed in 1968. Obviously, however, the data needed for the sequential economic programming model extend far beyond the basic input-output table, and will require additional time to develop.

Conclusion

We believe that the concepts and techniques of sequential economic programming which have been sketched herein represent a significant addition to the available tools for decision-making in a free, pluralistic economy. These techniques provide means for harnessing the power of the electronic computer and the concepts of systems analysis without the dangers inherent in centralized governmental planning and control. These techniques also provide means for reflecting, in the development of national policies and programs, a much closer representation of the diverse and complex ways in which the real world responds to external stimuli than is possible within either the framework of conventional econometric models, or the rigid optimizing strait jacket of mathematical programming. The techniques of sequential economic programming permit the model structure to be largely decoupled from the empirical work, thus making it possible to use a much wider spectrum of available data than is possible with alternative techniques, and to adapt the model structure to whatever empirical data are available.

REFERENCES

1. Wood, M. K., and Geisler, M. A.: *Development of Dynamic Models for Program Planning* In Activity Analysis of Production and Allocation, edited by Tjalling C. Koopmans, Cowles Commission Monograph 13, Chapter XII, 1951.

2. *Input-Output Analysis: An Appraisal.* Studies in Income and Wealth, Vol. 18. National Bureau of Economic Research, 1955.

3. Wood, M. K. PARM: *A New Model for Economic Projections.* Proceedings, American Statistical Association Annual Meeting, Dec. 1961.

4. Wood, M. K. PARM: *An Economic Programming Model.* Management Science, Vol. 11 No. 7, May, 1965.

5. Lowry, Ira S.: *Migration and Metropolitan Growth: two analytical models,* UCLA, 1966

6. Fox, Karl A. *Integrating National and Regional Models for Economic Stabilization and Growth,* paper presented at the Conference on National Economic Planning, Univ. of Pittsburgh, 25–26 March, 1964.

7. Berry, B. J. L. *Final Report on the SSRC Study of Metropolitan Area Classification,* Univ. of Chicago, May, 1967.

4. CAPITAL INVESTMENT DECISION MODELS FOR PUBLIC UTILITIES

E. F. MELLEN

CONTENTS

I. Introduction

In this paper the nature of public utilities is discussed. A highly significant feature of their operation is their dependence on large scale, irreversible capital investments. Models are described which explore the effect of different decisions. The importance of the objectives of the organisation and their relationship to the type of model structured is emphasised and a brief review is given of some of the current work undertaken in this field by the energy sector.

II. The nature of public utilities

No very exact definition can be given of public utilities. However, for the purposes of this paper public utilities can be regarded as the non-social part of the infra-structure of a modern economy. That is the services provided by transport, power, water and communications—those industries providing a service by means of wires, cables, pipes and rails, namely gas, water, electricity, telecommunications, sanitation, railways (see Figure 1).

They have one common requirement, large amounts of capital required for their initial provision of large quantities of expensive specialised equipment. Because of this large investment these industries tend to be "natural" monopolies. Since they supply essential goods and services they are generally subject to public regulations designed to ensure that they operate "in the public interest". This public regulation ranges from price control or limitation of the rate of profitability

59

E. F. MELLEN

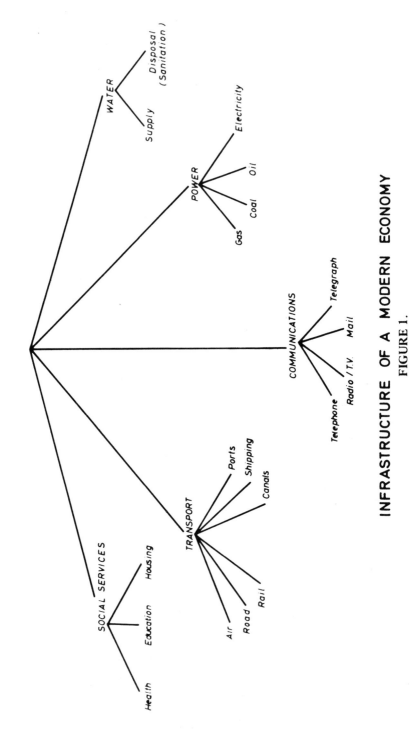

INFRASTRUCTURE OF A MODERN ECONOMY
FIGURE 1.

n invested capital to complete nationalisation (*cf.* App. II). The types of conrol under which these organisations operate has a fundamental bearing on their bjectives and thus of the constraints which are used in any model of their peration. A very significant feature of their operation is the irreversibility of many of the large capital decisions. For instance, a reservoir and the pipe system inking it to its consumers cannot be altered once it has been constructed. For his reason capital investment decision making is the key to successful operation of large utilities.

Generally speaking the financing of capital is the largest item in the cost tructure of utilities. Appendix I gives three examples from electricity, gas and water utilities, showing the proportion of this item to total revenue. This again ighlights the major problem of a utility—the optimisation of capital investment.

II. Objectives and constraints

Before we can construct a model or series of models to assist in capital investment planning or to fulfil other purposes we must consider the objectives or the goals of the system itself. This is essential if subsequent model structure is to be elevant. It will happen indeed that in our structuring of a model we continually eassess the objectives of the system as a whole and, in fact, when models have been developed and are being used to assist in the making of decisions the extra information supplied by the model may in fact cause us to alter some of the undamental objectives of the system as a whole.

We must be clear at the outset what we mean by an objective. With artificial henomena there is always a purpose, a goal, or a body of objectives which one lans to achieve. Every organisation has a purpose; the motives behind this purpose may be moral, material or a complex combination of factors. The escription of this purpose takes explicit form when one defines the objectives o be attained. In most cases there are several objectives, for instance to equal or etter a given output, not to exceed a certain investment level, not to exceed a iven percentage of overhead. These objectives are actually constraints and when we talk about optimising an *economic function* this will generally be some alanced combination of objectives.

By objective in this paper we shall indicate the goal to be achieved, the goal to e bettered, or the limit not to be exceeded (as the case may be) and note that here can be several objectives. By constraint we shall indicate a limitation over which we have, or do not have, control. The objectives and constraints taken ogether constitute mathematical restrictions. The function to be optimised, which represents the value associated with the system or the operation, we will all the economic function. This function is always unique. In certain problems he economic function can be an objective; for example, an industrialist may ake his own profit as his sole objective. In this case the other limitations are only onstraints.

In the case of public utilities which, as we have pointed out above, are genera constrained to operate "in the public interest" it is incumbent upon us to explor the governmental policy objectives which the given utility is expected to achieve e.g. in the case of the power industries, it is highly relevant to have a clear idea c the objectives of the government as regards the energy sector as a whole and still further an idea of governmental policy as regards the total economy in whose in structure the energy sector plays a vital role. In a similar way the objectives of t Federal Power Commission in America are highly relevant to the corporate obje ives set by American utilities in the gas and electricity sectors. (See Appendix I)

The statutory duties of nationalised industries are broadly to meet demand f their products and services in the most efficient way and to conduct their financ so that over time they at least break even, after making a contribution to reserve

However, in the past no guidance has been given on what is meant by efficien in economic terms and only a minimum standard of financial performance was prescribed. This was defined in terms of surplus (or deficit); it differs from the ordinary concept of profit (or loss) in that provision must be made for all items properly chargeable to revenue under the statutes. Later this requirement was made more specific and further guidance for nationalised industries was set out the White Paper on the Financial and Economic Obligations of the Nationalised Industries in 1961. This interpreted the statutory provisions as meaning that industry should aim to balance its accounts "taking one year with another" over a period of five years, after providing for interest, and depreciation at histo cost. Provision should also be made for the difference between depreciation at historic cost and replacement cost, and for allocations to reserve sufficient to make some contribution towards the Industry's future capital development pro- gramme and as a safeguard against premature obsolescence and similar contin- gencies. Financial objectives or targets were to be determined for each under- taking in the light of its needs and capabilities in relation to these criteria. In practice, targets have normally been expressed as a rate of return on the under- taking's assets though other methods of expressing them were not ruled out. Th Government's White Paper (Cmnd. 3437) has made the objectives more explicit:—

"The Government's objectives for industry are to increase the productivity o both labour and capital employed; to raise the rate of new capital formation to ensure that new equipment is as technologically advanced as possible and as effectively deployed; to increase the profitability of new investment; and to obtain the maximum return in terms of the production of goods and services.

Investment projects must normally show a satisfactory return in commercial terms unless they are justifiable on wider criteria involving an assessment of the social costs and benefits involved or are provided to meet a statutory obligation. Subject to these considerations the Government's policy is to treat the industries as commercial bodies and the underlying concept behind the control of nationalised industry's investment by rate of return is that the most efficient distribution of goods and services in the economy as a whole can be secured only if investments are made where the return to the economy is greatest. This holds true whatever the level of investment in the economy. The rate of return on new capital is not the same as the overall return on net assets; the two may diverge quite widely."

The Government has further requested that discounted cash flow techniques be used in assessing capital investment and that the test discount rate be 8%.

It is obvious that the criterion of operating 'in the public interest' is a difficult one to convert into mathematical terms, and particularly difficult to relate to a single economic function. However, as far as the nationalised public utility sector is concerned the Government has laid down as the principal objective, financial targets for the percentage return on the net assets of these undertakings.

Figure 2 gives an analysis of the problem areas facing the Gas Industry today and also the types of constraints that operate. Very similar problems and constraints apply to most public utilities: geographical, governmental, and resource availability (feedstocks, labour, plant construction etc). Within these constraints, decisions have to be made about the production or supply of the given product or service and about its marketing.

Having clarified our ideas about the objectives of the utility and explored their relationship to overall governmental policy we are now in a position to consider the purposes for which we wish to construct the model.

Objectives of a utility model

The model is an ordered representation of the system or a part of the system for one or other of the following objectives: —

      (a) Prediction
      (b) Exploring Policy alternatives
      (c) Optimisation

Different techniques will be used in structuring the model according to which of the above purposes we are particularly concerned with. This itself, is in part determined by the system objective which we have previously defined, therefore actual work on structuring a model cannot properly begin until the system objectives and then the model objectives have been clearly agreed.

The main problem we are concerned with is that of planning of a future which is only known imperfectly. At intervals in time decisions have to be made which will be implemented in succeeding years; some of these decisions are immutable; some can, to a very limited extent, be changed. If the future were known with precision then a set of decisions stretching many years ahead could be mapped out and adhered to quite closely. However, when the future is known with little precision and may hold great changes such long range planning loses its meaning and all that the planner can do at any one point is take the best set of decisions in the context of his knowledge of the future at that time. This is not to say that the

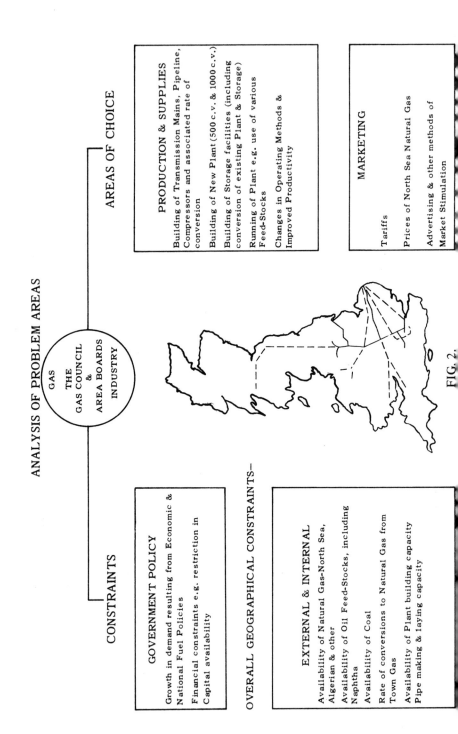

ANALYSIS OF PROBLEM AREAS

CONSTRAINTS

AREAS OF CHOICE

THE
GAS COUNCIL
&
AREA BOARDS
GAS
INDUSTRY

PRODUCTION & SUPPLIES

Building of Transmission Mains, Pipeline, Compressors and associated rate of conversion

Building of New Plant (500 c.v. & 1000 c.v.)

Building of Storage facilities (including conversion of existing Plant & Storage)

Running of Plant e.g. use of various Feed-Stocks

Changes in Operating Methods & Improved Productivity

MARKETING

Tariffs

Prices of North Sea Natural Gas

Advertising & other methods of Market Stimulation

GOVERNMENT POLICY

Growth in demand resulting from Economic & National Fuel Policies

Financial constraints e.g. restriction in Capital availability

OVERALL GEOGRAPHICAL CONSTRAINTS—

EXTERNAL & INTERNAL

Availability of Natural Gas-North Sea, Algerian & other

Availability of Oil Feed-Stocks, including Naphtha

Availability of Coal

Rate of conversions to Natural Gas from Town Gas

Availability of Plant building capacity

Pipe making & laying capacity

FIG. 2.

planner is taking an isolated set of decisions at any one instance. On the contrary he is taking one set of decisions now which are part of a whole decision sequence, which then constrain future decisions in the sequence.

Any mechanism constructed as an aid to planning must embody the recognition that consequent upon its planning decision, the Utility in the future will pass through a sequence of configurations or states determined with respect to the availability of resources and the demand upon them. There will be a best sequence of such states, and probably also a best set of "lower level" decisions with respect to the day to day operation of such a state. Further, a planning mechanism must be in such a form that the planner can assess quantitatively how dependent his decisions are upon his knowledge (or lack of knowledge) of the future.

The models described below are planning mechanisms which refer especially to the operation of public utilities. Many complex decisions have to be made and the models are structured in a form in which the interactions of decisions can be tested against external variables not entirely under the utility's control.

Feedback between model results and systems objectives

An important continuing use of models is in testing the effects of altering fundamental system objectives. This can provide a feedback of information to the governmental policy maker on the likely effects of certain changes in policy. This type of feedback will grow in industry as more companies develop overall business models, the results of which can be incorporated into total industry models, and thence into National Econometric Models.

IV. Some models for capital investment decision making

Figure 3 is a simplified representation of a general business model that probably applies to the bulk of private industry. In general the main objective of the business is to survive and this means, in money terms, earning a sufficient surplus to raise new capital or to continue to finance existing capital. As a result the structure of the model is such as to bring out clearly, so that it may be optimized, the relationship between surplus and capital, and therefore, the relationship between sales revenue and operating costs. It can be seen from the figure that there are three main functions which may themselves be looked at separately and, in fact, in many cases operational research models are applied to "sub-optimize" one of the systems; sales, operations or finance.

The simplest model, which gives a 'snapshot' of the firm is the Annual Account. Corporate mathematical models build into this both a time scale, and also mathematical relationships describing the operating structure and constraints of the organization. In this way the detail of the 'picture' is improved.

The following are brief descriptions of two methods of tackling the problem of

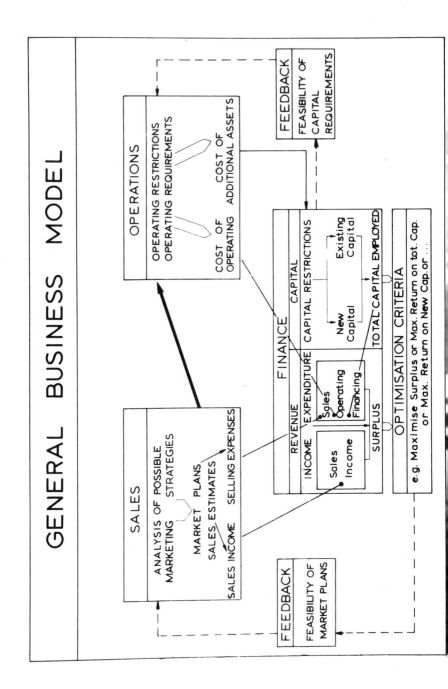

GENERAL BUSINESS MODEL

Capital Investment Decision Making. Essentially, these are planning models giving the best sequence or plan of investments to meet certain criteria. As has been mentioned above, in utilities nearly all capital decisions are irreversible and therefore at all times previous capital decisions form part of the constraints operating now. Capital investment decisions have to be considered as a complete integrated sequence rather than as individual projects.

A. Dynamic programming supply cost model

This model aims at minimizing investment and operating costs over a number of time intervals, e.g. years. During each of the intervals demand for the service may be satisfied in a number of different ways. The minimum cost 'route' over the whole planning period is therefore one out of a large number of possible ways. If for example in each of the years there were ten different states (combinations of plants or facilities) possible then the number of combinations in 20 years would be 10^{20}. It would be quite impossible to consider all these alternatives. The technique of Dynamic Programming gives us a means of reducing this number to manageable proportions.

It can be seen that each state, although it depends on the previous state in determining new facilities required, is independent of future states. Thus we start with the first year when there is only one state (the present set of facilities being used). Consider the second year, choose all feasible states for that year and the minimum cost route to each of these states. In the third year all feasible states are considered in turn with each of the feasible states of the second year and the minimum cost route determined. This is continued for each year. The economy of the method lies in that only the combinations between two successive years need be considered. The figure opposite gives a diagrammatic picture of the model. The final route chosen will be that leading to the state in the final year with the lowest minimum cost path. The number of cost comparisons made by this technique with ten different states in each year covering a planning period of 20 years would be 1910 which compares favourably with the 10^{20} comparisons that would be made if all possibilities were enumerated. This type of model is based on Bellman's Principle of Optimality which states:—

"An optimal policy has the property that whatever the initial state and initial decision are the remaining decisions must constitute an optimal policy with regard to the state resulting from the first decision".

References 8, 9, 10 describe the development and use of this type of model in the Gas Industry.

The main uses of this type of model are as follows:—

1. Exploring the effect on capital requirements, phasing and supply cost of changes in demand. Such changes in demand will be related to environmental changes, new technological uses, competitors' strategy, own strategy, etc.

2. Exploring the effect of changes in particular costs, either of plant construction and operation, or of raw material prices. New methods of supply can

also be introduced to test their effectiveness in the system as a whole (e.g. desalination plants, added to the complex of reservoirs).

3. Insofar as different plants or facilities within the undertaking will use different feedstocks the optimal interdependence between capital costs and feedstock costs can be evaluated—it may not always be best to use the cheapest feedstock.

B. Linear programming models

A linear program is a special case of the mathematical program in which the constraints and the objective function only use linear variables. A solution refers to a specific set of variables which satisfies all the constraints.

Over the last few years the increasing size and speed of computers has made feasible the solution of very large linear programs. A few years ago it was only possible to solve complex L.P. models which related to single time periods. Now multi-time period models are feasible.

Essentially this model is built round a flow chart of the operations of the utility, e.g. generation and distribution of electricity, material flow (oil, gas, water) distribution patterns (transport of people and goods, communication flows etc.).

These operations can be described approximately by equations describing the cost of capacities required to meet given demands. Constraints will generally refer to limitations on capacity in certain places or at certain times, and to limitations on capital available for new capacities.

In general we have a number N of activities which are considered in T time periods. Each activity, x_{nt}, (activity n, period t) will incur costs c_{rt} and be subject to constraints of the following form.

$$\sum_{n=1}^{N} a_{rnt} \; x_{rt} \quad b_{rt} \qquad \text{for the } r^{th} \text{ constraint and the } t^{th} \text{ time period.}$$

The linear programming model finds the lowest possible cost of the economic function

$$\sum_{n=1}^{N} \sum_{t=1}^{T} c_{rt} \; x_{rt}$$

subject to carrying out the activities required and permitted by the constraints.

The techniques used in tackling these L.P.s can also involve parametric, separable and integer programming.

The uses of this type of model are similar to those of the Dynamic Programming approach. Information is readily obtained on original costs and shadow prices. The main disadvantage is the larger computing facility required, though this is offset by ease in programming and the use of 'packaged' L.P. programs.

C. An optimization model

As well as the use of fairly complex models mentioned above, some policy decisions can be assisted by fairly simple but powerful optimization techniques. The following is an approach to optimizing transport fleet size when sub-contracting of work is possible. This is a problem of balancing the amount of traffic to be handled by one's own resources with the amount to be sub-contracted, taking into account the respective costs and profit margins in order to minimize the total cost.

The first requirement is knowledge of the pattern of demand. A simple case is that in which the distribution is Normal with a coefficient of variation 25%. This first approximation is accurate enough to draw general conclusions relating to the principles of fleet planning policy. The mathematical treatment of this problem is given in Appendix III together with tables to interpret the formulae as follows.

Table I — Guide to gross sub-contractors' earnings expected. If the proportion of traffic sub-contracted is on average more or less than this, then the fleet size is too small or too large.

Table II — Proportion of days in which some sub-contracting is required—again if this is on average more or less than that expected the fleet size is too small or too large.

Table III— Gives the fleet capacity in relation to average traffic demand. If the capacity is smaller or larger than this the fleet should be enlarged or reduced accordingly.

Figure 4 gives curves of the cost function for some values of sub-contractors' commission. The relationship of fleet capacity with demand is the main determinant of profitability and this model is an example of the power of relatively simple mathematical techniques in achieving an optimal or near optimal policy.

V. Review of some models being used in the energy sector

The oil companies have for a long time been major users of linear programming models. Initially the majority of these applications concerned the production programme for single refineries and were optimum mix problems. This is only a part

FIG. 4.

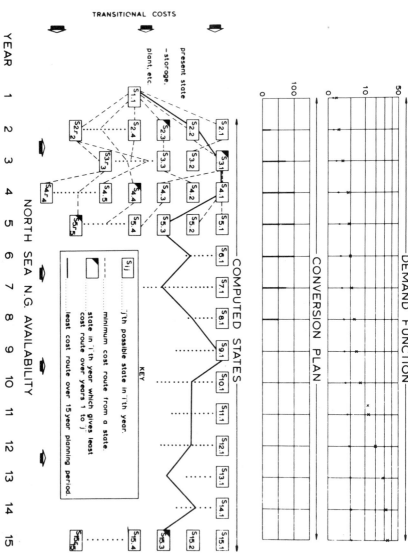

of the more general problem of supplying market requirements at minimum cost. In an integrated oil company operating crude oil fields in many parts of the world, transporting and refining and then supplying markets, again in many different parts of the world, the number of different plans which can be considered is very large. Fortunately computing power has expanded rapidly in the last few years and it is now possible to handle the very large computations required in a generalized L.P. Model of a complete oil company. However, in dealing with overall corporate problems it is found that smaller models, individually tailored to particular problems, can be used very effectively. The suite of models used by Esso's corporate planning department (Ref. No. 6 and *Fin. Times* 17.5.68) give the decision makers tools to explore the short term, medium term and long term results of certain decisions. Three models are used—an econometric model for short term environmental forecasting and economic analysis; a horizon year optimization model for long range corporate objectives setting; and a multi-time period simulation model for financial forecasting and planning both in the short and long term.

In the electricity and gas industries linear programming type models have been used successfully in multi-plant operation, where the programs have been used to minimize the costs of producing certain energy levels from a complex of inter-linked plants, whose operating characteristics and costs per energy unit (capital and operating) vary widely. Recently the advent of North Sea gas has increased the need for models taking a more comprehensive view of the gas industry (Ref. 8, 9, 10).

The National Coal Board uses linear programming techniques for distribution models and also in production models of various coalfields where over the medium term (5 years) the outputs required from different collieries are defined. A demand forecasting model has also been developed to assist in the marketing of domestic solid fuel (Ref. 11 and 12).

The Government itself, long recognizing the need for an energy infrastructure which makes optimal use of the energy resources available, has instituted the development of a National Fuel Model. It is likely that this model will be an "indicative" one, giving guidance to the policy makers on the effects of duties and subsidies in various parts of the energy sector.

In general, therefore, considerable skill and experience is being deployed in the energy sector, developing and using models, whose results are either directly concerned with capital investment decisions or are closely related to them.

VI. Conclusion

In this paper we have considered some of the large scale problems facing the decision makers of utilities. The setting of objectives has been stressed because without this preliminary work, subsequent model development may be irrelevant and valueless. The use of some techniques of mathematical programming has been described in relation to the capacity and investment decisions that have to be taken and a brief review (by no means exhaustive) has been given of some of the model work undertaken in the energy sector of the economy.

A final word of warning—just as the data processing experts say—"Rubbish in, rubbish out" so too an ill formed model will have little value, if it is not positively misleading. But, a carefully formulated model, with realistic objectives, assumptions and evaluation can give decision makers a valuable and powerful tool.

REFERENCES AND BIBLIOGRAPHY

1. *Dynamic Programming* – R. Bellman (Princeton).

2. *Applied Dynamic Programming* – R. Bellman and S.E. Dreyfus (Princeton).

3. *Methods & Models of Operational Research* – S. Kaufman (Prentice Hall).

4. *Management Models and Industrial Applications of Linear Programming* – A. Charnes an W.W. Cooper, Vols. 1 and 2 (Wiley).

5. *Scientific Programming in Business and Industry* – A. Vazsonyi (Wiley).

6. Models for Environmental Forecasting and Corporate Planning – B. Wagle; submitted to Operational Research Quarterly.

7. The Application of Linear Programming to Integrated Supply Problems in the Oil Industry – A.R. Catchpole. *O.R.Q.* Vol. 13 (2).

8. The Use of Long Range Planning Models in Determining the Capacity and Timing Program of a Gas Transport System – E.F. Mellen. E.C.E. Symposium on the Economics of Gas Transport (Budapest, Oct. 1967).

9. Operational Research in the Gas Industry – E.F. Mellen. *I.G.E. Journal* Vol. 8 and 6 (Jan. 1968).

10. Operational Research Models of the U.K. Gas Industry – E.F. Mellen. Research, Utilization and Marketing Conference, American Gas Association, February, 1968.

11. The Marketing of Domestic Solid Fuel – by D.A.V. Edmonds and R.G. Beatty. O.R. Conference Edinburgh, Sept. 1968.

12. Some Aspects of Planning in Coal Mining – W. Young, J.G. Fergusson, and B. Corbishley *O.R.Q.* Vol. 14 (1).

APPENDIX I
EXAMPLES OF COST STRUCTURES OF UTILITIES

Electricity utility cost structure

	£ mill.	%
Generation and Purchase of Electricity	466·6	44·1
Main Transmission and Distribution	66·3	6·3
Consumer Service, Collection, Research, Administration, Welfare etc. (less profit from sales of appliances)	97·9	9·2
Rates	32·8	3·1
Depreciation, Interest and Financing Expenses	373·9	35·3
Balance of Revenue	20·6	2·0
Total Income (Less Profit on Appliances)	1058·1	100

Source: Elec. Council Annual Report 1966

Bulk water supply cost structure

Supply Boards

	Coquet d/1000 gals.	%	Derwent Valley d/1000 gals.	%	River Dove d/1000 gals.	%
Working Expenses	8·73	36·7	4·17	41·6	10·83	35·4
Debt Charges	14·54	61·2	6·12	61·1	18·53	60·5
Appropriation/Net Loss or Investment Income	0·49	2·1	0·27 Cr.	(2·7)	1·27	4·1
Total Income	23·76	100	10·02	100	30·63	100

Source: Water Statistics 1966/7

Hypothetical future natural gas industry

	£ mill.	%
Total Gas and Materials (18·000 mill. therm.)	225 }	31·8
Cost of Manufacture (including storage)	25 }	
Distribution	100	12·7
Consumer Service, Collection. Admin., Welfare	82	10·4
Rates (as now)	19	2·4
Depreciation, Interest and Profit @ 12%	291	37·0
Unaccounted Gas	44	5·7
Total Cost	786	100

Source: The Future of the Natural Gas Industry in Great Britain—IGE Communication 717

APPENDIX II

FEDERAL POWER COMMISSION AND GAS PRICES (U.S.A.)

"Last week, when the Supreme Court upheld the prices fixed for gas at the well-head by the Federal Power Commission, the consumers of natural gas won a victory which has been 30 years in coming. The Natural Gas Act was passed in 1938; in 1954 the Supreme Court held that it required the commission to regulat the prices charged by the independent producers of the gas to the pipeline companies as well as those charged by these distributors. In 1963 the Court approved the commission's decision to fix ceiling prices, based on average costs, for whole producing areas rather than struggle with the impossible task of fixing prices for each producer. Three years ago a double standard, with higher prices for "new" gas, to encourage exploration, was finally laid down for the Permian Basin, in Texas and New Mexico, which supplies about 11 per cent of America's natural gas. Recently its price has been rising but now that the Court has over-ruled the producers' objections, lower costs are on the way for consumers in California and the Middle West, some $40 million is to be refunded and the FPC has a green light to fix permanent prices for almost all producers of natural gas. This will take time but the way the commission sets temporary maximums was upheld fully by the Court in the second decision this week."

Extract from The Economist: 11–17 May, 1968

APPENDIX III

OPTIMAL FLEET SIZE – MATHEMATICAL DERIVATION

Derivation of Total Cost of Own Fleet plus Sub-Contracting

Definitions

$\mathfrak{T}$ *(t)* — Function representing distribution pattern of daily traffic t.

F — Fleet Costs (varying directly with fleet size)

m — Average operating surplus (margin) obtained by a vehicle which does not incur idle time waiting for work, expressed as a fraction

s — Sub-contracting commission (margin) obtained

$\tilde{\jmath}$ — Capacity of traffic that can be handled by fleet (cost F) working at standard efficiency and incurring no idle time waiting for work

Capacities and costs are expressed in units of sterling.

By definition $\tilde{\jmath}\,(1 - m) = F$

Conditions Assumed

Each day traffic that cannot be handled is sub-contracted. Sub-contraction is always possible at a commission of $s\%$.

Costs independent of fleet size are not included.

As a first approximation for a given fleet size, fleet costs are considered fixed within the fluctuations of daily demand.

Total Cost of Handling Traffic

Costs are incurred by the operation of the fleet and by the charges made by sub-contractors.

For fleet size $\tilde{\jmath}$

$$\text{Fleet Costs } F = (1 - m)\,\tilde{\jmath}$$

Traffic demand in excess of $\tilde{\jmath}\left(= \dfrac{F}{1 - m} \right)$ must be sub-contracted.

Hence, charge by sub-contractors $= (1 - s) \int_{\tilde{\sigma}}^{\infty} (t - \tilde{\sigma}) \mathfrak{T}(t) dt$

Hence, Total Cost $= (1 - m)\tilde{\sigma} + (1 - s) \int_{\tilde{\sigma}}^{\infty} (t - \tilde{\sigma}) \mathfrak{T}(t) dt$ (1)

This expression varies with $\tilde{\sigma}$ and to be a minimum

$$\frac{d(\text{Total Cost})}{d\tilde{\sigma}} = 0$$

Now $\dfrac{d(\text{Total Cost})}{d\tilde{\sigma}} = (1 - m) + (1 - s)\dfrac{d}{d\tilde{\sigma}} \displaystyle\int_{\tilde{\sigma}}^{\infty} (t - \tilde{\sigma}) \mathfrak{T}(t) dt$

$$= (1 - m) + (1 - s) \int_{\tilde{\sigma}}^{\infty} -\mathfrak{T}(t) dt$$

$\dfrac{d(\text{Total Cost})}{d\tilde{\sigma}} = 0$ gives:—

$$0 = (1 - m) - (1 - s)\int_{\tilde{\sigma}}^{\infty} \mathfrak{T}(t) dt$$

or $\displaystyle\int_{\tilde{\sigma}}^{\infty} \mathfrak{T}(t) dt = \dfrac{1 - m}{1 - s}$ (2)

This expression indicates the average proportion of days on which sub-contracting will be required. It will be seen to decrease as m becomes greater in relation to s, i.e. the more efficient the fleet, the less sub-contracting required for a given traffic distribution.

Figure 5 gives graphs of the total cost function divided by the average level of earnings. The traffic distribution $\mathfrak{T}(t)$ is Normal with average T and coefficient of variation $\sigma/T = \cdot25$ or 25%

i.e. the graphs represent the function

$$(1 - m)\frac{\tilde{\sigma}}{T} + (1 - s) \int_{\tilde{\sigma}/T}^{+\infty} \left(\frac{t - \tilde{\sigma}}{T}\right) \frac{4}{\sqrt{2\pi}} e^{-8\left(\frac{t}{T} - 1\right)^2} d\left(\frac{t}{T}\right)$$

over values of $\tilde{\sigma}/T$ from 0 to 1·2 with values of sub-contracting margin (s) 0, ·1, ·2 (or 0%, 10%, 20%) and fleet operating margin (m) ·3 (or 30%).

These graphs show the total cost as a percentage of earnings and show that even when sub-contracting obtains no commission $(s = 0\%)$ it is still worthwhile to sub-contract to keep fleet size down and therefore to incur less waiting time. As the sub-contracting margin increases the optimum fleet size decreases.

Tables I, II and III have been worked out so that the formula can be easily interpreted directly for known values of s and m.

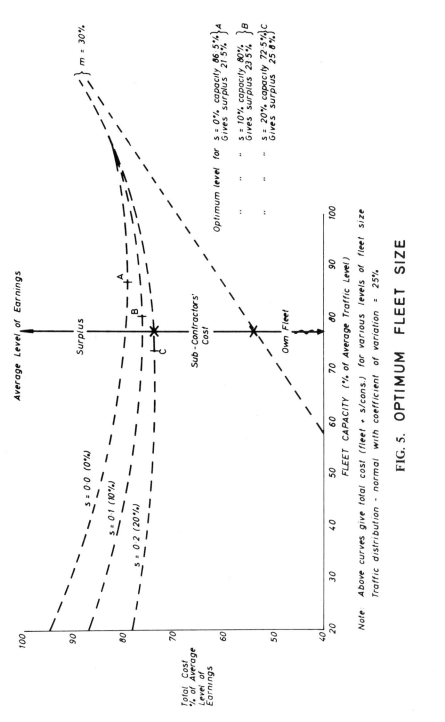

FIG. 5. OPTIMUM FLEET SIZE

TABLE I. PROPORTION OF TRAFFIC SUB-CONTRACTED AS % OF TOTAL TRAFFIC

	m%				
s%	25	30	35	40	50
0	21	17·5	15·5	13	10
5	23	19·5	16·5	14	10·5
10	26·5	22	18·5	15·5	11·5
15	30·5	25·5	21·5	17·5	12·5
20	38·5	30	25	20·5	14·0
25	100	38	29	23·5	16·0

TABLE II. PROPORTION OF DAYS SOME SUB-CONTRACTING REQUIRED, %

$$\left(= \frac{1 - m}{1 - s} \right)$$

	m%				
s%	25	30	35	40	50
0	75	70	65	60	50
5	79	74	68·5	63	52·5
10	82.5	77	71·5	66	55
15	88	82·5	76·5	70	59
20	94	87·5	81·5	75	62·5
25	100	93·5	87	80	65·5

TABLE III. OPTIMUM FLEET CAPACITY AS % OF AVERAGE TRAFFIC DEMAND

	$m\%$				
$s\%$	25	30	35	40	50
0	83	87	90	94	100
5	80	84	88	92	98
10	76	81	85	89	96
15	71	77	82	87	94
20	61	71	78	83	92
25	—	62	72	79	89

Note: Final Operating Surplus at Optimum Level of

$$\text{Capacity} = 100 - \left(1 - \frac{s}{100}\right)X_1 - \left(1 - \frac{m}{100}\right)X_3 \text{ where}$$

X_1 and X_3 are entries from Tables I and III corresponding to known s and m.

5. A MODEL OF BRAND LOYALTIES

GRAHAM PYATT

CONTENTS

Introduction

This paper is in two parts. The first is concerned with models of the pattern of repeat purchasing by households of brands of non-durable consumer goods. As such it is concerned with the same topic as the pioneering paper by Ehrenberg (4) and, indeed, follows directly from it. This paper by Ehrenberg was cited by Kendall (5) as an example of the fact that "quantitative patterns do exist in economics and can be brought out even where we have little quantitative knowledge about the causal system"*. The analysis presented here is largely the result of brooding over the existence of these patterns since Ehrenberg first brought them to light†. Since his paper was published, the same author has made many further contributions to which reference may be made through the bibliography of Chatfield, Ehrenberg and Goodhardt (3). In all this later work, however, the basic model of the first paper is maintained with modifications. This model describes the distribution of purchasing frequencies for a branded good by a negative binomial distribution. The distribution fits the data well subject to a phenomenon called by Ehrenberg "the variance discrepancy".

---

*   Kendall (5) p.10

†   I am grateful to Mr. K. Gribben for having brought Ehrenberg's first paper to my notice, and for emphasising its importance, when in 1960, I was temporarily employed by Unilever Ltd. Much more recently I have benefited greatly by being brought up to date with his work by Mr. Ehrenberg himself, and by discussing an earlier draft of this paper with him.

An alternative model is proposed here based on the compound binomial distribution. It is suggested that this will fit the data equally well and, indeed, might not be subject to the variance discrepency. However, these propositions are not tested empirically.

The material in the first part of this paper is presented in three sections. Ehrenberg's negative binomial model is explained in the first section and the compound binomial model is described in the second section. In the third section the two models are compared and the variance discrepancy problem is explored.

The second part of the paper is devoted to the formulation and discussion of a model of brand loyalties. This model also makes use of the compound binomial distribution and is concerned with the determination of the probability distribution of the number of times each brand of a commodity is bought, given the number of times the commodity is bought. It is called a model of brand loyalty since it not only yields expressions for the market share of each brand but also permits exploration of the extent to which a given market share is derived from a number of loyal buyers as opposed to a greater number of more casual customers.

The brand loyalty model is presented in four sections. In the first the model is defined for the duopoly situation of two competing brands. Alternative measures of loyalty are considered in the second section, use being made of the Lorenz curve analysis of concentration in deriving the second of these. The model is generalised to markets involving several brands in the third section. Finally, in the fourth section, there is a very brief discussion of some limitations of the model, including the fact that it applies only to a period of time during which tastes can be assumed to be constant.

I Models of purchasing frequency

1. *The negative binomial model*

The negative binomial model assumes that the number of times a particular product is purchased by a household during a finite time period has a Poisson distribution*. Thus denoting the number of purchases by X, it is assumed that

$$\Pr(x) = e^{-\mu}\frac{\mu^x}{x!} \quad \text{for } x = 0, 1, \ldots \infty$$

The model further assumes that the Poisson parameter μ varies between households, and that its distribution is of the Pearson Type III. Thus

---

* In Ehrenberg's paper (4) the random variable which is studied is the number of units of a product bought, and not the number of occasions on which it is bought. Which is the more appropriate formulation must depend on the purpose of the analysis and the "goodness of fit" of the alternatives.

$$f(\mu) = \frac{a^\lambda}{\Gamma(\lambda)} \mu^{\lambda-1} e^{-\alpha\mu} \quad \text{for } 0 < \mu < \infty$$

The Poisson probabilities are now averaged over the distribution of μ to yield

$$\Pr(x) = \frac{1}{x!} \frac{\Gamma(\lambda+x)}{\Gamma(\lambda)} \left(\frac{\alpha}{1+\alpha}\right)^\lambda \left(\frac{1}{1+\alpha}\right)^x$$

$$\text{for } x = 0, 1, 2, \ldots, \infty$$

which is the general term of the negative binomial distribution with parameters α and λ.

Some summary statistics which describe this distribution are as follows:-

$$E(x) = \lambda/\alpha$$

$$\text{Var}(x) = (1 + 1/\alpha) \lambda/\alpha$$

$$E(1 + t)^x = \left(\frac{\alpha}{\alpha - t}\right)^\lambda$$

$$\Pr(0) = \left(\frac{\alpha}{1+\alpha}\right)^\lambda$$

$$\Pr(x+1) = \frac{1}{1+\alpha} \cdot \frac{\lambda+x}{1+x} \cdot \Pr(x)$$

It can be shown that $x = 0$ is the mode of the distribution if the variance exceeds the square of the mean: if it does not, then the mode occurs at a non-zero value of x.

A common method of fitting the negative binomial is to equate the observed sample mean and the relative frequency at $x = 0$ to their theoretical values as stated above, and then to solve (iteratively) for α and λ. This method, due to Anscombe (2), is favoured by Chatfield, Ehrenberg and Goodhardt (3) in the present context.*

One implication of using this method to fit the negative binomial is that it yields estimates of α and λ which, when substituted in the formula for the variance of x, yield a variance estimate which is not necessarily.equal to the sample variance.

Comparison of variance estimates obtained in this way with the observed sample variance is one of the procedures used by Ehrenberg in his first paper to test the goodness of fit of the negative binomial model. After looking at over 150 examples it was concluded that "The agreement between the observed standard deviations and theoretical values of the fitted N(egative) B(inomial)

---

* See Chatfield, Ehrenberg and Goodhardt (3), p. 335.

D(istribution) was also generally good, for standard deviations up to 1 or 2. However, a systematic failure to fit also became apparent: for larger values of the standard deviation, the theoretical value is generally higher than the observed one. The most striking feature of the data . . . is that these discrepancies are themselves extremely regular and systematic."* It is this phenomenon which Ehrenberg calls "the variance discrepancy".

2. The compound binomial model

A model of the frequency of purchasing which is very similar to Ehrenberg's can be built up around the compound binomial distribution. In this model each household is assumed to conduct a series of N Bernoulli trials in which the probability of success, i.e. of purchasing the brand in question, is p. Thus

$$\Pr(x) = \binom{N}{x} p^x (1-p)^{N-x} \qquad \text{for } x = 0, 1, \ldots, N$$

Further, p is assumed to vary between households according to a β-distribution, i.e.

$$f(p) = \frac{1}{B(a, b)} p^{a-1} (1-p)^{b-1} \qquad \text{for } 0 < p < 1$$

so that, averaging over the population of households,

$$\Pr(x) = \binom{N}{x} \frac{B(a + x, b + N - x)}{B(a, b)} \qquad \text{for } x = 0, 1, \ldots, N.$$

which is the general term of the compound binomial distribution with parameters N, a and b.

Some summary statistics which describe the compound binomial distribution are:-

$$E(x) = \frac{Na}{a + b}$$

$$\text{Var}(x) = \frac{Nab}{(a + b)^2} \cdot \frac{a + b + N}{a + b + 1}$$

$$E(1 + t)^x = \sum_{R=0}^{N} \binom{N}{R} t^R \frac{\Gamma(a + b) \Gamma(a + R)}{\Gamma(a) \Gamma(a + b + R)}$$

$$\Pr(0) = \frac{\Gamma(a + b)}{\Gamma(b)} \cdot \frac{\Gamma(b + N)}{\Gamma(a + b + N)}$$

$$\Pr(x + 1) = \frac{a + x}{1 + x} \cdot \frac{N - x}{b - 1 + N - x} \cdot \Pr(x)$$

---

* See Chatfield, Ehrenberg and Goodhardt (3), p.330.

The compound binomial distribution is either positively or negatively skewed depending on which of the parameters a and b is the greater. It has a mode at $x = 0$ if

$$a < 1 + \frac{b-1}{N}$$

and at $x = N$ if

$$b < 1 + \frac{a-1}{N}$$

Otherwise the mode occurs at $x = M$ where

$$\frac{N(a-1) - (b-1)}{a + b} < M < \frac{(N + 1)(a-1)}{a + b - 2}$$

In fitting the compound binomial distribution two cases must be distinguished, namely the case when N is known and that when it is not known. Both are discussed by Skellam (7).

The question of whether or not N is known brings to the fore some ambiguities as to how this parameter should be interpreted. A simple interpretation of N would be that it is the number of times a housewife goes out shopping. Accordingly, on each such trip a Bernoulli trial is conducted, with "success" being achieved by buying the product in question. However, the compound binomial model assumes N is the same for all households, so that application of the model might have to be restricted to sub-samples of the population that go shopping with the same frequency. Alternatively, N could be thought of as the number of occasions on which a housewife *might* go shopping. It may be more reasonable to assume that N is the same for all households given this interpretation, but it is difficult to see how this view could be empirically tested.

The fact that the appropriate interpretation of N is not clear is a weakness of the formulation, and the above discussion by no means exhausts the possibilities. But perhaps it is a weakness which is not wholly regrettable, since there is some advantage in bringing issues involving shopping habits and facilities into discussion of the frequency of purchases.

3. *Comparison of the models*

As has been shown by Skellam (7), the negative binomial distribution is a limiting form of the compound binomial obtained by considering what happens as $N \to \infty$ subject to $a \to \lambda$ and $b \to \alpha N$. The result is most easily demonstrated in terms of the ratio of the probabilities of successive values of x. Thus

$$\frac{\Pr(x+1)}{\Pr(x)} = \frac{a+x}{1+x} \cdot \frac{1}{1+\dfrac{b-1}{N-x}}$$

$$= \frac{(\lambda+x)+(a-\lambda)}{1+x} \cdot \frac{1}{1+\alpha+\dfrac{b-\alpha N}{N-x}+\dfrac{\alpha x-1}{N-x}}$$

$$\to \frac{\lambda+x}{1+x} \cdot \frac{1}{1+\alpha}$$

under the conditions stated.

Skellam notes that "In many cases the (compound and negative binomial distributions) give almost identical results, even for moderate values of N".* Accordingly it can be assumed that the compound binomial distribution will fit data on the frequency of purchases fairly well.

Ehrenberg (4) has noted that, in using the negative binomial distribution, "The bias in the standard deviations is always positive and reasonably consistent.† This suggests that it should be possible to find another class of distribution which will fit these data better". The question arises, therefore, of whether or not the compound binomial is such a distribution.

If a distribution is to give a better fit to Ehrenberg's data in the sense that it does not have a "variance discrepancy" then it must necessarily have a smaller variance for given values of $\Pr(0)$ and $E(x)$. This is not a sufficient condition, however, since the variance of an alternative distribution might be too small, thus giving rise to a "variance discrepancy" in the opposite direction to that of the negative binomial.

The compound binomial distribution can be shown to satisfy the above necessary condition. The result to be proved is that if the parameter N of the compound binomial is increased to $N+1$, whilst the mean of the distribution stays fixed at some value m, then the variance must increase if the probability $\Pr(0)$ is to remain constant. In other words, as between different compound

---

*See Skellam (7), p. 250.

†In the later paper (3) it is suggested (p. 332) that the bias is described by

$$(\sigma^2-m)^{\frac{1}{2}}-(s^2-m)^{\frac{1}{2}} \doteqdot m$$

where s^2 is the sample variance and σ^2 is the value of the population variance calculated by using parameter values estimated from a sample mean and the proportion of non-purchasers.

binomial distributions with the same mean m, and the same $\Pr(0)$, the size of the variance is positively associated with the value of the parameter N. Since the negative binomial is obtained as the limit when N increases without bound it follows that a compound binomial distribution has a smaller variance than a negative binomial if each has the same mean and $\Pr(0)$. The proof is as follows.

Let a, b and N, and a^*, b^* and $N + 1$ be the parameters of two compound binomial distributions.

If the two distributions are to have the same mean, m, then

$$\frac{N a}{a + b} = m = (N + 1)\frac{a^*}{a^* + b^*}$$

from which it follows that

$$b = \frac{a(N-m)}{m} \; ; \; b^* = \frac{a^*(N + 1 - m)}{m}$$

The probability $\Pr(0)$ is given in each case by

$$\frac{\Gamma(a + b)}{\Gamma(b)} \cdot \frac{\Gamma(b + N)}{\Gamma(a + b + N)} = \prod_{R = 0}^{N-1} \frac{b + R}{a + b + R}$$

and

$$\frac{\Gamma(a^* + b^*)}{\Gamma(b^*)} \cdot \frac{\Gamma(b^* + N + 1)}{\Gamma(a^* + b^* + N)} = \prod_{R = 0}^{N} \frac{b^* + R}{a^* + b^* + R}$$

The second of these two probabilities involves an extra term, namely

$$\frac{b^* + N}{a^* + b^* + N}$$

which is necessarily less than one. Accordingly, if the two expressions for $\Pr(0)$ are to be numerically equal, then it follows that

$$\frac{b^* + S}{a^* + b^* + S} > \frac{b + S}{a + b + S}$$

or, from substitution for b^* and b,

$$\frac{a^*(N + 1 - m) + Sm}{a^*(N + 1) + Sm} > \frac{a(N - m) + Sm}{aN + Sm}$$

for all S. This last inequality can be reduced to

$$aa^* + Sam > S a^* m$$

which expresses a necessary condition for the two distributions to have the
same means and $\Pr(0)$'s.

The variances of the two distributions are given by

$$\frac{Na\,b}{(a+b)^2} \cdot \frac{a+b+N}{a+b+1} = m(N-m) \cdot \frac{a+m}{aN+m}$$

and

$$\frac{(N+1)\,a^*\,b^*}{a^*+b^*} \cdot \frac{a^*+b^*+N}{a^*+b^*+1} = m(N+1-m) \cdot \frac{a^*+m}{a^*(N+1)+m}$$

Consequently the second distribution has the larger variance if

$$(N+1-m)\frac{a^*+m}{a^*(N+1)+m} > (N-m)\frac{a+m}{aN+m}$$

which can be reduced to

$$a^*\,a + (N-m)\,Na + (a^*+m+am) > (N-m)\,N\,a^*$$

This relation will be satisfied if

$$a^*\,a + (N-m)\,Na > (N-m)\,N\,a^*$$

But it has already been shown that this last inequality holds, since

$$a^*\,a + S\,a\,m > S\,a^*\,m$$

for all S. Thus the result is established.

The theorem just proved suggests that if N is a parameter to be estimated from
the data, then the compound binomial distribution is likely to give a better fit
than the negative binomial. Indeed, if "fit" is judged by the variance discrepancy
for given mean and $\Pr(0)$, the compound binomial is sure to be better; it cannot
be worse because by assuming N infinite the two models become identical, and
it is likely to be better because the direction in which the variance is affected by
taking finite values of N is such as to offset the variance discrepancy which has
been found to hold with some consistency.

This conclusion is not very powerful in that a three parameter distribution,
(such as the compound binomial), would normally be expected to give a better
fit than a two parameter model, (like the negative binomial), especially when
the latter is a limiting form of the former. Further, the improved fit anticipated
for the compound binomial is likely to owe much to the fact that its range is
bounded, (by N), while the negative binomial has a "tail" which extends to
infinity. Introduction of a third parameter into the negative binomial by
truncation may remove the advantage which the compound binomial otherwise
has. However, much of the elegance of the negative binomial would be lost thereby

In the light of these considerations the choice between the two distributions must depend in part on their intuitive appeal: is it more helpful to think of consumers as conducting a series of Bernoulli trials with the probability of success being a variable between them, or is it more useful to see purchasing as a Poisson process going on at different rates in different households?

If some way of ascertaining the number of Bernoulli trials could be found other than by looking at the frequency of purchases, then the compound binomial might have a strong claim to being preferred. But as has already been discussed, the correct interpretation of N is by no means clear. Empirical examination of some actual estimates of N may shed light on this problem, but such estimates have not yet been explored. Meanwhile, however, a rather different reason can be given for considering the compound binomial model. It is that this model can be used to study the choice between brands and the loyalty to them of individual consumers. This topic is discussed in the next part of this paper.

II A Model of Brand Loyalties

1. A Two-Brands Model.

The model of brand loyalty to be presented here can be applied to markets in which a commodity is available in any number of brands. However, all the essential features of the model can be demonstrated in the duopoly case, i.e. in the case of two brands only. Since this is the simplest case, it is convenient to begin the exposition with a discussion of it.

Suppose that a commodity is available in two brands, A and B. Let the probability that the consumer shooses A be P_A and the probability that the consumer chooses B be P_B. In this case

$$P_A + P_B = 1$$

If the consumer's preferences remain constant throughout the course of N purchases, and if the choice between A and B is independent of previous choices, then

$$\Pr(X_A, X_B) = \binom{N}{X_A} P_A^{X_A} P_B^{X_B}$$

where X_A is the number of units of A chosen and X_B is the number of units of B chosen. Clearly

$$X_A + X_B = N$$

Assume now that P_A (and therefore its complement, P_B) varies between households, and that this variation is well described by a beta distribution with parameters a and b. As has been shown above in the model of purchasing frequencies, averaging over households will yield an expression for $\Pr(X_A, X_B)$ which is the general term of a compound binomial distribution with parameters N, a and b. Thus

$$\Pr(X_A, X_B) = \binom{N}{X_A} \frac{B(a + X_A, b + X_B)}{B(a, b)},$$

$$\text{for } X_A = N - X_B = 0, 1, 2, \ldots, N$$

This probability is symmetric in X_A and X_B since, of course, $\binom{N}{X_A} = \binom{N}{X_B}$

Again from earlier results, it follows that expected sales of A and B are

$$E(X_A) = \frac{N a}{a + b} \quad ; \quad E(X_B) = \frac{N b}{a + b}$$

Since total sales are N, the expected market shares for A and B are given by s_A and s_B where

$$s_A = \frac{a}{a + b} \quad ; \quad s_B = \frac{b}{a + b}$$

Consequently if $a > b$ then A can be expected to have the larger market share.

2. Measures of Loyalty

It would appear that two alternative concepts are involved in discussions of loyalty within a market. On the one hand loyalty can be understood to be a description of the whole market within which a collection of brands compete. It is not, therefore, a characteristic of individual products, but rather a property of consumer behaviour in relation to a product group which has its converse in brand switching. Quite apart from its intrinsic usefulness, such a concept has the great merit that loyalty is conceived of in a dimension which is oblique to that of market shares. Alternatively, loyalty can be thought of as a property of individual brands. According to this view the difference between two products which each have a half share of their markets, one being bought by everyone half the time, the other being bought by half the people all the time, is a difference of loyalty.

In this and the next section two measures of loyalty are discussed, which reflect the alternative concepts of loyalty. However, in the present section the measures are employed in the duopoly case of market made up to two products. In this context the distinction between alternative concepts of loyalty disappears since a decision to buy A is a decision not to buy B, and vice-versa. Thus if one product is bought by half the people all the time, then this must also be true of the other product : if A is bought by all the people half of the time then so is B. More generally, if the people who buy A are loyal to A then the people who b B must be loyal to B; otherwise they would be buying A some of the time and it would then not be true that all the people who buy A are loyal to A. It would seem to be a matter of logical necessity that in the duopoly case the two products have the same loyalty and any differences between them are differences in market share.

That part of the compound binomial model of the previous section which bears directly on loyalty is the beta distribution which describes how P_A (and hence P_B) varies between households. In terms of it the market share s_A can be broken down to permit examination of the extent to which it is derived from a few people who always choose A as opposed to more people who only buy A some of the time. Thus loyalty towards the product A can be examined as well as its market share.

It is well known that a beta distribution can take on a variety of shapes. If $a < 1$, then the distribution has a mode at $P_A = 0 (= 1 - P_B)$. If $b < 1$, there is a mode at $P_A = 1 (= 1 - P_B)$. Thus if both a and b are less than unity, the distribution is U-shaped. Such a situation would be one of high loyalties : there would be few households in the centre of the range where uncertainty is greatest and most households would be close to being sure about which product to buy. The limiting case in which there is no uncertainty is reached as a and b tend to zero.

An intermediate case arises when both a and b are unity. In this case the beta distribution reduces to a rectangular or uniform distribution. Households are uniformly spread over the whole range of possible values of P_A from 0 to 1.

If both the parameters a and b exceed one, then the distribution has a single mode somewhere within the range 0 to 1. The density function is bell-shaped but may be positively or negatively skewed depending on which of a and b is the greater. Another limiting case is reached as both a and b tend to infinity. In this limit, all the distribution is concentrated at a single point somewhere in the range 0 to 1. In such a situation all households have the same value of P_A, and hence of P_B. This value is equal to the market share of the product, and the compound binomial distribution for X_A reduces to the ordinary binomial form.

It is apparent from this discussion that the distribution of P_A, which is the distribution of loyalty, can vary a great deal even though the market share of A remains constant. This suggests that some measure of the variation in P_A should be used as an index of loyalty, and for this purpose the variance of P_A is an obvious candidate.

The variance of P_A is given by

$$\text{Var}(P_A) = \frac{ab}{(a + b)^2 (a + b + 1)}$$

and is equal to the variance of P_B. Thus the variance satisfies one useful criterion for a loyalty index in that it gives the same value for both products as a description of the market in the duopoly case. It has a deficiency however, in that its range depends on the market shares of a and b. This range is the interval 0 to $s_A s_B$. Its lower limit is reached as $a, b \to \infty$, and its upper limit as $a, b \to 0$.

Accordingly, a preferable index of loyalty is

$$\frac{\text{Var}(P_A)}{s_A s_B} = \frac{\text{Var}(P_B)}{s_A s_B} = \frac{1}{a + b + 1}$$

The variance $\text{Var}(P_A)$ can be computed directly from estimates of a and b, or it can be estimated indirectly from an analysis of brand switching.

In a simple analysis of brand switching it can be assumed that households are asked which of two products they purchased this week and last week. The expected relative frequencies for the four possible answers are set out in the table below.

		Last Week		
		A	B	Total
This week	A	$\dfrac{a(a+1)}{(a+b)(a+b+1)}$	$\dfrac{ab}{(a+b)(a+b+1)}$	$s_A = \dfrac{a}{a+b}$
	B	$\dfrac{ab}{(a+b)(a+b+1)}$	$\dfrac{b(b+1)}{(a+b)(a+b+1)}$	$s_B = \dfrac{a}{a+b}$
Total		$s_A = \dfrac{a}{a+b}$	$s_B = \dfrac{b}{a+b}$	1

It can be noted from the table that the diagonal elements exceed the product of their row and column totals in the general case. The two are equal in the limit as a and b tend to infinity, which corresponds to zero loyalty. This is to be expected since the differences are in fact the (equal) variances of P_A and P_B. Thus denoting the body of the table by a matrix T, and by s a column vector with elements s_A and s_B, a further matrix $T - s\,s'$ can be formed which is the variance-covariance matrix of P_A and P_B. Further let i be a column vector the elements of which are all unity, and let s be the matrix which has the elements of s along its diagonal and all other elements zero. Then the diagonal elements of

$$\hat{s}^{-1}(T - s\,s')\,\hat{s}^{-1} = \hat{s}^{-1}\,T\,\hat{s}^{-1} - ii'$$

are equal to the loyalty index for A and B.

As an alternative to working with the variance of the distribution of P_A, a (different) index of loyalty can be derived from direct consideration of the extent to which purchases are concentrated among households.* For this purpose it is useful to work with the Lorenz curve.

In the present application the Lorenz curve plots a cumulative proportion of purchases against a cumulative proportion of households. The accumulation of households starts with those for whom P_A is the lowest. Thus Y, the cumulative proportion of households, is the distribution function of the beta variate P_A, i.e.

$$Y(\pi) = \frac{1}{B(a, b)} \int_0^\pi P_A{}^{a-1} (1-P_A)^{b-1} dP_A$$

The cumulative proportion of purchases is the distribution function of the first moment distribution of the beta variate P_A. Denoting this proportion by Z, it follows that Z is the proportion to total sales of A which are accounted for by the proportion of households Y. Hence

$$Z(\pi) = \frac{1}{E(X_A)} \cdot \frac{N}{B(a, b)} \int_0^\pi P_A{}^a (1-P_A)^{b-1} dP_A$$

$$= \frac{1}{B(a+1, b)} \int_0^\pi P_A{}^a (1-P_A)^{b-1} dP_A$$

and the Lorenz curve is the graph of $Z(\pi)$ against $Y(\pi)$.

There is a straightforward relationship between $Y(\pi)$ and $Z(\pi)$. It can be obtained by noting that

$$\int P^a(1-P)^{b-1} dP = \frac{-P^a(1-P)^b}{b} + \frac{a}{b} \int P^{a-1}(1-P)^b dP$$

$$= \frac{a}{b} \left[\int P^{a-1}(1-P)^{b-1} dP - \int P^a(1-P)^{b-1} dP \right] - \frac{P^a(1-P)^b}{b}$$

whence

$$\int_0^\pi P_A{}^a (1-P_A)^{b-1} dP_A = \frac{a}{a+b} \int_0^\pi P_A{}^{a-1} (1-P_A)^{b-1} dP_A - \frac{\pi^a(1-\pi)^b}{(a+b)}$$

Substituting this result in the expression for $Z(\pi)$ yields

$$Z(\pi) = Y(\pi) - \frac{\pi^a(1-\pi)^b}{(a+b) B(a+1, b)}$$

It follows from this that $Z(\pi)$ is always less than $Y(\pi)$, which is to be expected since households are accumulated starting with those for whom P_A is lowest.

---

* The discussion in the rest of this section owes much to the parallel discussion of income distributions in Chapter 11 of Aitchison and Brown (1).

From the definitions of $Y(\pi)$ and $Z(\pi)$ it can be shown that

$$dY(\pi) = \frac{\pi^{a-1}(1-\pi)^{b-1}}{B(a, b)} d\pi$$

and

$$dZ(\pi) = \frac{\pi^{a}(1-\pi)^{b-1}}{B(a + 1, b)} d\pi$$

Therefore the slope of the Lorenz curve is given by

$$\frac{dZ}{dY} = \pi \frac{(a + b)}{a} = \frac{\pi}{s_A}$$

From this result it follows that the slope of the Lorenz curve is one when $\pi = s_A$. This means that the proportion of the population that consume less than the average amount of A, i.e. $Y(s_A)$, can be read off from the Lorenz diagram as shown in Figure 1.

Some further and more interesting results can be deduced. First, note that the slope of the Lorenz curve increases as π increases, and therefore as $Y(\pi)$ increases. From this it follows that the Lorenz curve is strictly convex. Secondly when π is zero and therefore when $Y(\pi)$ is zero, the Lorenz curve has zero slope. Finally, when π is one, and therefore when $Y(\pi)$ is one, the slope of the Lorenz curve is $1/s_A$. Thus the lorenz curve is asymmetric, and s_A can be read off from it by simple geometric construction as shown in Figure 2.

Lorenz (6) originally devised the curve named after him to yield a measure of the concentration of the distribution of wealth. The measure he used was the ratio of the area α in Figure 2 to the sum of the areas α, β and γ. If this area is zero, then all households have the same wealth holding so that there is no concentration. If it is one, then all wealth is owned by one household so that concentration is at its ultimate limit.

In the present context the measure used by Lorenz is not entirely appropriate since it has an upper bound of $1-s_A$. This follows from the fact that the Lorenz curve is bounded from below by the convex hull OCD. Thus a more appropriate concentration index for present purposes is $\frac{\alpha}{\alpha + \beta}$.

To evaluate this index it is necessary to obtain measures of the areas α and β. These can be derived from the fact that

$$\beta = \int_0^1 Z(\pi) \, dY(\pi) - \gamma$$

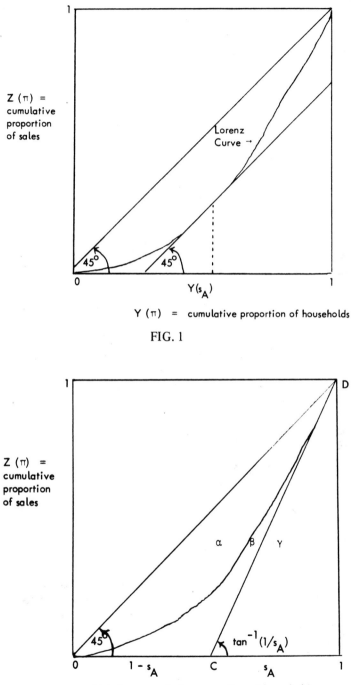

Z (π) = cumulative proportion of sales

Lorenz Curve →

45°   45°

Y(s_A)

Y (π) = cumulative proportion of households

FIG. 1

Z (π) = cumulative proportion of sales

α   β   γ

D

45°   tan⁻¹(1/s_A)

1 − s_A   C   s_A

Y (π) = cumulative proportion of households

where $\gamma = \dfrac{s_A}{2} = \dfrac{a}{2(a + b)}$

It has already been shown that

$$Z(\pi) = Y(\pi) - \frac{\pi^a(1-\pi)^b}{(a + b) B (a + 1, b)}$$

so that

$$\int_0^1 Z(\pi) \, dY(\pi) = \frac{1}{2} Y^2 (\pi) \Big|_0^1 -$$

$$- \frac{1}{(a + b) B (a + 1, b) B (a, b)} \int_0^1 \pi^{2 a-1}(1-\pi)^{2 b-1} d\pi$$

$$= \frac{1}{2} - \frac{B(2a, 2b)}{(a + b) B (a + 1, b) B (a, b)}$$

Consequently

$$\beta = \frac{b}{2(a + b)} - \frac{B(2a, 2b)}{(a + b) B (a + 1, b) B (a, b)}$$

Similarly α can be deduced from the fact that

$$\alpha + \beta = \frac{1}{2} \frac{b}{a + b}$$

$$\text{Thus } \alpha = \frac{B(2a, 2b)}{(a + b) B (a + 1, b) B (a, b)}$$

The alternative loyalty index based on the Lorenz curve is therefore

$$\frac{\alpha}{\alpha + B} = \frac{2 B(2a, 2b)}{b B(a + 1, b) B (a, b)}$$

$$= \frac{2(a + b)}{ab} \cdot \frac{B(2a, 2b)}{\{B(a, b)\}^2}$$

Like the index considered earlier, this alternative index is symmetric in a and b, and can take any value between zero and one irrespective of the values of the market shares s_A and s_B. However, whilst the Lorenz curve analysis leads to some insights into the composition of sales in terms of loyalty, the index of loyalty which it yields is more cumbersome than that considered earlier.

3. Generalisation to Several Brands

Much of the analysis of the duopoly case considered so far extends to the more general case in which a commodity is available in several brands.

In the case where there are K brands it can be assumed that an individual makes N purchases, the probabilities with which each brand is purchased on each occasion being $P_A, P_B, \ldots$ and P_K. Thus the numbers of units of each brand which are purchased, i.e. $X_A, X_B, \ldots, X_K$, are given by a multinomial distribution. In other words.

$$\Pr(X_A, X_B, \ldots, X_K) = \frac{N!}{X_A! X_B! \ldots X_K!} P_A^{X_A} P_B^{X_B} \ldots P_K^{X_K}$$

$$\text{for } X_A, X_B, \ldots X_K = 0, 1, \ldots, N$$

$$\text{subject to } P_A + P_B + \ldots + P_K = 1$$

$$\text{and } X_A + X_B + \ldots + X_K = N$$

The probabilities $P_A, P_B, \ldots, P_K$ can be assumed to vary between households according to a generalized beta distribution, so that

$$f(P_A, P_B, \ldots, P_K) = \frac{\Gamma(a + b + \ldots + k)}{\Gamma(a)\, \Gamma(b) \ldots \Gamma(k)} P_A^{a-1} P_B^{b-1} \ldots P_K^{k-1}$$

$$\text{for } 0 < P_A, P_B, \ldots, P_K < 1$$

$$\text{subject to } P_A + P_B + \ldots, + P_K = 1$$

Averaging the multinomial probabilities over households yields an expression for the general term of the resultant compound multinomial distribution which is

$$\Pr(X_A, X_B, \ldots, X_K) = \frac{N!}{X_A! X_B! \ldots X_K!} \cdot \frac{\Gamma(a + b + \ldots + k)}{\Gamma(a + b + \ldots + k + N)}$$

$$\cdot \frac{\Gamma(a + X_A)}{\Gamma(a)} \cdot \frac{\Gamma(b + X_B)}{\Gamma(b)} \ldots \frac{\Gamma(k + X_K)}{\Gamma(k)}$$

$$\text{for } X_A, X_B, \ldots X_K = 0, 1, \ldots, N$$

$$\text{subject to } X_A + X_B + \ldots + X_K = N$$

The generalised model reduces to the two-brand model if all brands other than A are consolidated into a single brand A. Accordingly the structure of a market can be analysed either in terms of the general model, or by repeated application of the duopoly model, taking each brand, and the complementary set of all other brands in turn.

This facility to aggregate brands is potentially most useful. For example, it implies that a market composed of two major brands and several minor ones can be analysed in terms of a three-brand model in which all the minor brands are grouped together as one.

Since the k-brand case can be reduced to the two-brand case by considering brands A and $\bar{A}$, it follows that either of the indices of loyalty developed in the duopoly case can be applied in the more general situation.

In the case of the standardized variance index, which is the first of the two indices considered earlier, the index will have the same value

$$\frac{1}{a + b + \ldots + k + 1}$$

for all brands in the market. Accordingly it corresponds to the view that loyalty is a property of the market and not of the individual products within it. The alternative index based on the Lorenz curve for each product, will be different for each product in the general case and is therefore more appropriate if loyalty is conceived of as a dimension of a brand which is additional to its market share.

4. Some Concluding Comments

Perhaps more than anything else, the model of brand loyalties requires empirical testing before it is persevered with further. It is likely, however, that some of the difficulties which would be revealed in fitting the model to data can be anticipated. To this extent it is possibly useful to comment on the limitations of the formulation which might be revealed.

The model is concerned with frequency of purchases for particular brands given the total number, N, of purchases made. Obviously, in data collected from a panel of households over, say, a month, N will vary. Accordingly the parameters a, b, c, etc. might vary with N. Such a result is quite consistent with tastes being constant throughout the period of observation, and would imply that the extent to which consumers discriminate between brands of a product depends on their rate of consumption. The effect might go either way: heavy buyers might require more variation than occasional buyers, or they may, perhaps as a result of experience, have more polarised preferences.

The possibility that consumers learn by experience must be allowed for in any general model of choice, but is not accomodated here. The present model simply assumes that the over-all distribution of preferences remains constant. This is inconsistent with "learning-by-consuming" in so far as it results in changing market shares. But it is not inconsistent with changes in the purchasing probabilities for individual households. It may well be that these individual parameters are always on the move within a constant aggregate framework, but if this is so, then it is likely to be revealed by observing that the model of brand switching given above, does not, in fact, explain observed behaviour.

As an alternative to "learning-by-consuming", changes in preferences may come about by changes in the character of brands due to price changes, advertising, etc. Again it is not clear how these should be brought into the model, although empirical evidence on the effects of advertising might be interesting. For instance, does heavy advertising help consumers to distinguish products, or does it confuse them? The answer might come in the form that the more heavily advertised a commotity is, the lower (or higher) are the values of the parameters a, b, c, etc. associated with the different brands of it.

It might be that these potential difficulties will be offset by a potential gain representing a link between the model of purchasing frequency in the first part of this paper and the model of brand loyalties in the second. In the model of purchasing frequencies it is clear that a limitation of the compound binomial formulation is the need to estimate and interpret N. This does not arise in the brand loyalty model since N is known as, say, the number of tins of soup bought. It might emerge that in studying purchasing frequencies for different brands of soup the parameter N is not only equal as between brands but also is equal to the total number of tins of soup bought. If this was so, then a powerful link would have been forged between the two models from which might develop an objective definition of the market within which a particular brand exists.

REFERENCES

1. Aitchison, J., and Brown, J.A.C. (1957). *The Lognormal Distribution,* University of Cambridge, Department of Applied Economics Monographs, No. 5., Cambridge University Press.

2. Anscombe, F.J. (1950). "Sampling theory of the negative binomial and logarithmic distributions", *Biometrika,* 37, pp. 358-382.

3. Chatfield, C. Ehrenberg, A.S.C., Goodhardt, G.J. (1966). "Progress on a simplified model of stationary purchasing behaviour". *J. Roy. Statistical Society,* A, 129 pp. 317-367.

4. Ehrenberg, A.S.C., (1959). "The pattern of consumer purchases", *Applied Statistics,* 8, pp. 26-41.

5. Kendall, M.G. (1960). *New prospects in economic analysis* (Stamp memorial lecture) Athlone Press, University of London.

6. Lorenz, M. (1905). "Methods of measuring the concentration of wealth", *Publications of the American Statistical Association,* 9, pp. 209-19.

7. Skellam, J.G. (1948). "A probability distribution derived from the binomial distribution by regarding the probability of success as variable between the sets of trials", *J. Roy. Statist. Soc.* Series B (Methodological) 10, pp. 257-261.

6. COMPUTABLE MODEL FOR THE ASSESSMENT OF MEDIA SCHEDULES

P. A. B. HUGHES

Introduction

The construction of an economic model essentially involves the formal representation of human behaviour. Usually this is done implicitly rather than explicitly For example, any model which includes retail sales is representing the sum of individual consumer behaviour patterns. But usually the model will relate aggregate series of sales to various other aggregate series, such as income per head: the pattern of individual behaviour is not considered as such. Sometimes relationships are proposed to represent certain aspects of human behaviour, for example, consumption functions or savings functions. Aggregate series are used to statistically determine the coefficients in the proposed functions. This is one step nearer to including human behaviour directly into the model, but still working with highly aggregated series.

An alternative approach is to incorporate directly into the model individual behaviour patterns. The starting point of all such models is the market research survey or panel. Detailed data are obtained from a small sample, and this sample is then used to represent the total population. The final aggregate projections are produced from the bottom upwards—starting with the individuals and summing, rather than dealing throughout with the aggregate figures. Such models have usually developed out of the straightforward tabulation of market research questionnaires. They attempt to go a stage beyond the analysis of past behaviour to deal with the question 'what will happen if . . .?' Their field of application is nearly always marketing. They have occasionally been used in other fields. One such example is politics, where they have been used in the planning of campaigns in the U.S.A. Their use in this context has aroused considerable controversy.

Marketing models

The model described in this paper uses as its starting point the individual, and from there builds up the expected response of the total population. The purpose of the model is to plan advertising schedules so as to maximize their effectiveness.

This is just a part of the overall decision process associated with marketing operations. To tackle that part on its own begs a number of questions. It takes as given
the overall money allocation to be spent on the advertising campaign. It does not
attempt to decide *how much* should be spent on advertising, but only *how best* to
spend the money allocated. Also it does not deal with the 'true' measure of
effectiveness in terms of extra sales, but only with a limited representation of
effectiveness as described below.

This model, and others like it, have been criticized for their limitations, in that
they are sub-optimizing. Why concentrate on trying to decide how best to spend
an agreed budget when the 'real' problem is to decide how much to spend? These
criticisms are unreasonable. By tackling a part of the marketing problem rather
than the whole one is making a start. In the past the whole field has been woefully
neglected by model builders, operational research workers and the like, and there
are very few examples of effective marketing models.

The reasons are not hard to find. It is difficult, very difficult. The fundamental data require the observation and measurement of consumer behaviour
patterns, about which little is known. But the whole field of marketing cannot
continue to be neglected by the model builders, as it constitutes such an important part of industrial activity: it could be argued that in relative terms it is a more
important part than manufacturing. And so no apologies need be made for starting by modelling just one part of the marketing process. Large sums of money
are spent on advertising (somewhere between £200 million and £400 million per
annum in the U.K.) and it is a very important objective to try and spend this
money as effectively as possible.

The media scheduling model

The original purpose of the model was to assess the effectiveness of advertising
schedules in the press and television in the U.K. and hence assist in their planning.
Since the model was first put into operation (early 1966) it has been generalized
so as to enable it to deal with a wide variety of source populations and of advertising media. This has required no structural change, merely a generalization of
the data handling. The original form of the model is dealt with here as this illustrates some of the difficulties and worries that we had in the design, construction
and implementation.

The model assists, it does not automate. The model is not intended to replace
the media planner. It is a tool for him to use, a tool without which he could not
hope to assess the effectiveness of any chosen schedule. He chooses the base
schedules, the starting points, and the model assesses how these could be improved
upon. We could have constructed a model that would have completely automated the process and constructed 'optimum schedules'. We rejected this for two
reasons. Firstly, for mathematical computational reasons it would have meant
aggregating the data and not keeping the detailed representation of individuals:
secondly, because the media planner has great experience in the balance and form

that schedules should take and this experience should be incorporated. Thus the model simulates over a chosen set of the population to calculate the effectiveness of a set of trial schedules. At the same time it assesses the change in effectiveness that would occur if modifications were made to these trial schedules. These assessments are then used by the media planner to draw up the final schedule.

The population

The crux of the problem of planning a media schedule is to consider the effects of overlapping readership (and viewership). Given tabulations obtained from processing suitable market research surveys, single readerships are easily taken care of. The problems start with a more detailed analysis. What is the overlapping readership between the *Daily Express* and the *Daily Mail*? and how does this vary by age groups? and what is the expected pattern of TV viewing of these readership groups? etc. These overlaps are not just a small perturbation on the whole, they are of fundamental importance. Take a very simple example. From tabulations both the *Daily Express* and the *Sunday Express* might seem very good buys for a particular campaign. However, taken together they would have a very large common readership. Hence though the *Sunday Express* might appear on its own as a better buy than the *People*, the combination of the *People*, together with the *Daily Express* may be much better than the *Sunday Express* with the *Daily Express*. So as to take into consideration the detailed effects of overlapping it is necessary to simulate the effect of the schedule over a sample population.

The population that we used was derived from two sources. The main source was the very detailed survey which is the standard in the U.K. for press readerships. It is known as the National Readership Survey (NRS). It is a continuous survey with over 17 000 interviews a year. As well as asking the readership habits of some 90 publications, each interview covers a number of demographic, product usage and other characteristics. But it has only very limited data on television viewing habits. Whilst it forms an excellent base for assessing press schedules it is virtually useless for TV schedules.

So we had to turn to another source for detailed data on TV viewing habits. We used the data derived from panels that were run by Television Audience Measurement Ltd (TAM). These provided very detailed viewing characteristics for about 2 700 individuals covering a four-week period. Each quarter a new set of observations were used. Although the data from these panels was very detailed (i.e. quarter hour segments) for viewing, as far as other characteristics were concerned it was limited to only simple demographic breakdowns. It had no details whatsoever of press readership.

The two basic sets of media data—on reading and on viewing—came from completely different samples of the population. We wish, however, to assess mixed schedules, i.e. schedules using both press and television. To do so we need detailed information about media exposure of both types on the same individuals. This did not exist, so we constructed it artificially.

The only information from the NRS about the individuals' habits of viewing ITV was contained in two questions. From these we classified individuals viewing frequently on a five point scale. We used this measure, and the demographic information available in both sets of data, to associate particular NRS individuals with particular TAM individuals. We call this process 'marriage'. For later work it is convenient to have a population of total size about equal to the total number of people in the TAM panels, about 2 700. The procedure adopted was to select a stratified sample of the required size from the relevant NRS survey, and then associate or 'marry' each TAM individual with a different member of the reduced NRS population. The demographic characteristics of each member of the married population are taken as those of the corresponding NRS individual in all cases. If we define a numerical measure of the discrepancy between the demographic and viewing characteristics of an NRS individual and any TAM individual to whom he might be married, then the problem of doing all the marriages to minimize the sum of these discrepancies is a classical assignment problem of linear programming.

Individuals are aggregated into 120 groups with similar characteristics, so the linear programming computations are carried out as a 120 x 120 transportation problem for each of the three main TV regions. The 120 different groups are derived from classifying individuals within five separate categories—Sex, Age, With/Without Children, Social Grade and Television Viewing Intensity. Before solving the transportation problems we need to generate a full 120 x 120 matrix of penalty costs for mismatching. The diagonal elements of this matrix must all be zero, for these cells correspond to marrying together like individuals. The off-diagonal elements are calculated from a set of five small sub-matrices. For each of the demographic category groups there is a matrix which gives the penalty costs for mismatching within the category, whilst matching correctly within all of the other four categories. If individuals that are married together mismatch within more than one category, the penalty costs are taken from the relevant sub-matrices and added together to derive the total penalty cost. The elements in these sub-matrices were so chosen that a mismatch within the television viewing intensity category was more serious than mismatches within any of the other four categories.

Since the model was constructed a new survey has become available which contains very detailed information covering *both* press and TV, as well as a wide variety of product use groups. This means that it is no longer necessary to carry out the marriage procedure. But in behavioural models the need will often arise to combine detailed information from a number of sources to construct a base population. Clearly the procedure has dangers if taken too far, but it may prove more practical than trying to gather an extremely detailed set of data on an individual by individual basis.

Effectiveness and Response

The data in the model varies from that which is firm and can be clearly measured (i.e. demographic) to that which is very difficult to measure and could almost be considered as subjective (i.e. 'response' which is described below). This is bound to occur in any behavioural model. Our present state of knowledge does not allow us to accurately observe and measure certain factors. Indeed, we may have to introduce notional factors to represent the way that we believe individuals to react. This is completely defensible as long as we clearly separate out such factors and assign to the numerical values, knowing that these values are to a large extent subjective measures. What is not defensible is to pretend such factors do not exist because we cannot observe them sufficiently accurately.

In this model a number of such factors are incorporated, three of which are described. Firstly there is *perception*. The readership and viewership data provide the probability of reading or viewing for each medium for each individual. But it is clearly unreasonable to assign as high a probability to 'seeing' an advertisement in a paper as it is to being a 'reader'. There is a fair body of research on this subject for measuring advertising noting (that is the proportion of readers who say that they have seen particular advertisements).

A much less definite factor is that of *impact*. This goes beyond the 'noting' or 'seeing'. It is an attempt to measure on a relative scale the impact value of the advertisement. For example, it is always assumed that a colour advertisement is more effective than one in black and white, and that on TV a longer 'spot' is of greater value than a shorter 'spot'. But by how much? Clearly this is a factor which must be brought into consideration, but which is very difficult to measure.

Of even greater importance is the notion of a *response* function. This is an evolution of the relative usefulness to the advertiser of causing an individual to receive his first impression, second impression . . . and so on. (An impression is taken to be the seeing and noting of an advertisement of maximum relative value, i.e. maximum impact). Again it is clear that we must have a response function. The nature of any advertising campaign is to aim to produce a cumulative response from individuals receiving a number of impressions.

It is extremely difficult to measure in practice what we have just defined as a response function, although some advertising experiments have attempted to do so (see Broadbent and Segnit, 1967, for an excellent review of this subject). It is unlikely that, in most of the campaigns for which we write schedules, there will be any explicit research data on this point. However, in an actual problem the agency will be prepared to state how they expect the advertising to act. We are able to say whether we feel the advertising had done nearly all it can after an individual has seen a small number of our best advertisements in our best vehicle (i.e. a small number of impressions). This might apply for example to a schedule supporting the launch of a new product. Or we might feel that repeated impressions will continue to be of high value to the advertiser.

In this model the response function is not defined to have any set mathematical form. However, some particular forms are used frequently and are worth recording.

(i) Step functions: these state that at one or two or three impressions the job of the campaign is done and further impressions are unnecessary.

(ii) Linear functions: these state that response rises steadily, each successive impression being equally valuable. There may be a limit, after which there is no further increase in response, or the increase may be unlimited.

(iii) S-shaped functions: these are popular in the literature and correspond to the notion that a few impressions do little good, while after a certain number there is little additional response; in the middle range response increases more rapidly.

(iv) Geometric functions: these state that each additional impression adds to response a constant fraction of the amount added to by the previous impression.

The assessment of schedules

To use the model the media planner first specifies the target population that he is aiming to reach. He can specify different weighting factors for different cells in a multi-way breakdown. He then writes several trial schedules. He bears in mind the natural restraints imposed by the vehicles, their cost structures and the total budget. He also has the response function as a guide to the length of the schedule. If the response function lays stress on cover (a step function at one impression is the extreme case) there is no point in too many insertions in any one vehicle and a long list of publications should result. If the response function states that large numbers of impressions on one individual are still valuable, he knows that he should buy mainly in the best vehicles; a short list of media will result. What the media planner cannot take into account completely is the overlapping between pairs and other groups of vehicles. He makes an attempt to use what he knows intuitively and from analyses of duplication, but he can achieve only an approximation.

We select from the basic data a panel which is representative of the target population. We go through each schedule for each individual in this panel in turn. For each individual we construct his impression distribution. The weighted sum of these over the panel is the overall impression distribution for that particular schedule. That is, we know how much of our target received no impression at all, how much received just one, just two . . . impressions. We have stated the relative usefulness of each of these, in the cumulative response function. Therefore if we weight the impression distribution by the response function we get a single figure for the effectiveness of the schedule.

To get the marginal rates of return for a specified change in the schedule we find the corresponding new impression distribution. From this we find a new figure for effectiveness. The increase (or decrease) in effectiveness divided by the change in cost is the marginal rate of return for the change specified.

An example:

The use of the model is best illustrated by an example of a typical job. The product concerned is sold to motorists and motor-cyclists. A budget of about £350,000 was available for a national advertising campaign for which both television and press are considered suitable.

The target population

The following sets of weighting factors were decided upon to define the target group weights.

TABLE 1

Definition	Weighting factor
Motorist	100
Non-motorist	10
Male	100
Female	25
Aged 16–24	85
Aged 25–44	100
Aged 45 +	65

These factors are treated as multiplicative, i.e. a female motorist aged over 45 has a weight of:

$$100 \times \frac{25}{100} \times \frac{65}{100} = 16 \cdot 25$$

The schedules

The media planner considered that a television schedule supplemented by press was likely to be the best approach. He was uncertain how large the press share should be. He wrote one schedule in which press takes 13 per cent of the appropriation and another in which it takes 21 per cent; we called these Schedules 1 and 2. He also wished to check his opinion that this emphasis on television is correct. He wrote a press-only schedule costing £306 000 which we called Schedule 4. Schedule 3 was the television portion of Schedule 1 and had the same cost as Schedule 4.

Additions and deletions

The media planner prepared a list of 35 publications for consideration as possible additions to schedules basically involving television. He used nine of these publications in Schedule 1. He wished to know if any of those he had included should be omitted, or, alternatively, whether more advertisements should be taken in them. He also wished to know if any of the other 26 publications should be substituted. He required similar evaluations for Schedule 2 and for the television portions of both these schedules. In all 283 possible additions and deletions were to be assessed.

Judgement factors

Three different response functions were specified. Each of these attached less value to the first few impressions received compared with those received subsequently. The accent in the campaign was on obtaining a large number of impacts rather than a high cover.

The impact of a 45-second spot (the only length considered) was considered to be 100; a half-page press insertion was considered to be 50.

Conclusions

We give an outline of the main conclusions drawn from this run.

1. Was emphasis on television correct? We compared Schedule 3 (television only) with Schedule 4 (press only). The effectiveness figures with the 'best' response function were 12·0 and 7·8 respectively. This indicated that with the judgement factors as chosen, television appeared to be the better medium for the campaign. This conclusion was the same with all three response functions tried. The two media produced quite different shapes of impression distribution. If the response function had given greater emphasis to impression cover, i.e. the percentage of the target receiving one impression, then press would have been chosen as the following table shows:—

TABLE 2

	No impressions (%)	1–20 impressions (%)	At least 24 impressions (%)
Television	15	58	27
Press	3	92	5

2. How much press should be added to the television schedule? Schedule 1 had an effectiveness of 14·1 compared with 14·0 for Schedule 2. The difference was hardly significant, but it indicated that if anything the press element should be small as in Schedule 1.

3. Improvement of Schedule 1. The program prints out for each base schedule full lists of the additions and deletions that have been evaluated, sorted in order of their marginal rate of return.

Consideration of the table of deletions indicated that the late Saturday spots in Region 6 (South Wales and West and the North-east) and Region 5 (Scotland, North-east Scotland and Border) could be dropped with least loss in effectiveness.

The next television spots on this table all had about the same marginal rate of return; we picked one in Region 2 (Midlands) as the table of additions shows there is a good segment here in which to reinvest: we deleted some of the 8.0– 8.30 p.m. Friday spots.

In press, the *Daily Express, TV Times* and *Reader's Digest* could be dropped with least harm to effectiveness. Thus we arrived at the list of deletions shown in Table 3. They removed about £46 000 from the schedule and dropped effectiveness by only 10 per cent.

TABLE 3 DELETIONS

Description	No. of spots or advertisements Original	Deleted	Marginal rate of return	Saving (£)	Percentage loss in effectiveness
Region 2, Friday, 8.0–8.30 p.m.	18	8	0·8	8 800	2·1
Region 5, Saturday, 11.0–11.30 p.m.	12	12	0·7	3 948	0·8
Region 6, Saturday, 11.0–11.30 p.m.	12	12	0·5	4 860	0·7
Daily Express, ½ page	6	6	0·8	18 000	4·0
TV Times, full page	3	3	0·8	5 400	1·2
Reader's Digest, full page 4-colour	4	4	0·9	4 900	1·2
			Totals	45 908	10·0

We reinvested the £46 000 where it did most good as indicated by the table of additions. We noticed that *Practical Motorist* and *Car Mechanics* are outstanding and we added here up to the maximum (8, since this is an 8-month schedule). We increased the number of insertions in four other publications, particularly the *Daily Mirror*. We also added some of the best television spots. We arrived at the list of additions shown in Table 4, which increased effectiveness by about 23 per cent.

Because the marginal rates of return for the additions we made were higher than for the deletions, the net result of all these changes was an increase in schedule effectiveness. The increase was approximately 13 per cent. While there is no exact cash equivalent, as a proportion of the appropriation this was over £40 000.

TABLE 4 ADDITIONS

Description	No. of spots or advertisements Original	Added	Marginal rate of return	Cost of change £	Percentage gain in effectiveness
Region 1, Saturday to 3.45 p.m.	27	7	2·7	2 100	1·6
Region 1, Saturday, 11.0–11.30 p.m.	12	3	2·1	2 025	1·2
Region 1, Friday, 6.30–7.0 p.m.	–	2	1·6	1 950	0·9
Region 2, Saturday, 11.0–11.30 p.m.	12	15	1·7	6 975	3·3
Region 4, Saturday, 11.0–11.30 p.m.	12	14	2·1	2 395	1·5
Region 5, Saturday, 5.15–5.45 p.m.	–	16	1·8	3 072	1·5
Daily Mirror, ½ page	6	10	1·5	16 240	7·1
Daily Sketch, ½ page	6	10	1·4	4 250	1·7
Reveille, ½ page	3	7	1·3	4 130	1·5
Do-it-Yourself, full page, face matter	4	4	1·6	1 012	0·5
Car Mechanics, full page, face matter	4	4	4·3	960	1·2
Practical Motorist, full page, face matter	4	4	6·2	840	1·5
			Totals	45 949	23·5

Assumptions

In making these calculations we have assumed that the effect of the additions or deletions in individual media as calculated in the program can be added together. How justified is this assumption in practice? Obviously in pathological cases we could not do this. There is, of course, an easy test: we can rerun the program to reassess the amended schedule. We have done this for various early trial runs and this gave us sufficient confidence in our assumptions. The total change, as calculated by summing the separate efforts (applying in effect a series of partial derivates of effectiveness with respect to the various media in turn, all measured at the same point on the response surface), turned out to be close to the exact change.

We have also calculated the effects of adding (or deleting) a varying number of insertions in a particular medium. In most cases the change in total response was very nearly proportional to the change in the number of insertions, within a sensible range.

Conclusions

This media selection model has been described here in outline to illustrate one type of behavioural model (a fuller description of the model is given in Beale, Hughes & Broadbent, 1966. The main credit for this work belongs to Dr. S. R. Broadbent who specified the form of the model and defined the factors and relationships used, and to E. M. L. Beale who developed most of the detailed mathematical treatment). It is in essence a very simple model, though in execution it involves a set of fairly large and complex computer programs. It does not contain causal relationships. It is essentially a model for assessment, rather than forecasting. It does, however, attempt to represent in a limited way the behaviour of individuals. In this respect it is a primitive forerunner of a whole area of model building that is likely to fast develop as our knowledge in the behavioural sciences grows, both in theory and in practice.

REFERENCES

E. M. L. Beale, P. A. B. Hughes and S. R. Broadbent (1966). 'A Computer Assessment of Media Schedules', *Operational Research Quarterly*, Vol. 17, No. 4.

S. R. Broadbent and S. Segnit (1967). *'Response Functions in Media Planning'*, The Silver Medal Award Paper of the Thompson Awards for Advertising Research, 1967.

7. MODEL BUILDING IN MANPOWER PLANNING AND STAFF MANAGEMENT

PART 1 MANPOWER PLANNING
E. S. M. CHADWICK

When I was invited to address this symposium, I had, being neither a mathematician nor a statistician, considerable reservations about the usefulness of the contribution I could make. I have, however, taken comfort from Dr. Kendall's definition of a 'model' as "a specification of the inter-relationships of the parts of a system, in verbal or mathematical terms, sufficiently explicit to enable us to study its behaviour under a variety of circumstances and, in particular, to control it and predict its future". I propose to outline, in verbal terms, the system that interests us, namely the planning of the manpower and employment aspects of the operations of the British Petroleum Company, and to leave Mr. Duffett to discuss an example of a mathematical application.

Perhaps I should give some sort of background to our interest in manpower planning. There are two arguments in favour of manpower planning at the level of the firm which have particularly influenced us. Firstly, there is considerable evidence to indicate that, for some time to come, there will be a shortage of manpower, particularly of high-quality manpower, which will be in even greater demand. Secondly, changes in manpower requirements are likely to be much more rapid in the future than they have been in the past, when there was usually adequate time to make adjustments in skill requirements. No longer will a man be able to learn, in his youth, a skill which will carry him through the whole of his working life. It is probable that both the young man and the not so young may have to change his skill once, or even twice, in the course of his working life.

The oil industry is particularly sensitive to such a situation in that the people who go to make up its manpower form a group that at all levels and in all areas is heavily weighted with skill in the broadest sense. An industry that handles liquids and gases in vast quantities does not need thousands of unskilled men to carry the product around; instead it needs comparatively large numbers of good engineers and good operators who can make the best use of the expensive equipment that replaces unskilled manpower in a modern "capital intensive" industry.

This emphasis on formal "quality" is not the only characteristic of the manpower employed by BP. The Company does not employ very large numbers of people concentrated in one immediate area; even its largest installations are comparatively modest in employment terms. Instead there are a considerable number of people scattered around the globe in quite small groups, either running a refinery, working in an exploration or production area or helping to man a marketing company.

It is at this stage that, in Dr. Kendall's sense, the concept of a model really arrived on the personnel scene. In many ways, of course, models have been used for some time to deal with complex managerial problems in the oil industry. For example, many of you will be familiar with Mr. Newby's paper on the application of model building to the very complicated issues of an integrated oil company. In the field of personnel management, however, the idea of measurement in anything but the crude sense of measuring discrete trends is almost unknown. So far as personnel people have normally measured at all, it has been to measure the parts of the system in isolation; very rarely have they attempted to specify the interrelationships of the parts of the system with which they are professionally concerned. Indeed, we have found that, although there is now a growing and vigorous interest in manpower planning in this sense, we had to start from scratch. Even now, in the growing literature on model building for long range corporate planning, manpower is largely neglected.

It is against this background, that manpower planning in BP has been developed with two objectives:—

(i) To establish requirements for manpower in the Company, both quantitatively and qualitatively over the next five years and to consider requirements up to fifteen years ahead.

(ii) To establish how these needs may be met.

It should be understood that, while there is a global company plan in terms of production, shipping and refining, this must be translated into the contribution which each Associate or Subsidiary Company makes to the total and, since there is no significant interchangeability of staff of different nationalities, each Company in manpower terms, must stand on its own. Manpower planning in BP has therefore to be applied both to the small marketing company, employing less than 500 people and to the large integrated company employing 5 – 6 000.

Our first thoughts were that we should consider what sort of Company we would be in the future, in terms of production, refining and sales and from that we would be able to deduce what numbers and categories of manpower we would require. It soon became evident that manpower forecasting was not as simple as that, if that could be called simple, and that many other, external, factors needed to be taken into the reckoning. The factors affecting manpower demand and supply fall into four main groups which are, nevertheless, closely inter-related.

A. Trading and production patterns

This includes gross tonnages (e.g. production, throughput, sales) range of products handled, distribution methods, organisation and Company policy, and any changes which can be foreseen such as expansion, contraction, diversification and introduction of new products—the Company Plan. Preliminary studies showed that there was very little direct correlation between gross figures of sales, tonnages and throughputs with gross manpower needs. It was soon evident that it would be more realistic to study individual sections (production, manufacturing, distribution and sales) and individual categories (chemists and engineers).

B. Technological change

This group includes the factors most likely to affect our requirements of men and skills. The impact of automation and of data processing; the application of operational research techniques and of computers to the overall Company operations; the effect of technological evolution on operating methods; market demand, the development of new products and the improvement of existing products.

C. Economic change

This includes such factors as fiscal policy; prices and incomes; and the state of the economy, which, although entirely outside the control of the Company, are becoming more and more influential as Governments enter the field of national economic planning. Economic factors can only be studied in the short-term, because Government regulation of the economy is conditioned by political considerations. On the other hand, the development of national plans may at least indicate the desired future of the economy towards which stimuli or regulators may be applied.

D. Social change

This includes the impact of change in the fields of education, hours of work and holidays, retirement pensions, retirement and school leaving ages, all of which can affect manpower, either in terms of availability or cost.

Following preliminary work and discussion, it was decided, in September 1965, to take three courses of action.

Firstly, to prepare, company by company, five-year manpower plans linked with Company plans and forming an integral part of them.

Secondly, to study, at the level of the firm, the impact on manpower of such matters as automation, automatic data processing and other specific technological developments.

Thirdly, to investigate mathematically-based prediction techniques in order to discover whether it is possible to assist in policy decisions on recruitment patterns, retraining, staff movements and retirements. The developments in this particular area, which are perhaps most familiar in the mathematical sense, will be dealt with by Mr. Duffett.

As work progressed it became increasingly clear that it is convenient to think of manpower planning as comprising three phases:—

Phase 1 – Overall Planning

Planning for total numbers, skilled groups, organizational groups, costs, etc.

Phase 2 – Individual Planning

Planning in the context of Phase 1 for management succession, career planning, recruitment, training, etc.

Phase 3 – Review and Audit

Regular review and audit of phases 1 and 2.

Phase 2 of this progression is familiar in many areas of industry and is often taken to be synonymous with "manpower planning". Phase 1, on the other hand, although familiar enough on the broad national level in the planning of educational facilities, is comparatively uncharted territory at the level of the firm. Any manpower planning activity must embrace all three phases and to do one without the others is unlikely to achieve any worthwhile results. The aim is to evolve not one plan, but a series of plans—the overall (or strategic) plan, concerned with total activities and total numbers and a series of individual (or tactical) plans embracing recruitment planning, career planning, management succession, training plans, etc.

THE PREPARATION OF COMPANY MANPOWER PLANS

A. Present position

The starting point of any plan must be a careful analysis and description of the existing position in terms both of the manpower currently employed and also of the needs and pressures that have led to this position.

1. Present manpower

This can conveniently be expressed as:—

(a) Numbers and costs by sex, grade, age, length of service, function/department, progression/skill/qualification.

(b) Numbers related to sales, throughput etc.

2. *Present organization and policies*

The pressures that have produced the present manpower situation include: —

(a) National considerations

(i) The general position of the Company in relation to national policies, both economic and social.

(ii) The Company's market share in relation to that of other Companies.

(iii) The position in the labour market for the various categories employed.

(b) Company considerations

Changes in: —

(i) Organization

(ii) Manning schedules

(iii) Tonnages and range of products

(iv) Supply and distribution patterns

(v) Sales objectives

B. Analyses of trends

Analyses of manpower trends in terms of distribution between and within departments, of movement and of costs, are essential to any attempts to make forecasts. These analyses can only be carried out if a systematic historical data bank is available. The retrievability of data related to groups rather than to individuals is not a familiar feature of staff work and data banks of this type are all too rare.

C. Anticipated changes

On the basis of the anticipated influences of company planning, and technological, social and economic changes, forecasts can be made of the establishment of jobs necessary to carry out the Company's business. An example of a summary of anticipated total changes is shown in Table 1. This relates to one of our continental companies and summarises into a simple table a great deal of analysis along the lines I have been discussing, and certainly emerges from an examination of the inter-relationships of the parts of their system. This example has been slightly disguised, but it is interesting to note that, although the total establishment is expected to increase by 536, this is the nett result of the creation of 1 133 new jobs and of the removal of 677 old jobs. In addition to the 536 extra posts to be filled, a replacement of 3 104 will be required to balance wastage. In all, this represents a considerable amount of manpower movement over 5 years. The increase in jobs is almost wholly accounted for by the commissioning of a new refinery (in 1969) and by the extension of the research activity.

TABLE 1

	1968	1969	1970	1971	1972	1973	Totals
Establishment at beginning of year	5 129	5 222	5 482	5 554	5 593	5 650	—
Anticipated + changes in	346	426	138	139	63	21	1 133
establishment −	253	166	105	100	47	6	677
Increased require-ments due to shorter work-ing hours +	—	—	39	—	41	—	80
Establishment at end of year	5 222	5 482	5 554	5 593	5 650	5 665	—
Anticipated + nett changes in establish-ment −	93	260	72	39	57	15	536
	—	—	—	—	—	—	—
Replacements + due to wastage	264	552	566	568	576	578	3 104

D. Prediction

Prediction techniques are useful not only in providing a clear insight into the dynamics of the manpower situation but also in indicating the probable outcome of present, or possibly of alternative, courses of action. The approach has been to use the trends of the past five years to forecast the position within the next five years. This, of course, can only be done with the full realization of the assumptions involved. Just because there has been a certain promotion pattern over the last five years, it will not necessarily be the same for the next five years. The aim indeed is to examine the effect of a variety of trends and see whether the projected position achieved by these trends is satisfactory or not. The executive decision lies in deciding what position is desirable, what trend produces this position and what action, if any, is necessary to produce this trend. There is no method of establishing a staff position which, in five years time, *will inevitably* be achieved; decisions can be made which, in all probability, will approximate to this position—the accuracy of the approximation depending, not only on the accuracy of the prediction method, but also on the unpredictable effect of outside influences.

SUMMARY AND CONCLUSIONS

The study of the totality of manpower by categories and skill groups (Phase 1) such as I have described has four main purposes:—

1. The gaining of insight into and understanding of situations and the relationships that brought them about.

2. The assessment of the effect of the various factors on demand, supply and cost.

3. The assessment of those areas which are controllable by the organization and those which are not.

4. The isolation of problem areas which require action.

The complexity of many factors, not all of which are precisely measurable, precludes a total model but not a series of smaller models of parts of the whole. These, to date, have been fairly simple in concept, and restricted to two or three variables, yet even these have posed considerable problems of taxonomy.

I have already referred to studies of mobility and career patterns; other problem areas which have emerged include:—

(a) The changing pattern of skills required within comparatively stable total numbers of manpower.

(b) The high cost of manpower and the consequent need to achieve optimum manpower utilization.

We are currently engaged in defining and identifying individual skills, the results of which will be ultimately included in our historical data bank.

Whereas inclusion of skills is a most desirable addition to our data bank, the question of costs is fundamental to all manpower considerations. *Per capita* costs have been rising sharply over the past five years and all our forecasts point to a comparable increase over the next five years. In one of our Associate Companies, for example, the *per capita* cost rose by 85% between 1960 and 1965, and a further increase of 62% is expected between 1965 and 1970. Analyses of the make-up of total *per capita* costs (salary, pensions, statutory charges, fringe benefits, services) are comparatively simple to make, but provide disquieting information. In general, for staff in our Head Office, the *per capita* cost is about double the salary, yet this is something over which a Company has little control, being almost entirely dictated by external pressures.

Limited control over costs and the imbalance between supply and demand for skilled manpower emphasise the need for improving utilization. As, ultimately, the performance of a company must be expressed in financial terms, so also must manpower utilization. No great problems arise in a unit production situation where output can be precisely measured and directly related to human effort, but this represents only about 25% of the total work force in this country, and in the oil industry is almost non-existent. We have a need for meaningful manpower cost/performance criteria.

There is, as I hope I have demonstrated, considerable scope for the application of model building to manpower. Our models, although we have not up to now used that term, have been essentially simple, but adequate for our immediate needs. I see no virtue in complexity for its own sake; nevertheless, as a layman, I do not think we have yet considered all the possibilities.

REFERENCES

1. Kendall, M.G. "Model building and its problems", from *Mathematical Model Building in Economics and Industry, First Series.* Griffin, London (1968).

2. Chadwick, E.S.M. "An approach to manpower planning". *Personnel,* Sep. 1970.

3. Chadwick, E.S.M. "Corporate Planning and its implication for staffing", presented at the University of Bradford, Jan. 1968.

4. Newby, W.J. "An integrated model of an oil company", from *Mathematical Model Buildin in Economics and Industry, First Series.* Griffin, London (1968).

7. MODEL BUILDING IN MANPOWER PLANNING AND STAFF MANAGEMENT

PART 2 STAFF MANAGEMENT
R. H. E. DUFFETT

Quantitative Approach

It is convenient to think of manpower planning as comprising three phases:-

>Phase   I. Overall Planning. Planning for groups.
>Phase II. Individual Planning. Planning for individuals
>in the context of phase I.
>Phase III. Review and audit. Continual auditing of plans
>as circumstances change.

Our attempts at model building have been confined to Phase I which is normally, and illogically, neglected in favour of Phase II. Quantitative studies of the past behavioural patterns of groups of employees have been examined in order to decide to what extent these patterns will be reproduced in the future and in what way they are liable to be changed. It has then been possible to estimate the disposition of a group in, say, 5 years time if certain actions are taken. Although problems of numerate communication in staff work normally obviate discussion about the confidence limits of forecasts, at least it can be pointed out that if assumptions about behaviour are incorrect or if the prescribed actions are not taken, then the situation may well be very different from that predicted. Forecasting of manpower is not fundamentally different from forecasting of anything else, but emotional involvement makes it essential to be more careful about detail and it soon becomes apparent that:-

1. Staff data must be in impeccable order. Only the simplest and least equivocal information should be used in Phase I.

2. Groups of employees must be carefully defined so that they are homogeneous within the context under study.

3. Groups larger than 100 can be handled with confidence; groups less than 50 need only be discussed semi-quantitatively. Between 50 and 100 the scope for numerical manipualtion depends on the characteristics of the group.

4. The behaviour of a group should be examined over at least the last 5 years (but probably not more than the last 10 years) before reasonable forecasts can be made up to 5 years ahead.

5. If any substantial organizational changes have taken place recently, or are envisaged within 5 years, quantitative work may well be unreliable.

6. A useful forecast can only be made if either it is assumed that present practices will be continued or if anticipated requirements and actions are made known by the person responsible for the group.

7. Patterns of behaviour and parameters of patterns vary from group to group.

It is convenient to illustrate the terms group, behaviour, pattern and parameter as follows:-

(a) Group

e.g. Research Chemists. A chemist is defined as an individual having a degree, or a qualification equivalent to a degree, in a chemical subject. A research chemist is a chemist who is currently fulfilling a role in research or technical development.

(b) Behaviour (Fig. 1)

In this context behaviour is considered to be synonymous with the movements of individuals into, out of and within a defined group. i.e.
Movements into the group by:-

(i) Recruitment from outside the company.

(ii) Transfer from another group within the company.

Movements out of the group by:-

(i) Termination (wastage, retirement or death).

(ii) Transfer to another group within the company.

Movements within the group by:-

(i) Promotion.

(ii) Demotion.

(c) Pattern

The pattern is the way in which the behaviour is distributed throughout the group i.e. the variation of behaviour as a function of one or more defined parameters.

(d) Parameter

The parameters associated with manpower forecasting are normally age, length of service and status (salary or grade).

Ability to study group behaviour depends heavily upon the availability of information in a systematic form. During the evolution of these investigations our staff data system has been converted from Hollerith punch cards to computer tape but the main emphasis is naturally on up-to-date information for individuals rather than historical information for groups. It has been necessary to devise an additional, parallel, system specifically for manpower planning. The information

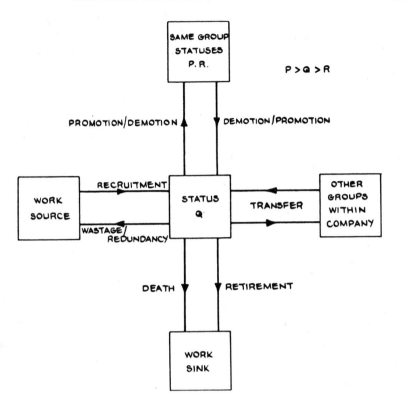

MANPOWER   MOVEMENT

FIGURE I

very simple but is in a form which can be readily manipulated. It consists
or each individual of:-

    (a) Name and Initials
    (b) Sex
    (c) Company Registered Number
    (d) Date of birth   STATIC
    (e) Date joined company
    (f) Date left company
    (g) Degrees and Qualifications

(h) Department
(i) Grade (or Status)
(j) Skill Zone
(k) Salary

DYNAMIC

The static data can be supplemented at any time from the main computer record. The dynamic data is updated at the end of each year, again from the main record, and is currently available from year end 1960 onwards. Item (k), although readily available, has only recently been included; item (j) is still under development but is intended to contribute to the better definition of homogenous groups.

This rudimentary, although extensive, bank of information has proved more than adequate for investigations undertaken in Phase I. It must be emphasized that this particular arrangement and time scale (annual update) is suitable for the major group of Career Staff on which interest has been focused. In a similar study of the movements of typing staff it was necessary to alter the time scale and to modify the form of the data bank; likewise it is obvious from the literature (References 1, 2) that studies of labour have their special data requirements.

For the group of Career Staff that has been studied, it has been found that the parameter of age is much more important than either status or length of service; this is an interesting distinction from labour studies where length of service is of prime importance. It is also a particularly convenient feature because age is normally the least equivocal piece of information available; length of service is frequently confused by apprenticeship schemes, broken service or change of job within the company and status may be more subjective than is immediately obvious. In many cases, however, as a result of company practices, there is a high degree of correlation both between age and length of service and between age and grade. As a result of this, and because the size of group under study is usually not more than 2-300, the forecasting model has been built on the basis of distribution by age.

A. AGE DISTRIBUTION IN FORECASTING

The aim is to analyse population Q (Figure 1) in terms of age, to assign probabilities to the different types of loss from population Q, to interpret from managerial policies the gains required and to examine the outcome at fixed points of time in the future.

(a) Analysing Population Q in terms of Age

The main problem is always to define population Q satisfactorily. A convenient example, already defined, is "Research Chemists". In this case there is no higher status P and relationship with status R is simply by transfer from R to Q of recently qualified individuals. The individuals currently in population Q are divided into 5-year age groups. This elementary detail is the source of much error and confusion. The age groups are defined as 20-24, 25-29 etc. and an individual born at any time in 1943 is said to be aged 24 at the year end 1967

ıd remains at that age until year end 1968. This definition is not important
xcept at the boundaries of age groups which, although artificial, are necessary
ɔr simplifying quantitative work.

*) *Assigning Probabilities to Loss from Population Q*

It is normally assumed that loss is by accident rather than by design and is
ıerefore expressed in terms of probability. However, deliberate policies of
:dundancy or transfer to other groups can be recognised and are not normally
robabilistic. For simplicity this aspect is disregarded in this paper but does
ot present any problems. An example of the probabilities of wastage and
ansfer out is shown in Figure 2; these probabilities have been derived from
ıe historical information for population Q and the height of the boxes is a
ıeasure of annual variation. No distinct trends are detectable in any age group
ıd there is no known reason why these should not apply in the immediate
ıture. One aspect of wastage is that it is assumed that an individual is not
ıbject to wastage in the year he is recruited; this is partly because recruiting
:nerally occurs late in the year and partly observation on past behaviour.

·) *Interpreting from Managerial Policies the Gains Required*

Intake to population Q is the sum of external recruitment and internal transfer.
ıture action is interpreted in terms of the total intake needed for replacement
ıd for meeting any expansion. A desirable distribution by age of the intake is
:rived from the amount of outside experience required by status Q.

ℓ) *Examining the Outcome of Calculations*

This is a question of matching the anticipated outcome of current policies with
ıme preferred distribution in, say 5 years time. This is discussed in more detail
ter in the paper.

, **Theoretical**

Calculations are based upon 5-year age brackets and forecasts are made for 5
ears ahead, by annual iterations, working from the general statement that:-

$$
\begin{bmatrix} \text{The number of} \\ \text{people in} \\ \text{Status } Q \text{ aged} \\ i \text{ at time} \\ (t+1) \end{bmatrix} = \begin{bmatrix} \text{The number of} \\ \text{people in} \\ \text{Status } Q \text{ aged} \\ (i-1) \text{ at time } t \end{bmatrix} - \begin{bmatrix} \text{The number of} \\ \text{people in} \\ \text{Status } Q \text{ aged} \\ (i-1) \text{ at time} \\ t \text{ who have left} \\ \text{between } t \text{ and} \\ (t+1) \end{bmatrix} + \begin{bmatrix} \text{The number of} \\ \text{people aged } i \\ \text{at time } (t+1) \\ \text{who have joined} \\ \text{Status } Q \text{ between} \\ t \text{ and } (t+1) \end{bmatrix}
$$

The number in each age group is calculated by summing the results for each
f the individual 5 years in the group.

g.
$$
F_{i+2} = \left[A_{i-3} \, x_b^3 \, x_c^2 \right] + \frac{K}{5} \left[n_b (x_b^2 \, x_c^2 + x_b \, x_c^2) + n_c (x_c^2 + x_c + 1) \right] \tag{i}
$$

ıd
$$
F_{i+3} = \left[A_{i-2} \, x_b^2 \, x_c^3 \right] + \frac{K}{5} \left[n_b (x_b \, x_c^3) + n_c (x_c^3 + x_c^2 + x_c + 1) \right] \tag{ii}
$$

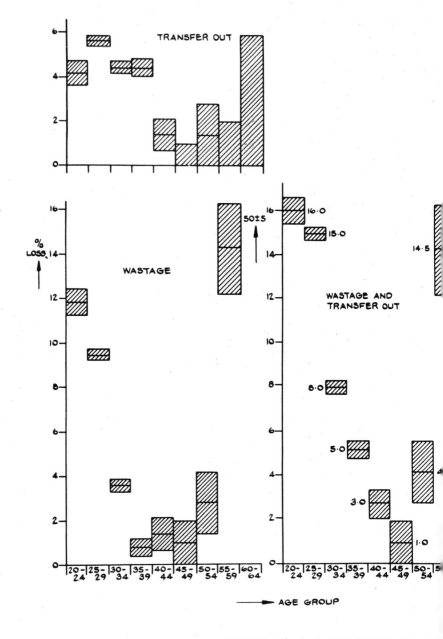

ANNUAL LOSS FROM STATUS Q AS A FUNCTION OF AGE

FIG

where the 5-year age group is for ages i to $i + 4$.

A_{i-3} is the number of people aged $(i-3)$ at time t.

F_{i+2} is the number of people aged $(i + 2)$ at time $(t + 5)$.

x_b, x_c are the wastage factors for age groups $(i-5)$ to $(i-1)$ and i to $(i + 4)$ respectively.

n_b, n_c are the recruitment factors for age groups $(i-5)$ to $(i-1)$ and i to $(i + 4)$ respectively.

K is the annual number of recruits.

Note:

(a) It is assumed that the recruitment is constant (i.e. K/year) for each of the 5 years.

(b) Wastage factor (more accurately retention factor). If the wastage is $w\%$ per annum, the wastage factor is $(100 - w)/100$.

(c) Recruitment factor. n_c is the proportion of the intake aged i to $(i + 4)$ and $\Sigma n_j = 1$.

(d) For simplicity of calculation it is assumed that
$F_i = F_{i+1} = F_{i+2} = F_{i+3} = F_{i+4} = 1/5$ of total in 5-year age group.

The basic equations for predicting age distributions can therefore be summarised as:-

$$F_j = \alpha_j A_{j-1} + K(\beta_j n_{j-1} + \gamma_j n_j) \quad \text{(iii)}$$

where F, A, K, n, are as previously defined,
$(j-1)$, j are consecutive 5-year age groups.

α_j, β_j, γ_j, are constants peculiar to age group j and are calculated from wastage factors for groups $(j-1)$ and j.

An important feature of equation (iii) is that the predicted number of people is obtained as the sum of those employed at time t who remain in the group at time $(t + 5)$, referred to as the 'core' and of those recruited in the intervening 5 years who remain at time $(t + 5)$. Thus, by adjusting the recruitment pattern it is theoretically possible to obtain an infinite variety of different distributions, and to provide an infinite choice for managerial decision. By expressing wastage as an array of constants in equation (iii) there is the danger that the influence of changes in wastage pattern will be forgotten. However, equation (iii) can in no way be utilised until the whole question of wastage has been carefully examined and numerical values assigned.

2. Preferred Distribution

It is not a particularly difficult problem to calculate the number of recruits required to meet a desired total at some time in the future. Indeed it is only slightly more involved to achieve a defined distribution by age as well as a given total. The question invariably arises as to what age distribution is desirable and why this should be preferable to any other. Certainly in a bureaucratic situation the preferred distribution is likely to be the one which is stable within the working environment. A stable distribution is one which reproduces itself annually as the result of balancing anticipated wastage with a fixed recruitment pattern; in a stationary situation the numbers in each age group stay the same, in an expanding or contracting situation the number in each age group is multiplied by a common factor (the ratio of the overall totals). Under these conditions for stability excessive numbers in narrow age bands are avoided. The concept of 'age bulge' is a familiar feature which has the undesirable side-effects of a disproportionate increase of cost with time, blockage of promotion possibilities involving loss of experience and, eventually, a massive need for replacement, which usually re-creates the original problem.

A stable age distribution can be defined at a point in time by the expected subsequent wastage pattern, recruitment distribution and total number required. It is always theoretically possible to achieve such a distribution, especially over a period of 5 years, but it is not always practical to do so; at worst it is possible to compare the preferred stable distribution with the distribution expected on the basis of declared policies, and to see what problems are liable to arise from such policies.

3. Example (Figure 3)

A major problem in manpower forecasting, which has not hitherto been mentioned, is the difficulty of forecasting the managerial policies which influence the input to any model. Unless there is any striking evidence to the contrary, the first forecasts are made on the basis of unchanged wastage and recruitment patterns. For the purpose of illustration two trends in total number are considered; firstly the continuing rate of expansion and secondly no further increase, or decrease.

On the basis of the loss pattern derived from information for year end 1962 to year end 1967 (and shown in figure 2) the equations for forecasting 5 years ahead become:-

$$F_a = (2 \cdot 432)(Kn_a) \qquad \text{(iv)}$$

$$F_b = (0 \cdot 428)(A_a) + (1 \cdot 218)(Kn_a) + (2 \cdot 464)(Kn_b) \qquad \text{(v)}$$

$$F_c = (0 \cdot 523)(A_b) + (1 \cdot 343)(Kn_b) + (2 \cdot 698)(Kn_c) \qquad \text{(vi)}$$

$$F_d = (0 \cdot 704)(A_c) + (1 \cdot 612)(Kn_c) + (2 \cdot 808)(Kn_d) \qquad \text{(vii)}$$

$$F_e = (0 \cdot 807)(A_d) + (1 \cdot 753)(Kn_d) + (2 \cdot 883)(Kn_e) \qquad \text{(viii)}$$

$$F_f = (0 \cdot 895)(A_e) + (1 \cdot 863)(Kn_e) + (2 \cdot 960)(Kn_f) \qquad \text{(ix)}$$

$$F_g = (0 \cdot 895)(A_f) + (1 \cdot 883)(Kn_f) + (2 \cdot 845)(Kn_g) \qquad \text{(x)}$$

$$F_h = (0 \cdot 649)(A_g) + (1 \cdot 583)(Kn_g) + (2 \cdot 464)(Kn_h) \qquad \text{(xi)}$$

$$F_i = (0 \cdot 200)(A_h) + (0 \cdot 860)(Kn_h) + (1 \cdot 613)(Kn_i) \qquad \text{(xii)}$$

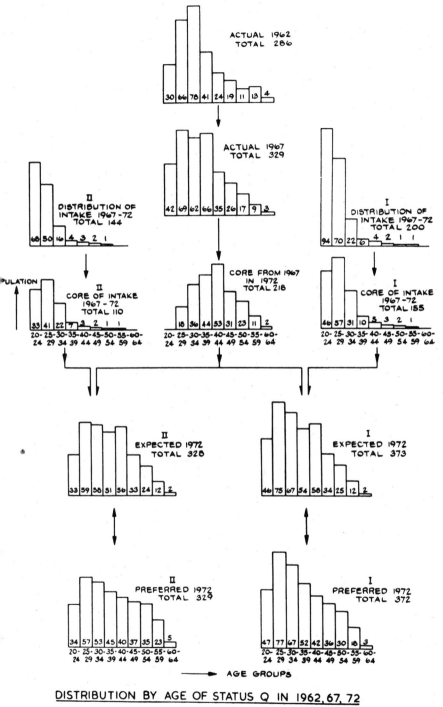

DISTRIBUTION BY AGE OF STATUS Q IN 1962, 67, 72

FIGURE 3

where F_a is the number of people in age group a in 5 years time

A_a is the number of people in age group a now

n_a is the recruitment factor for age group a

K is the total annual recruitment

Age groups $a, b, \ldots$ are for ages 20-24, 25-29, $\ldots$

The recruitment distribution (1962-1967) is expected to remain (at this stage indefinitely):-

$$n_a = 0\cdot47 \quad n_c = 0\cdot11 \quad n_e = 0\cdot02 \quad n_g + n_h = 0\cdot01$$
$$n_b = 0\cdot35 \quad n_d = 0\cdot03 \quad n_f = 0\cdot01$$

Equations (iv) $-$ (xii) are simplified to:-

$$F_a = (1\cdot143)\,(K) \tag{xiii}$$
$$F_b = (0\cdot428)\,(A_a) + (1\cdot435)\,(K) \tag{xiv}$$
$$F_c = (0\cdot523)\,(A_b) + (0\cdot767)\,(K) \tag{xv}$$
$$F_d = (0\cdot704)\,(A_c) + (0\cdot262)\,(K) \tag{xvi}$$
$$F_e = (0\cdot807)\,(A_d) + (0\cdot110)\,(K) \tag{xvii}$$
$$F_f = (0\cdot895)\,(A_e) + (0\cdot067)\,(K) \tag{xviii}$$
$$F_g = (0\cdot895)\,(A_f) + (0\cdot033)\,(K) \tag{xix}$$
$$F_h = (0\cdot649)\,(A_g) + (0\cdot020)\,(K) \tag{xx}$$
$$F_i = (0\cdot200)\,(A_h) + (0\cdot004)\,(K) \tag{xxi}$$

For various reasons it is convenient to calculate the core of people currently in the group who will remain in 5 years time. This is obtained in equations (iv) - (xii) by putting $K = 0$. The annual number of recruits required is then calculate from equations (xiii) - (xxi) by:-

$$\sum F_j = \sum \alpha_j A_{j-1} + 3\cdot841K \tag{xxii}$$

Total required   Core   Annual
in 5 years time   Recruits

Having obtained a value for K the anticipated age distribution can be determined The stable (preferred) distribution for 5 years ahead is the distribution which will subsequently reproduce itself annually. (Note: The time scale is simply convenient for the group of career staff). It is assumed that the wastage and recruitment distributions will be unchanged and that in one case expansion wi continue steadily while in the other case there will be no expansion. The general equation, comparable to equation (iii) becomes:-

$$L_j = \alpha_j F_{j-1} + K^1(\beta_j N_{j-1} + \gamma_j n_j) \tag{xxiii}$$

where L_j is the number of people in age group j in 10 years time.

F_{j-1} is the number of people in age group $(j-1)$ in 5 years time.

$\alpha_j, \beta_j, \gamma_j, n_{j-1}, n_j$ are numerically identical with previous equations.

K^1 is the annual number of recruits over the period 5-10 years ahead.

Equation (xxiii) can be simplified to:-

$$L_j = \alpha_j F_{j-1} + \delta_j K^1 \tag{xxiv}$$

where δ_j is a constant defined by the wastage and recruitment patterns.

The condition for stability is that $\qquad L_j = uF_j$ for all j (xxv)

where u is a constant and:- $\qquad \sum L_j = u \sum F_j$ (xxvi)

In the illustrated example $u = 1 \cdot 13$ for an annual expansion of $2 \cdot 5\%$ (roughly 13% expansion over 5 years), $u = 1$ for no expansion.

These various steps are shown in Figure 3.

The conclusions that can be drawn from comparisons of the anticipated and preferred distributions are as follows:-

CASE I

Expansion $2 \cdot 5\%$ per annum

TABLE 1

Preferred and anticipated numbers in 1972. Case I.

AGE GROUP	NUMBERS IN 1972		
	PREFERRED[(P)] DISTRIBUTION	ANTICIPATED[(A)] DISTRIBUTION	(P) – (A)
20–24	47	46	+ 1
25–29	77	75	+ 2
30–34	67	67	0
35–39	52	54	− 2
40–44	42	58	–16
45–49	36	34	+ 2
50–54	30	25	+ 5
55–59	18	12	+ 6
60–64	3	2	+ 1
TOTAL	372	373	− 1

The bracketed groupings in the (P) – (A) column give: + 1 (for 20–24 to 35–39), − 16 (for 40–44), + 14 (for 45–49 to 60–64).

In this case the distribution between the first four age groups is satisfactory. There is, however, a large excess in the age group 40–44 and a similar shortfall distributed over the last four age groups. It can be seen that this excess is present in the core and is therefore already a fault in the present age distribution of the group. The shortfall in the older age groups is the result of excessive recruitment in the younger age groups in the past. The situation is one of a group with insufficient experience (if equated with age) and with all the potential problems of an age bulge.

CASE II

No Expansion.

In this case the problems of Case I are simply exaggerated. It is extremely difficult to suggest a practical solution to such a series of problems which have arisen from past actions.

TABLE 2

Preferred and anticipated numbers in 1972. Case II.

AGE GROUP	NUMBERS IN 1972			
	PREFERRED(P) DISTRIBUTION	ANTICIPATED (A) DISTRIBUTION	(P) – (A)	
20–24	34	33	+ 1	} – 1
25–29	57	59	– 2	
30–34	53	58	–5	
35–39	45	51	– 6	} – 27
40–44	40	56	– 16	
45–49	37	33	+ 4	
50–54	35	24	+ 11	
55–59	23	12	+ 11	} + 29
60–64	5	2	+ 3	
TOTAL	329	328	+ 1	

There is no reason why the anticipated recruitment pattern for 1967–72 should not be altered in order to bring the anticipated distribution closer to the preferred distribution for subsequent years. However there is a much bigger managerial problem in both cases arising from existing excesses which can only be solved, in the quantitative sense, by transfer-out or redundancy.

B. FORECASTING BP PROMOTION PROSPECTS

There are references in the literature (Ref. 3, 4) to the use of forecasting by status distribution, specifically in academic and civil service environments. In industry where status is not so clearly defined and where, as already indicated, age is often the primary parameter, forecasts of promotion chances are better made in the light of conclusions from forecasts of age distribution. There are many unsatisfactory aspects of the approach which will be outlined but these arise partly from the relatively small size of the groups and partly from the unstable nature of the internal structure of the group. Within the population of status Q four sub-statuses are defined:-

A Senior Management

B Middle Management

C Junior Management

D Junior Staff

These sub-statuses are related directly to the grading system which is linked to the salary structure. In the group already illustrated, the distribution by age and status is shown in Table 3 in which it can be seen that there is a general increase of status with age.

TABLE 3

Distribution by age and sub-status

AGE GROUP	NUMBERS IN STATUS GROUP BY AGE				
	D	C	B	A	TOTAL
20–24	41	1	-	-	42
25–29	60	8	1	-	69
30–34	28	22	12	-	62
35–39	11	34	20	1	66
40–44	4	7	13	11	35
45–49	-	6	8	12	26
50–54	-	4	1	12	17
55–59	-	1	1	7	9
60–64	-	-	-	3	3
TOTAL IN 1967	144	83	56	46	329
CORE IN 1972	70	65	51	32	218

Using a combination of wastage by age and by grade it is possible to deduce the distribution by status of the core in 1972. Likewise on the basis of past experience it is possible to assess the distribution by status of the core in 1972 of the intake during 1967–72. The major problem is to forecast the overall distribution of statuses in 1972; the possibilities are endless and in Figure 4 only four cases are considered.

As in the age distribution discussion, Cases I and II correspond to continued expansion and no change respectively. Within each case there are two status distributions, A and B; distribution A for 1972 is the same as for 1967,

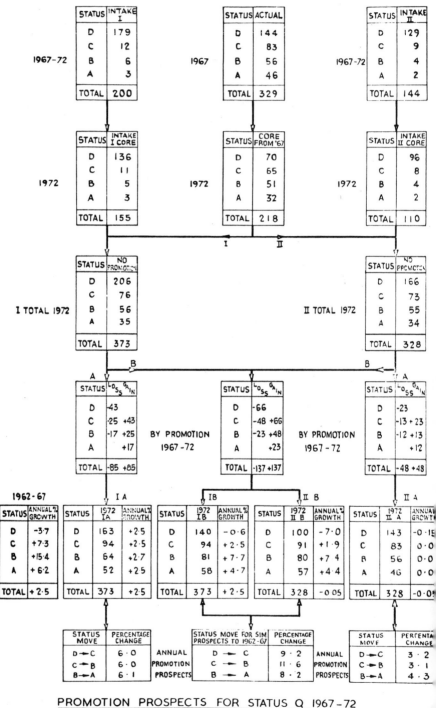

PROMOTION PROSPECTS FOR STATUS Q 1967–72

FIGURE

distribution B for 1972 is the distribution which will give comparable promotion chances to those which were available during 1962—67. Promotion chances are expressed as the percentage of the population of a status who can expect to be promoted annually.

It can be seen that for distribution A the promotion prospects are worse for 1967—72 than they were for 1962—67; this arises because of the status inflation that occurred, represented by a decrease in status D and increase in statuses C, B, A.

An important aspect of forecasting promotion prospects, which in many respects is simply an embellishment on age distribution forecasts, is the lack of information normally available to managers who offer careers in industry. The promotion probabilities calculated in Figure 4 give an indication of the career chances in status Q. It is obvious that, except for the most gifted, progress will be slow and not everyone can expect to reach sub-status A. The calculations are, however, particularly sensitive to changes in status distribution, either of status Q as a whole or of the intake to status Q and to changes in overall size.

C. Concluding Remarks

This paper has been intended to expose the extent to which it can truly be said that model building is being applied to the problems of staff management. On one hand the mere ordering of staff data into a series of statements of present position is a practice which is insufficiently general but which is extremely useful to managers in assessing the situation. On the other hand, analysis of past trends and forecasting of future possibilities seems to raise problems, rather than solve them. However, in these calculations it is often all too easy to see the repercussions of ill-advised decisions in the past; if these situations can be made clear to the decision makers it will indeed be a step towards solving some problems and avoiding others. Our model, if it can be dignified in this way, is clearly of the simplest type but we have taken heart from a remark by Dr. Kendall (ref. 5) ".... model building should start with simple and modest models, and work towards the more complicated systems by integration, rather than start with attempts at comprehensive models .... the layman is fully entitled to distrust a crude model which leaves out of account features of the system which he knows to exist and believes to be important". The laymen in Staff Management are distrustful of even the most modest models.

REFERENCES

1. SILCOCK, H. (1954). 'The Phenomenon of Labour Turnover' *J.R. Statist. Soc., A*
    117, 429–440.

2. LANE, K.F., and ANDREW, J.E. (1955). 'A Method of Labour Turnover Analysis'
    J.R. Statist. Soc., A, 118, 296–323.

3. YOUNG, A., and ALMOND, G. (1961). 'Predicting Distributions of Staff' *Comp. J.,*
    3, 246–250.

4. YOUNG, A. (1965). 'Models for Planning Recruitment and Promotion of Staff' *Br. J.
    Ind. Rel.* Vol III, 301–310.

5. KENDALL, M.G. (1967). 'Mathematical Model Building in Economics and Industry'.
    C.E.I.R. Conference July, 1967.

8. MICROANALYTIC MODELS AND THEIR SOLUTION*

GUY H. ORCUTT

CONTENTS

I. Why model national economies?

Accurate and dynamic models of economic systems are needed to forewarn policy-makers of impending developments and to enable them to evaluate policies by trying these policies on a model before applying them to the economy. Forecasts about future development have a direct relevance to policy formulation. The present situation is known only with a lag and instruments work only with a lag. Therefore, if policies are to be applied with optimum timing, policy-makers must be forewarned of impending developments. If we had a realistic dynamic model of an economic system, it could be used to generate forecasts of future economic developments. The accuracy of forecasts obtained in this way would depend on how adequately the dynamic behavior of the economy was represented as well as on the assumptions made about outside events that impinge on the economy.

Forecasting is sometimes done solely on the basis of such things as businessmen's intentions to invest or consumers' intentions to buy durables. Intentions of various components of our economy have a bearing on subsequent behavior, but

*This is a draft of a talk given to the C-E-I-R Ltd Model Building Symposium held in London in June 1968. It is drawn rather directly from earlier works of the author and from parts of chapters by the author in *Forecasting on a Scientific Basis*, Do Instito Gulbenkian de Ciencia (1968). This book by H. Wold, G. Orcutt, E. Robinson, D. Suits, and P. de Wolff is an outcome of the NATO Advanced Summer Institute on Forecasting on a Scientific Basis, held at Curia, Portugal, September 1966. The research behind this paper was financed by the National Science Foundation.

there is nothing which requires that intentions be mutually consistent. Accurate forecasting must take account of interactions and thus requires the use of a model of the economy.

Predictions derived from a realistic model of an economy are needed as a basis for selection of governmental policies relating to taxation, spending, debt management, etc. If policy-makers are considering one tax law as compared to some other tax law, or one spending policy as compared to some other spending policy, they should know what the consequences are of the policies under consideration. One way to find out would be to try out the policies on the economy, but it would not be very satisfactory from the standpoint of the participants. Policies should be selected on the basis of their fruit; but it would be preferable to sample the fruit before applying policies to the real world. If a sufficiently accurate model of the economy were available, it would make such sampling possible.

II. Alternative approaches

The oldest and most widely utilized approach to the construction of quantitative models of the United States economy dates back to the path-breaking work of Tinbergen (1939). Models used in this approach may be referred to as aggregate-type national income models. These models use major sectors, such as the household and business sectors, as basic components. Macroeconomic relationships for these components are estimated and tested on the basis of annual or quarterly time series data of such variables as aggregate consumption and income of the household sector. The relationships developed have been finite difference equations of a stochastic nature. Both recursive and simultaneous equation systems have been developed. Examples of models of this general type include those conducted by Tinbergen, Clark (1949), Klein (1947, 1950), Klein and Goldberger (1955), Duesenberry, Eckstein and Fromm (1960), Smithies (1957) and Suits (1962), to name only a few. The current SSRC-Brookings econometric model building effort (1965) represents the latest and most ambitious attempt in this general direction. The model being developed contains several hundred equations and the industrial sector has several subsectors.

The second oldest and the second most widely utilized approach to construction of models of the United States stems from Leontief's highly important work (1951, 1953). Industries are used as basic components in these models. Emphasis is placed on the cross-sectional structure of the economy rather than on its dynamic features. Physical outputs of industries are assumed to be strictly proportional to physical inputs classified by industry of origin. Models of this type have been stated in a non-probabilistic form. Solution of such models with as many as 100 industries has been achieved by the numerical inversion of a matrix of the same order.

The newest and least developed approach to construction of models of the United States economy is the microanalytic approach, Orcutt, Greenberger,

Korbel and Rivlin (1961). While being of the same general statistical type as other models of economic systems, microanalytic models are, nevertheless, the most general in terms of their statistical structure. Each major type of model of a national economy may include stochastic elements, each may use lagged dependent variables as part of what is treated as given, and each may be expressed as a system of finite difference equations. However, microanalytic models are more general in that they may contain a population of any kind of component instead of but a single case of each kind, as is true with both Leontief type and aggregate-type national income models.

III. The need for microanalytic models

Up until about three decades ago, it was widely believed that economics, perhaps like mechanics, should consist of an elegant deductive structure resting upon a few simple premises about the behavior of microcomponents. It also was believed that simple introspection, self-observation, and casual observation of familiar components would be adequate for achieving the essential inductive substructure. However, three factors led to the abandonment of the microanalytic approach to the modelling of national economies.

In the first place it came to be appreciated that households and firms are too complicated to yield the essential secrets of their behavior to unsophisticated, inductive attempts based on introspection and casual observation. In the second place, it began to be apparent that as models of microcomponents became more complex, deduction of the results of their interaction would become extremely formidable if not impossible with available tools. In the third place, governments responded to pressing problems, and a growing general belief in the value of information, by accumulating data about those economic aggregates of concern.

Economists, being unable to deliver what was needed by the microanalytic approach, turned to a more direct approach which we will refer to as the national account approach. This approach has been based upon the rapidly growing body of national income data. These data, being already at the level of aggregation of central interest from the standpoint of stabilization and growth policies, seemed to permit the econometrician to sidestep the intractable problems associated with the microanalytic approach. The development of these data also permitted the econometrician to retreat from the painstaking and substantial effort associated with data collection.

However, a gradual realization of the inadequacy of national accounts, as a satisfactory data base for predicting the effect of governmental actions, has been taking place during the last one to two decades. This has been coupled in time with two major technological developments which are bringing about substantial changes in economic research and which now make the more indirect microanalytic approach feasible. The first of these developments is the emergence of improved sample survey techniques and instruments. The second is the development, during the last decade, of computational facilities which are thousands of times more powerful than anything previously available. The first of these greatly increases the opportunity for collection of data about microcomponents. The second of these revolutionized the possibilities for solution and analysis of large scale microanalytic models of an economy. The need to develop microanalytic models of economic systems, given the feasibility of doing so, arises because of the following considerations.

1. A substantial part of the theory and of the output of current research cannot be applied effectively in models restricted to macro-components and macro-relations. Much of our theory and research relates to the behavior of individuals, families, and firms. However, while it is a simple matter to aggregate behavior of micro-components, we do not know how to aggregate micro-relations appropriately

2. Satisfactory estimation and testing of highly aggregative models cannot be achieved because of the relatively few macro time series observations available for testing implications of such models against actual developments. Multicollinearity autocorrelation, feedbacks, and errors of observations only serve to complicate and worsen what is already a very precarious situation insofar as satisfactory testing is concerned. The information available for estimation and testing can be enormously increased by appropriate use of data relating to micro-components.

3. Models built only in terms of the interaction of major sectors cannot yield several important kinds of predictions. For example, not only is it important to predict how unemployment or income would be affected by alternative policies, but it is also important to predict how unemployment and income would be distributed among individuals by various characteristics. Such characteristics might well include previous unemployment, age, sex, race, and family size.

IV. Outlines of a microanalytic model of an economy

Both for research purposes and for convenience of presentation, it is important and perhaps even essential to consider an overall model of an economy as an ensemble of interacting building blocks. Each type of block becomes a focus of research activity, and presentation of the overall model is facilitated by presentation of submodels of each type of block along with a description of the way in which interaction between blocks is to take place.

Alternative ways of breaking an overall model into blocks are possible, but some ways seem definitely preferable. In general, the objective is to select blocks in such a way that each block or type may be studied with a minimum of concern about interrelationships with other blocks.

The major building blocks are called "components". In microanalytic models of an economy the components represent recognizable entities met in everyday experience. The type of component occupying center stage is called a "decision unit". Decision units include such components as individuals, nuclear families, spending units, household units, manufacturing firms, retailers, banks, insurance companies, labor unions, and local, state, and federal government units. Individuals are regarded as imbedded within more extensive family or household units. Firms are thought of as being imbedded within industry units.

The decision units in microanalytic models interact with each other either directly or indirectly through a second major type of component called a "market". The markets in a model represent markets in the economy, and it is through them that the third type of component flows from decision unit to decision unit. For brevity, components of this last type will be referred to as "goods". But it must be noted that such components include money, bonds, shares of stock, deeds, mortgages, and various other things which may be produced, held, sold, bought, or consumed by decision units.

Variables used in the submodel of a component but given time from outside of the component are referred to as "input variables for that component". Variables that flow from or are emitted by a component are called "output variables of that component". Variables that are stored in a component are called "status variables of that component". Input, status, and output variables may refer to either stocks or flows, and of course all variables appearing in a dynamic model are dated.

A description of any component would include a listing of its own input, status, and output variables along with those relationships which are used in updating status variables and in generating output variables. The behavioral relationships used to generate values of the updated status variables and of the output variables, given the predetermined status variables and the input variables, are called "operating characteristics of that component". Other relations of a definitional or tautological character may be used as convenience dictates.

Finally, any variables used by an operating characteristic may be referred to as an "input of that operating characteristic" and any variable determined by an operating characteristic may be referred to as an "output of that operating characteristic".

Let us now consider interactions between decision units. Some outputs of operating characteristics are end products and only require aggregation. Most outputs of operating characteristics, however, update status variables, and are directly used as inputs into other operating characteristics of the same component, and/or are outputs of the component. As will be recalled, the second major class of components in microanalytic models are markets, and the specific function of these components is to transmit the outputs of decision units and to distribute them as inputs to other decision units.

The information received by potential buyers is used as inputs into their operating characteristics, and in some cases orders to buy are the resulting outputs. These orders enter as inputs into the appropriate markets. Operating characteristics of each market summarize and classify the orders by region of origin, price accepted, etc. Other operating characteristics of the market then use this

summarized information about orders, along with information about each poten
seller considered in turn, to distribute the orders among potential sellers. Decisi
units respond to the orders which they receive as inputs and generate various ou
puts among which in due course will usually be deliveries. These deliveries show
as inputs into an appropriate market, are transmitted and distributed by the mai
appear as outputs of the market and as inputs into the appropriate decision unit:
These decision units then make payments or promises to pay which are again dis
buted through the market to the appropriate sellers.

Figure 1 shows how the outputs of an entire set of N decision units may be
visualized as transmitted and distributed by the M markets. The outputs of the
decision units become inputs into the markets. After being summarized and dist
buted they appear as outputs of the markets. These market outputs then becom
inputs into the decision units again.

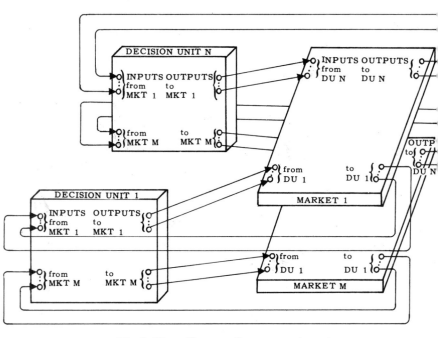

Fig. 1. Flow diagram of an economic system.

V. Solution of models

Solution of a model consists of deriving implications from it or by use of it.
Solutions may be more or less complete, and a wide variety of ways of solving a
model may be possible. The various approaches to model solution may be classi
fied into three broad classes, which for present purposes will be referred to as th

analytic approach, the transitional matrix approach, and the Monte Carlo simulation approach.

The analytic approach.   In the analytic approach an attempt is made to deduce a relationship for each endogenous variable that will express it explicitly as a function of parameters. The set of such relationships is the general solution of the model. Specific solutions of a model are obtained by evaluating these functions for specific sets of endogenous variables for specific time periods, and for given values of the parameters. The parameters referred to include initial conditions and the values of exogenous variables.

When feasible, the analytic approach has much to commend it and is greatly preferred by mathematicians. However, this approach has not been successfully applied to any models of even moderate complexity and realism. Either it has proved impossible to deduce general solutions or, if they can be deduced in a formal way, they are too complicated to understand or even to use as a basis of calculation for specific numerical solutions.

In some cases in which a full analytic solution cannot be obtained, researchers lower their objectives and instead seek to analytically determine the dependence of expected values of dependent variables on parameter values, including initial conditions and exogenous variables. Conditional density functions are replaced by conditional expected value functions, and expected values of endogenous variables are sought instead of their probability distributions.

The approximation of probability distributions by their means is certainly a sensible idea for arriving at a first approximation. And, if expected values of endogenous variables are all that are needed, this approach may be adequate in some cases. In fact for single period prediction it may be ideal. The major difficulty with this approach arises in the following way. In general, it is essential, for purposes of estimation, to regard the derived joint conditional density function of endogenous variables as the product of a long chain of conditional density functions. Moreover, the variables taken as given in some of these density functions will be the dependent variables in others of these density functions. Thus some expected values will depend upon the full distribution of other endogenous variables rather than merely on the expected values of these other variables. If only the expected values of these other variables are used, then unknown and possibly large biases will be introduced into the calculated expected values of variables dependent upon them.

Transitional matrix approach.   A numerical approach, which has been used very effectively in obtaining specific solutions for some models, might well be referred to as the *transitional matrix approach.* It has been used frequently by demographers, among others, and is the computational technique used by the United States Bureau of the Census in making population projections.

For purposes of illustrating this approach, let us consider a population of *m* components which may be classified adequately according to a single, three-valued variable. The state of this population at time t is given by a specification of the number of components having each value of the variable. The state of the population at time $t + 1$ is to be calculated, given the state of the population at time t and a model which serves to link the state of the population at any point in time to its state one period earlier.

The transitional matrix is a matrix which, when multiplied by the vector of frequencies representing the state of the population at any time t, yields the vector of frequencies specifying the state of the population at time $t + 1$. The transitional matrix in this case would be a matrix of transitional probabilities. There would be one transitional probability for each combination of initial and final values of the variable by which components are classified. In the simplest case the model specifies that the transitional probabilities remain constant from period to period, and each of the transitional probabilities is estimated directly on the basis of some available body of data.

The following diagram may help in seeing how this technique might be used to update the state of the model population from t to $t + 1$. X is the single variable. The P_{ij} are the transitional probabilities.

Matrix of Transitional Probabilities

X_t	$f(X_t)$	$X_{t+1} = 1$	$X_{t+1} = 2$	$X_{t+1} = 3$
1	$m_{1,t}$	P_{11}	P_{12}	P_{13}
2	$m_{2,t}$	P_{21}	P_{22}	P_{23}
3	$m_{3,t}$	P_{31}	P_{32}	P_{33}
		$m_{1,t+1}$	$m_{2,t+1}$	$m_{3,t+1}$ $f(X_{t+1})$

$m_{1,t}$ is the number of components at time t that have the first of the three values of X_t. $m_{1,t+1}$ is the number of components at time $t + 1$ that have the first of the three values of X_{t+1}. $m_{1,t+1}$ is the sum of products, $P_{11}m_{1,t} + P_{21}m_{2,t} + P_{31}m_{3,t}$ and similarly for $m_{2,t+1}$ and $m_{3,t+1}$. The state of the model population at time $t + 1$ is thus obtained as the product of a vector of frequencies times a matrix of transitional probabilities.

When feasible, this particular class of approach is highly attractive. In the first place, it is easily specified in terms of repetitions of simple matrix operations. Secondly, this technique groups components so as to effectively minimize computation costs, if the number of components is very large relative to the number of cells into which components are classified. The difficulty, which prevents this method of solution from being a satisfactory one for models of the economy, arises because the number of cells essential for a suitable specification of the state of an economy are many times larger than the number of components in the economy.

The transitional matrix technique seems attractive because it appears to avoid unnecessary repetition of calculations by grouping those components which are to be similarly treated. However, this grouping and regrouping becomes less and less attractive as the number of groups into which a population must be classified becomes large relative to the size of the population.

Even an extremely modest model of the economy would involve at least 10 endogenous variables. And, even if only 10 values were permitted for each variable, the number of possible cells into which components might be classified would be 10^{10} or 10 billion. The full matrix of transitional probabilities would have $(10 \text{ billion})^2$ elements! No doubt if one were determined to use the transitional matrix technique he would look for methods of avoiding the handling of empty cells and the calculation of transitional probabilities which would apply only to empty cells. He, of course, would have to abandon any notion of direct estimation of each transitional probability from any conceivable body of data no matter how large. His problem would be increased by the fact that while most of the cells would be empty at any point of time, it would not be the same set which would be empty in successive time periods. Even if he were able, without great cost, to reduce the number of cells at time t to one millionth of 10 billion, he would still have 10 000 cell frequencies and the matrix of transitional probabilities would have 100 million elements. Since current attempts to model the economy involve several times as many variables as used in the above example, and since one digit specification of variables would be highly unsatisfactory, it seems clear that the transitional matrix technique will not be suitable for carrying out simulations of a national economy.

The simulation approach

Simulation is a general approach to the study and use of models. As such it furnishes an alternative approach to that offered by conventional mathematical techniques. In using conventional mathematical techniques to solve a model the objective is to determine, deductively and with generality, the way in which the model implicitly relates endogenous variables to initial conditions, parameters, and time paths of exogenous variables.*

Simulation techniques also are used to solve models, but in any single simulation run the solution obtained is highly specific. Given completely specified

---

*There are many areas in which simulation is of importance to social scientists and to policymakers and the interested reader is referred to such useful starting points as provided by Adelman (1968), Clarkson and Simon (1960), Guetzkow (1962), Orcutt (1960), Shubik (1960a, 1960b).

initial conditions, parameters, and exogenous variables, a single simulation run yields only a single set of time paths of the endogenous variables. To determine how the behavior of the endogenous variables is more generally dependent on initial conditions, parameters, and exogenous variables may require a very large number of simulation runs; and even then induction from specific results to general solutions will be required.

An individual simulation run may be thought of as an experiment performed upon a model. A given experiment involves operating a model after first completely specifying a set of initial conditions appropriate to the model, a set of values of the parameters used in specifying relations contained in the model, and the time paths of those variables used in the model and treated as exogenous. Additional experiments would involve operating the model after respecifying the initial conditions, the parameters, and/or the exogenous variables. The problem of inferring general relationships from specific results obtained in individual experiments performed on a model is the same as that of inferring general relationships from specific experimental results in any of the inductive sciences. The scientist studying natural phenomena has no alternative. The research worker, studying or using a model, could conceivably use a purely deductive approach, but this alternative may not be attractive or it may not prove feasible with known mathematical methods.

In practice, the word simulation is used in a variety of related but somewhat different senses. For example, if someone refers to the simulation of an economy or of some other set of real phenomena, he probably is referring to the combined activity of building a model of that set of phenomena and also of studying and/or using the model by means of the kind of simulation approach defined above. While building a model it is, of course, important to give some thought to its eventual solution and use. However, any particular model might be expressed in any one of various languages and might be solved and used by means of more than one approach.

Not only is the term simulation used in different senses, but also a number of other words are used to identify activities or methods which might properly be regarded as specialized uses of a simulation approach. Both gaming and Monte Carlo methods are cases in point. The former may be characterized by the fact that contestants are used as components in models studied by simulation techniques. The latter may be characterized by the fact that probability models are studied by simulation techniques.

The Monte Carlo–simulation approach

Since simulation is the construction and operation of a model, both the transitional matrix approach, and the Monte Carlo-simulation approach, could be thought of as simulation approaches. The distinguishing feature of the Monte Carlo-simulation approach is, as suggested by our choice of a name, the use of the Monte Carlo method. This unsophisticated yet powerful method is one which has come into wide use along with the development of the modern computer. It and sample representation of populations provide the main methods for successfully solving microanalytic models by means of a simulation approach.

The Monte Carlo method capitalizes on the following two basic facts:

1. It is possible to empirically approximate a probability distribution as closely as desired on the basis of an adequate number of random drawings from the distribution.

2. It frequently is a great deal easier to obtain random drawings from a distribution than it is to analytically deduce the form of the distribution.

The following very simple example may be of help in seeing the potentialities of the Monte Carlo method in solving microanalytic-type models.

Example. Suppose that the density functions, or some moment of the density function, of x/y is desired. Let this density function be denoted by: $g(x/y)$. Also, let the following two single variate density functions be known:

$$f_1(x) \text{ and } f_2(y \mid x).$$

By the usual rules relating to density functions it is obvious that the joint density function of x and y may be expressed as the product of these two density functions. Thus,

$$f(x,y) = f_1(x). \ f_2(y \mid x).$$

A Monte Carlo procedure for obtaining an empirical approximation of $g(x/y)$ would be as follows:

1. Draw random samples of x from the distribution specified by $f_1(x)$.

2. Use each such sample x to obtain a random drawing of y from the conditional distribution specified by $f_2(y \mid x)$.

3. Each x and associated y obtained in this way will be the coordinates of a point drawn at random from the bivariate distribution specified by $f(x,y)$.

4. For each point drawn from the bivariate distribution, calculate the ratio x/y.

5. Form a relative frequency distribution of values of x/y and use it as an empirically derived approximation of $g(x/y)$. The approximation may be made as close as desired, in a statistical sense, by use of a sufficiently large number of random drawings.

Sample representation of populations.   The Monte Carlo method used with a simulation approach does permit, in principle at least, the solution of models of

economic systems. However, one serious difficulty remains. How shall multivariate distributions of many variables be represented? This problem is particularly acute for microanalytic-type models but is serious enough even for aggregate-
type national income models.

In the case of aggregate-type national income models it occurs because, while
sample points may be drawn from multivariate conditional distributions of
endogenous variables, it may not be feasible to obtain an adequate, empirically
derived, functional description of such distributions. This may well be the case
even if a fairly large number of random drawings are obtained.

In the case of microanalytic-type models it is not even feasible to obtain
drawings from the joint conditional distribution of endogenous variables until
this problem is handled. This arises because the initial conditions include the prior
values of microvariables for micro-components. In other words, the initial joint
distribution of the components must be obtained and specified. But how can it
be specified if it involves say 100 variables for each of say 100 million components?

The solution is as simple as it is obvious. Any multivariate distribution may
be represented by a random sample drawn from it. And the larger the sample
the better the representation. Means, variances, covariances, and other functions
of the sample will be estimates of the corresponding functions of the parent
population. The properties of samples and of sample statistics in relation to
populations and population statistics have been extensively investigated and are
readily available. The initial population may be satisfactorily represented by a
sample and so may the population at subsequent points in time. Population
statistics may be estimated as desired on the basis of such sample representations.

VI. Simulation of a microanalytic model

As one step in demonstrating the feasibility and potential usefulness of the
Monte Carlo-simulation approach, in connection with the development and use of
models of economies built in terms of micro-components, Orcutt, Greenberger,
Korbel and Rivlin (1961) constructed and carried out computer simulations of a
demographic model of the United States household sector.

The basic components of the model are individuals and combinations of
individuals such as married couples and families. The family units form, grow,
diminish, and dissolve as married couples have children and get divorced and
individuals age, marry, and die. These outputs of the basic components in a given
month depend on the status variables that characterize each component as of the
beginning of the month and on the inputs into each component during the month.
The operating characteristics, which serve to relate outputs of components to
input and status variables, are stochastic in nature; i.e., it is the probabilities of
occurrence of certain outputs rather than the outputs themselves which are
regarded as functions of input and status variables. For example, the probability

that a woman will give birth to a child during a given month was estimated, on the basis of available data, to depend on a nonlinear, multivariate function of her marital status, age, number of previous births, interval since previous birth or since marriage, month, and year. The model is recursive in that the probabilities determined for the possible outputs of each component in any period depend only on previously determined input and status variables.

Solution of the model was achieved by simulation on a large electronic computer. An initial population of over 10 000 individuals was made to be representative of the United States population as of April 1950 by appropriate assignment to these individuals of sex, race, age, marital status, parity, interval since marriage or previous birth, and family composition. Assignment of these status variables was based on information contained in tabulations of the Bureau of the Census and in various sample surveys carried out by the Survey Research Center of the University of Michigan for the Federal Reserve Board and for a family planning study by Ronald Freedman, Pascal Whelpton, and Arthur Campbell.

The simulations carried out proceeded in one-month steps. Data relating to specific individuals and families were stored on magnetic tape. Operating characteristics, summary information and variables nonspecific to microcomponents were stored in high-speed core storage. In each "month" the members of each family were considered in turn. For each possible output of each component a probability of occurrence was specified by use of the relevant operating characteristic and the appropriate status and input variables. Whether the output occurred or not was then determined by a random drawing from this probability distribution. For example, if the probability that a male with a particular initial status will die during the month was calculated to be 0.0002, then, in essence, a random drawing was made from a bag containing two black balls for every 9 998 white balls. The man either died and was eliminated from the population (and from his family) or he lived through the month depending on the outcome of the draw. In practice, however, random numbers generated by the computing machine provided a less cumbersome method of making the random drawings than balls in a bag.

When each possible output for each unit had been considered in this way, the first "pass" or month was complete. The whole procedure was then repeated for the second month and as many more as desired. Each succeeding month was begun with a population of components which was slightly different both in size and composition from the preceding one, since some individuals had died or married, some couples had divorced, some babies had been born and all surviving individuals were one month older.

Several simulation runs covering part or all of the interval from April 1950 to April 1960 were carried out using operating characteristics estimated on the basis of data from available sources. Simulation runs, involving systematic variations in critical operating characteristics, also were carried out.

As each simulation run was carried out the computer was used to summarize the micro-changes taking place and to feed out aggregative monthly information about births, deaths, marriages and divorces. At selected intervals cross-sectional tabulations of the developing populations also were produced by the computer. The aggregative time series and frequency distributions produced in this way were then blown up to provide estimates relating to the real population and where appropriate these estimates were compared with available aggregative data about the United States population and its composition.

The use of simulation techniques by the authors of this demographic study does not, of course, offer any guarantee in itself that they have produced an acceptable and useful population model. However, by producing a feasible means of solution it permitted them to introduce a variety of interactions, variables, non-linearities and stochastic considerations into their model which they otherwise would have been forced to leave out despite strong evidence of their importance. In addition, by providing a means of solution it made possible comparison of generated results with observed time series and cross-sectional data and thus permitted testing of a sort that would not otherwise have been possible.

VII. Simulation of large-scale systems

Economic systems are complex organizations involving the behavior of hundreds of millions of complicated decision units and their interaction. Models involving hundreds of millions of components can be conceived but their construction and use pose problems that appear insuperable both from the standpoint of completely specifying such models and from that of studying and using them if they could be constructed. There are, however, various means by which satisfactory computer simulation of large-scale systems can be made feasible. Some of the more important means are as follows:

1. *Building-block approach.* One rather simple but essential procedure is that of using a building-block approach. Construction of a large-scale model and of a large-scale computer program requires an extended effort over time by many individuals with many skills. Extensive testing of individual pieces must be carried out before the pieces are assembled, and even after they have been assembled, it frequently may be necessary to modify some pieces. Also in finding and eliminating the errors in a large and complex computer program it is important to be able to do it piece by piece. And even after it is assembled, it frequently may be desirable to alter a particular operating characteristic, or parameter, or the initial composition of components and their status variables. For these reasons, it is highly useful to take the individual components of a model as building blocks and construct them and the overall model so that they are like the fully plugable components of a modern piece of electronic equipment.

2. *Use of block-recursive models.* Given that a building-block approach is to be used in constructing and simulating a large-scale model on a computer, it is of considerable practical importance that the model be block-recursive, at least in its broad outlines. If it is assumed for purposes of illustration that individual families are treated as blocks, then in order for a model to be block-recursive it

is necessary, for example, that a family's expenditure on clothing during a month should not have such an immediate chain of consequences as both to alter income payments to the family and also thereby alter the family's expenditure on clothing during the same month. This is thus a much less restrictive requirement than that of full recursiveness. Wold makes an impressive case for the use of recursive models, Wold and Jureen (1953) and all of Tinbergen's models have this property. Models of Klein, however, must be put in a reduced form before they have this property. Whether or not a real economy can be adequately represented by a block-recursive model depends upon the choice of blocks and how short time lags can be without being represented as zero time lags. Given flexibility in choice of blocks and the use of very short time lags where appropriate, it is difficult to see how the requirement of block-recursiveness places any series limitations on the model builder. The advantage of working with models which are block-recursive is that digital computers, now available, all perform their operations in a sequential fashion. This does not prevent solving sets of reasonably small numbers of linear simultaneous equations. It does make extremely difficult or impossible the handling of large numbers of nonlinear simultaneous equations. Use of block-recursive models does limit any given set of simultaneous equations to those needed in generating the output of a single block and thus greatly facilitates computer simulation with computer equipment that is or will be available within the next few years.

3. *Replication of components.* Given a building-block approach, another major method of facilitating the design and computer simulation of large-scale complex models is to replicate components. This means that while large numbers of components may be used in a model these components are restricted to a relatively small number of major types. Components of the same major type will have identical operating characteristics but may of course, have different series of values for their input variables. The advantages of this kind of replication in terms of saving labor in developing and programming a model are obvious and important. There are, however, more subtle advantages to such replication that relate to estimation and testing of the operating characteristics of the basic components. A full discussion of these is beyond the scope of this paper, but it may be pointed out that replication has essentially the same importance for learning about the behavior and response mechanism of components that it has for experimental design in general.

4. *Treatment of model as a probability sample.* A fourth basic method for achieving effective computer simulation of models that, conceptually at least, involves millions of micro-components, is to regard components used in computer simulations as probability samples of the components in more extensive conceptual models of economic systems. This can reduce the number of components actually handled in a computer simulation to something less than the hundred thousand or so that are manageable with computers now available. The results obtained from the computer models may then be appropriately blown up in the same way that results obtained by sample surveys are blown up to yield figures appropriate for the populations sampled.

REFERENCES

Adelman, I. (1968). "Economic Processes", in *International Encyclopedia of the Social Sciences,* David L. Sills Ed., Macmillan Co. and the Free Press, Vol. 14, p. 268–274, 1968.

Clark, C. (1949). "A system of equations explaining the U.S. trade cycle 1921–41". *Econometrica,* Vol. 17, 93–124.

Clarkson, G., and H. Simon (1960). "Simulation of Individual and Group Behavior, *American Economic Review,* Vol. L, December, 1960.

Duesenberry, J., O. Eckstein, and G. Fromm (1960). "A Simulation of the United States Economy in Recession", *Econometrica,* October, 1960.

Guetzkow, H. (1962). Editor of *Simulation in Social Science: Readings,* Prentice Hall, 1962

Klein, L. (1947). "The use of Econometric Models as a Guide to Economic Policy", *Econometrica,* April, 1947, 15, 111–51.

Klein, L. (1950). *Economic Fluctuations in the United States 1921–41,* Cowles Commission Monograph 11, London, 1950.

Klein, L., and A. Goldberger (1955). *An Econometric Model of the United States, 1929–1952.* North-Holland Publishing Company, Amsterdam.

Leontief, W. (1951). *The Structure of the American Economy,* Second edition, Cambridge, Massachusetts, 1951.

Leontief, W. (1953). "Static and Dynamic Theory", *Studies in the Structure of the American Economy,* New York, 1953.

Orcutt, G. (1960). "Simulation of Economic Systems", *American Economic Review,* Vol. I December, 1960.

Orcutt, G., M. Greenberger, J. Korbel and A. Rivlin (1961). *Microanalysis of Socioeconomi Systems: A Simulation Study.* Harper & Row Publishers, Inc., New York.

Shubik, M. (1960a). "Simulation of the Industry and the Firm", *American Economic Review,* Vol. L, December, 1960.

Shubik, M. (1960b). "Bibliography on Simulation, Gaming and Allied Topics", *Journal of American Statistical Association,* Vol. 50, December, 1960.

Smithies, A. (1957). "Economic Fluctuations and Growth", *Econometrica,* January, 1957, 25, 1–52.

Suits, D. (1962). "Forecasting and Analysis with an Econometric Model", *American Economic Review,* Vol. 52, March, 1962, 104–132.

Tinbergen, J. (1939). *Statistical Testing of Business-Cycle Theories,* Society of Nations, Geneva.

Wold, H. in association with L. Jureen (1953). *Demand Analysis,* John Wiley & Sons, Inc., New York.

9. PRODUCTION MODELS

J. GRATWICK

CONTENTS

Introduction

The core of a production operation is an activity that changes materials. Materials can be considered as moving through a number of stages of a process, whether the material actually flows through, as in a refinery, or whether the processes move to the material, as in a shipyard. The concept can be extended to include services in addition to physical products, so that a production process can include enterprises such as hospitals, beauty parlours and insurance companies.

Production management is concerned with the integrated human groups and associated physical facilities that are engaged in activities directed to the creation and distribution of goods or services. The management task includes designing, predicting the results of, providing resources for, and controlling, the activity. In examining production models we will be interested in those concepts and techniques that can be of assistance to the manager in performing these tasks.

Production processes tend to be more fully under the control of management, and generally accessible for examination. To the extent that industrial operational research can be said to have started with the work of F. W. Taylor, the production component of industry has been the subject of scientific study longer than finance or marketing, although the dividing lines between these three components are themselves far from distinct.

Much recent work on models for production decision-making highlights another aspect of their use. In a relatively static or stable situation, the emphasis is on the design of the system. With a more fluid, dynamic environment, the emphasis shifts to the responsiveness of the system, and the usefulness of the models to the decision process is measured by their ability to be manipulated and applied frequently and eventually continuously. They can thus become part of the control system of the production process.

Increasingly, models of the various components of the production process are being combined to give a representation of the complete production system. This aggregation can in turn be linked to models of the other elements of an enterprise, finance, marketing, research and development, so that simulation of the complete corporation becomes possible.* Production models can thus be considered as tools for the plant manager for the operation and improvement of the production process, and as representations of that process in a corporate model available to assist top management in its role.

It is intended to examine several basic model structures that are relevant to various aspects of the total production process. No obvious sequence suggests itself, partly because any given activity which is a production entity in itself may also have to be considered as a component in a larger production sequence.

Inventory Models

While problems of inventory are primarily considered as within the production area, they are clearly related to both finance and marketing. Their pervasiveness throughout an organization is also emphasized by the fact that in addition to raw materials, in-process stocks, finished goods and spare parts, it is equally valid to consider inventories of cash, people and energy resources.

The basis of analysis of a stock level control problem is the identification of relevant costs. Where the expected demand for an item is relatively constant, and the stock replenishment process is predictable, there are two basic groups of costs associated with an inventory of any sort.

   a) *Set-up (or ordering) costs* – in the case of a production run to manufacture the item, this includes the time (and thus cost) of preparation for the run; where the item is being ordered from an external source, it includes the administrative costs of preparing, placing and expediting the order. Basically, these costs are independent of the size of the order or run;

   b) *Carrying costs* – the capital tied up in goods and materials in stock, and the loss of its use is a real cost. In addition, holding stock may incur storage costs and perhaps additional costs due to deterioration, loss or obsolescence.

---

* For example, the approach of Imperial Chemical Industries Ltd., is indicated in "Coming: the Instant Five-Year Plan", Conway, A, *New Scientist*, August 7, 1969; "A Systems Approach to Management", G.M. Jenkins and P.V. Youle, *Op. Res. Quart.,* Vol. 19, April 1968. (Special Conference Issue).

The fundamental inventory model minimizes the total of these inventory costs y making the derivative of the expression for total cost with respect to order or run) quantity equal to zero.

$$T_c = \frac{QC_h}{2} + \frac{YC_p}{Q} \tag{1}$$

here:

$_c$ = total inventory cost

* = order quantity

$_h$ = annual cost of holding one item

$_p$ = set-up cost

* = annual requirement for item

Then $\quad \dfrac{dT_c}{dQ} = \dfrac{C_h}{2} - \dfrac{YC_p}{Q^2} = 0$

$$\text{giving } Q = \sqrt{\frac{2YC_p}{C_h}} \tag{2}$$

ften referred to as the economic lot size or Economic Order Quantity (E.O.Q.)

Most applications involve some modification or elaboration of this basic model. When the production run to produce the required replenishment quantity takes significant length of time in relation to the time between successive orders, then the expression for the E.O.Q. becomes:

$$Q = \sqrt{\frac{2YC_p}{C_h\left(1 - \dfrac{r}{p}\right)}} \tag{3}$$

where r = consumption rate; p = production rate. It can be seen that when the production rate is very high in comparison to the consumption rate,

$$\frac{r}{p} \longrightarrow 0$$

and the expression reverts to the initial form.

When the usage rate of an item is constant, and the time between ordering replenishment stock and its receipt is also unvarying, the stock level at which a replenishment order should be placed to avoid a run-out is calculable and no uncertainty exists. In most real applications, both usage rates and lead times are subject to unpredictable fluctuations. The re-order point has to be raised to provide protection from this uncertainty, and the inventory cost equation (1) becomes:

$$T_c = C_h\left(\frac{Q}{2} + R - M\right) + \frac{YC_p}{Q}$$

where R is the re-order level, and M is the average usage during the lead time.

The size of the buffer stock, $R - M$, determines the degree of protection again a stock-out condition. It must in some way be chosen to reduce the adverse effects of an out-of-stock condition to an acceptable level. While some of these effects, such as loss of profit or idle time, can be measured directly in dollar terms, it is often the case that the full effect cannot be so measured. It is sometimes helpful to relate the probability, P, of a run-out to the interval between run-outs X, i.e.

$$X = Q/YP$$

Management may find it easier to make a decision or choice for the value of X. The inventory model used by the C.N.R. incorporates this concept into tables giving re-order points and re-order quantities for various usage rates and item values, with a choice for average interval between run-outs, depending on an assessment of the sensitivity of the item.

Allocation Models

One of the most ubiquitous characterizations of the production management process is that of the allocation of scarce resources. Equipment, materials, man power, money and space are never available in unlimited quantities, and the production process consists of combining them, within the limitations they impose, in the most effective manner according to some criterion of value, which may be profit, cost or time. There are a number of techniques available to solve or to assist in the resolution of this class of allocation problems.

In many situations, the number of ways of making the allocation is infinite; even where the choices are finite, enumeration is rarely a practical method of arriving at the optimum. The assignment of twenty jobs to twenty work station can be made in 20! different ways; it is unlikely that a computer will ever exist that could search all these alternatives in less than a year. Where the resources are linearly related to both the measure of effectiveness and the restraints, *linear programming* techniques are available to develop solutions.

The *assignment model* is appropriate when a group of jobs have to be allotted to a similar number of machines, or men, one job to each, where each is capable of performing any of the jobs, but with varying effectiveness. It is desired to make the assignments of jobs to men or machines that maximizes the total effectiveness over all the jobs.

In formal terms, if (C) is an $m \times n$ matrix of numbers C_{ij} each representing the value associated with making an assignment to that position, it is required to find among all permutations of $(i_1\ i_2 \ldots \ldots i_n)$ of the set of integers

, 2, ... n) the one for which

$$C_1 i_1 + C_2 i_2 + \ldots C_n i_n \text{ takes the optimal value.}$$

n example will indicate the method of solution

Four jobs have to be assigned to four machines; the time that each machine would take for each of the jobs is given in the matrix.

Machine

		A	B	C	D	
	1.	8	11	12	10	
Job	2.	7	6	8	2	Fig. 1
	3.	9	5	8	4	
	4.	6	9	6	9	

The first step to the solution is to reduce the rows and columns by the smallest value in each row or column; it can be seen that this does not affect the selection of the best assignment.

The matrix reduces to:

Machine

		A	B	C	D	
	1.	0	3	4	2	
Job	2.	5	4	6	0	Fig. 2
	3.	5	1	4	0	
	4.	0	3	0	3	

nd then by further reducing column B, to:

Machine

		A	B	C	D	
	1.	[0]	2	4	2	
Job	2.	5	3	6	[0]	Fig. 3
	3.	5	[0]	4	0	
	4.	0	2	[0]	3	

If an assignment can be found with a zero total for this reduced matrix, it will be an optimum assignment for the original matrix. This is clearly possibl￼ in this case, as indicated. In cases where a complete assignment cannot be made among the zeros, an algorithm exists* that selects additional assignmen￼ on the basis of least possible opportunity cost.

For small matrices, it is likely that an intuitive solution may well be at, or nea￼ to the optimum; for larger problems, intuition fails, and even a manual calculati￼ becomes too time consuming, so that a computer will be required.

The so-called *transportation method* is applicable not only to many transport￼ tion and distribution problems, but also to analogous problems of an origin/ destination nature, even where physical movement is not involved. The basic structure of the problem can be stated as follows:

$$\text{Minimize} \quad C = \sum_i \sum_j C_{ij} x_{ij} \qquad (i = 1, \ldots n; \, j = 1, \ldots n)$$

$$\text{subject to} \quad \sum_j x_{ij} = b_i$$

$$\text{and} \quad \sum_i x_{ij} = a_j$$

$$\text{where} \quad \sum_i b_i = \sum_j a_j$$

$$\text{and} \quad x_{ij} \geqslant 0$$

C_{ij} represents the cost of shipping one unit from source i to destination j; b_i is the total available at source i and a_j is the total requirement at destination j.

There always exists a basic feasible solution to satisfy the requirements of the destinations from the m sources that will use no more than $m + n - 1$ cells in the array. Starting with any initial basic feasible solution, algorithms exist for adjusting the allocations, still satisfying the a_j and b_i conditions, until the least cost allocation is reached.

A simple numerical example will make the method clear. Suppose three plant￼ have production capacities for the same product, and have to ship to five ware-houses with differing requirements, and the unit shipping cost varies between plants and warehouses. The information can be summarized in an array (Fig. 4)￼

---

* Flood, M.M., "The Travelling-Salesman Problem," *Op. Res.* Vol. 4, No. 1, February, 1956.

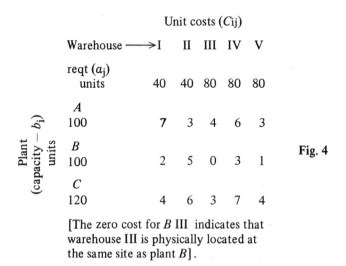

Fig. 4

Unit costs (C_{ij})

Warehouse $\longrightarrow$	I	II	III	IV	V
reqt (a_j) units	40	40	80	80	80
A 100	7	3	4	6	3
B 100	2	5	0	3	1
C 120	4	6	3	7	4

Plant (capacity — b_i) units

[The zero cost for *B* III indicates that warehouse III is physically located at the same site as plant *B*].

Figure 5 shows a basic feasible solution satisfying the capacity/requirement constraints.

	I	II	III	IV	V
A	40	40	20		
B			60	40	
C				40	80

Fig. 5

A systematic evaluation of all unoccupied cells of a basic feasible solution, each of which is a possible shipping alternative, is the basis of the algorithm. Row and column values u_i and v_j are established (the initial u or v is set at zero arbitrarily) so that

$$C_{ij} = u_i + v_j \quad \text{where } x_{ij} > 0 \text{ (i.e., occupied cells)}$$

For an unoccupied cell, if $C_{ij} < u_i + v_j$, then re-allocation to include it will give a lower total cost than previously. After adjusting the u_i and v_j values, the process is repeated, until $C_{ij} \geqslant u_i + v_j$ for all unoccupied cells, and the optimum value is thus reached. The sequence of steps to an optimum solution, starting from the basic feasible solution of Fig. 5, is shown in Fig. 6.

It is worth noting that some of the lowest cost moves are not utilized in the optimum solution; it is also obvious that individual warehouses do not appear to be receiving goods from the plants that have the cheapest shipping costs to them. The application of this type of model can generate difficulties with local management if the form of financial decentralization in the organization inhibits acceptance of the best overall solution.

This model is applicable to production scheduling over a number of time intervals, with storage costs from one period to another entering as the cost variable. Some machine and man assignment problems, where jobs can be shared, are also amenable to the method.

	I	II	III	IV	V	$\downarrow u_i$
1. A	40	40	20		*	0
B			60	40		− 4
C				40	80	− 4
$v_j \rightarrow$	7	3	4	7	8	

$$* \text{ for } A \text{ V}, C_{ij} - (u_i + v_j) = -5$$

	I	II	III	IV	V	$\downarrow u_i$
2. A	40	40			20	0
B			80	20		− 3
C	*			60	60	1
$v_j \rightarrow$	7	3	3	6	3	

	I	II	III	IV	V	$\downarrow u_i$
3. A		40			60	− 1
B			80	20		− 4
C	40		*	60	20	0
$v_j \rightarrow$	4	4	4	7	4	

	I	II	III	IV	V	$\downarrow u_i$
4. A		40			60	− 1
B			20	80		− 3
C	40	60		20		0
$v_j \rightarrow$	4	4	3	6	4	

Fig. 6

Both the assignment model and the transportation method can be considered to be special cases of the general *linear programming model*. In situations where there are a number of possible products, each of which requires differing quantities of limited resources, and the potential profit from each product is known,

---

* $C_{ij} \geqslant u_i + v_j$ for all unoccupied cells − optimum reached.

the object is to find the production mix that will maximize the profit from the resources available. Where products are made by mixing or blending a number of ingredients, each of which varies in specifications, the result may be to maximize the total quantity of end product that can be produced from the ingredients available while meeting a necessary output specification. The structure of the general problem is as follows:

$$\text{Maximize} \quad Z = c_1 x_1 + c_2 x_2 + \ldots + c_n x_n$$

$$\text{subject to} \quad a_{11}x_1 + a_{12} x_2 + \ldots + a_{1n} x_n \leqslant b_1$$

$$a_{m1} x_1 + a_{m2} x_2 + \ldots + a_{mn} x_n \leqslant b_m$$

$$x_j \geqslant 0 \qquad j = 1, \ldots n$$

x_j is the quantity j^{th} product, that has a unit profit of c_j associated with it.

The usual method of solving this problem is the simplex procedure, which is described fully in many texts.* Some idea of the principle of the method can be obtained from a simple example that can be portrayed graphically; (see Edge's Paper, p. 202).

The arrowed polygon is the feasible solution space. If the iso-profit line is moved away from the origin, the last point of contact it has with the polygon will represent the quantities of the two products that meet the restraints of process capacity and yield the maximum profit.

It can be seen that in general, the point will be a vertex of the polygon (it is possible that a range of values will satisfy the conditions if the slope of the iso-profit line matches one of the restraint equations). It is thus possible even in an n-dimensional problem to determine algebraically all the vertices, and then test each in the objective function to find the optimum. When the number of variables and restraints increases to the level met in practice, however, the number of vertices would be too large. The simplex routine provides a more efficient procedure by starting at any vertex (generally the origin), and successively moving along edges to adjoining vertices where such a move improves the value of the objective function. When no move remains that makes this improvement, the optimum has been reached.

While the simplex method can be performed by hand computation, it is impractical to do so when the number of variables or restraints exceeds twenty or so. With many applications involving hundreds or even thousands of variables and restraints, the real value and power of this technique has grown with computer availability. Daily, or even more frequent, updating of production schedules is now both possible and increasingly common.

---

* See, for example, Bowman, E.H., and Fetter, R.B., *Analysis for Production and Operations Management,* Irwin, 3rd Edition, 1967; Vajda S., *Mathematical Programming,* Reading, Mass., 1961.

An extension of the general linear programming model is needed when the variables must be integers. Rounding out the optimum values obtained by the simplex method can lead to grossly erroneous results, and alternative methods have been devised. The 'cutting plane' method uses the simplex optimum, then successively adds further restraint equations that do not exclude any feasible integer values.

Much current work is directed to non-linear programming. While no general solutions exist, there are a number of approaches to finding acceptable, if not optimal, solutions.

Sequencing Models

A common production situation is where a number of jobs have to be processed through a fixed sequence of machines or operations, and where the time for each job at each stage is known. The problem is to choose, and perhaps modify, the sequence in which jobs should be handled, in order to optimize some objective. Optimum solutions to the problem are only possible for simple cases of two or three machines and jobs; no general algorithms exist; Mellor * reviews the status of the topic and gives additional bibliography. Practical results have mainly come from the development of heuristics ('rules') based largely on intuition and experience, that have been modified and tested by computer simulation, enabling the individual characteristics of a particular production situation to be included. Elementary rules that may be compounded and elaborated include:

— first come, first served

— job with least operations first

— job with most operations first

— job with shortest total time first

— highest value job first

The objective has to be defined, and may be in terms of plant utilization, or cost reduction, or job completion time.

Critical Path Methods

A remarkable improvement over previous methods of work planning, scheduling and control has come into common use in the last ten years. The limitation of Gantt charts, and their many variations, has been their failure to highlight schedule interference resulting from inherent restraints on the order in which jobs must be performed. These restraints, on a large, multi-activity project tend to be the prime regulator of completion times. The complementary problem is to have some indication of spare time available so that re-allocation of resources can be considered.

---

* Mellor, P., "Review of Job Shop Scheduling", *Op. Res. Quart.* Vol. 17, No. 2, June 1966.

The new methods, embodying network models of events or activities, capture all precedence relationships and permit the calculation of schedule limits. They offer further extensions in terms of resource levelling and minimum cost scheduling, which converts them from purely descriptive models to optimizing tools.

Two main streams of development, starting in about 1957, led to PERT and CPM. CPM (Critical Path Method) was developed by du Pont, initially for the overhaul of large chemical plants. Emphasis was on performance of the individual jobs making up the project and CPM is thus a deterministic, activity oriented approach, suited to the manager who must control and perform the work. PERT was a U.S. Navy development, initially to plan and control the Polaris missile project. Its emphasis was on the uncertainty of the duration of the research and development components of the project, the need to monitor and co-ordinate the work of a large number of individual subcontractors, and the requirement to summarize progress reporting. PERT emerged as a probabilistic, event oriented approach, concerned with the occurrence of events – generally completion of a particular component, rather than the planning of the actual jobs involved.

There has been a tendency to merge the two approaches, and many critical path programs now incorporate the best features of both PERT and CPM. Common to them both is the representation of all component activities of a project shown in their correct logical sequence as the arrows in an arrow diagram, or network model.

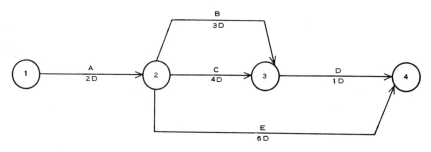

Fig. 7

In the diagram, activity A *must* precede activities B, C, E, and activity D cannot start before B and C are completed. Determining the strict logical sequence of activities is an essential ingredient of the method, and is not always a simple matter. The discipline this requirement invokes has proved to be a valuable contribution to the work planning process. The nodes ①, ②, ③ and ④ are events, and may well represent clearly defined stages in the project.

The activity durations shown enable the calculation of the earliest time at which an event can occur; it is established by the activity chain of longest duration to the node from the origin node of the project. Thus, in the example, the earliest event times are:

node   ①   – 0
node   ②   – 2 days (activity A)
node   ③   – 6 days (A, C is the longest chain)
node   ④   – 8 days (A, E is longest chain)

thus the total project length is 8 days, set by activities A and E, and they form the *critical path* for the project. By making a reverse pass through the network, and starting with the completion time, the latest event times can be determined. These represent the latest time that it is possible to reach a particular node without delaying the completion time. In the example the latest event times are:

node   ④   – 8 days (Terminal event)
node   ③   – 7 days (activity D is the
                            longest backward chain)
node   ②   – 2 days (activity E is the
                            longest backward chain)
node   ①   – 0   (activities E and A)

For any activity, the maximum time available during which it must be performed is given by the difference between the latest event time of the successor node and earliest event time for the predecessor node. The 'float' or 'slack' available is the amount by which this time exceeds the activity itself. In the example for activity B, the time available is

$$7 - 2 = 5 \text{ days}$$

as activity B only takes 3 days, it has 2 days 'float' which enables it to be scheduled in relation to other work without affecting the project duration.

A network may include activities for which the duration is not known with certainty. The PERT system accommodated this by requiring three time estimates for each activity:

m, the modal, or most likely, time;

a, an optimistic estimate, and

b, a pessimistic estimate.

These three are combined to give an expected value for the elapsed time E:

$$E = \frac{\alpha}{2}(a + b) + (1 - \alpha) m$$

where the weighting factor α is generally taken as $1/3$. The same estimates can be used to give an estimate of variance for E, and some applications of the method combine the activity variances to develop a total project time variance.

In developing a network model for a project, it may well be that some external constraint makes the initial estimate of total duration unacceptable. The network diagram is a useful tool for examining the arrangement of the work in the project, and by concentrating on those activities that form the critical path, alternatives may be discovered. In addition, an activity may well be speeded up, though generally at some additional cost. By relating the possible time savings on different activities to these costs, possible reductions in total duration time can be evaluated.

Network diagrams containing more than 200 – 300 activities become unwieldy to calculate manually, particularly if the updating during the progress of the work is required frequently. Many packaged computer programs exist for handling the computation and updating process; most of them produce reports that are designed to meet the various needs of management.

While initially developed for one-shot project management and control, with particular benefits to major construction or modification programs, critical path methods have found wide application to many production areas; maintenance, change overs, machine replacements, shop layout changes and organization and training programs. It is used as a basic means of communication between contractors and sub-contractors on many major contracts.

Quality Control

Statistical sampling methods underlie the whole field of quality control, and to an extent, the relevant statistical theory on which quality control decision models are based has been developed from the needs of industrial quality control.

The familiar 'control charts' of production processes are based on the use of small samples of measurements to establish estimates of mean and variance for those parameters considered appropriate for monitoring the process. Successive sample readings over time are plotted on a chart (Figure 8) that has control limits established based on acceptable standard performance.

Variations beyond the control limits serve as warning or action signals for correction or adjustment of the production process. The continuing view provided by successive sample readings, and the comparisons between mean and variance changes can be used by a skilled operator as a diagnostic tool as well as a mere warning mechanism.

Acceptance sampling, is as the name implies, used to evaluate incoming goods or materials, whether they are purchased from external source, or arriving from an earlier stage in the production process. The requirement is for a decision rule that will reject all lots that are below the acceptable quality standards, and accept all lots that are at or above the standard. Perfection can only be obtained by inspection of every item, or the total material if it is in bulk form. Apart from cost and physical infeasibility, which would make 100% inspection impossible, in many cases, the necessary inspection destroys or damages the item, so that sampling inspection is generally the only practicable method. The operating characteristic curve of a sampling scheme is an indication of its effectiveness; ideally, it would look like Figure 9.

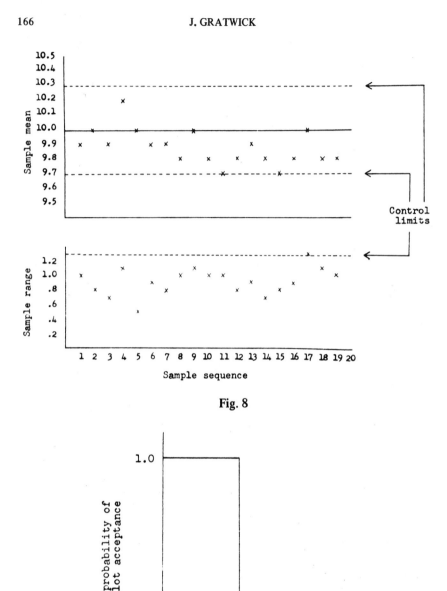

Fig. 8

Fig. 9

Lots meeting, or bettering the acceptable 'lot fraction defective' level would be certain to be accepted; those containing any higher fraction of defective items would be rejected.

In practice, a sampling plan is based on two variables; the size of the samples to be drawn, and the allowable number of defectives within a sample for the lot as a whole to be accepted. The operating characteristic curve takes the form

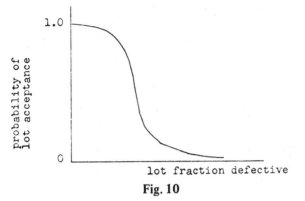

Fig. 10

The larger the sample size, the more closely the curve takes the ideal 'Z' form. The decisions to be made to define an appropriate plan are the acceptable quality standard, the allowable risk that an acceptable lot will be rejected, and the allowable risk that a defective lot will be accepted.

Many extensions of the basic sampling scheme have been developed for particular applications. Double sampling models, where a larger sample is taken if a first small sample does not give a definite decision, can be more effective where the operation of such a plan is possible. In the limit, multiple sampling models reduce to sequential single sampling, continued until a decision point is reached.

Waiting Line Models

Items to be processed by a machine, a machine requiring repair, operation of a tool crib, can all be considered as instances of the provision or receipt of a service. In cases where both the demand and the service rate are variable, the problem has some similarity to the inventory situation under conditions of uncertainty. It differs, however, in the fact that the equivalent, in the servicing case, of a buffer stock is excess servicing capacity. Such excess capacity consists of man or machine time, and is not capable of being stored. The examination and analysis of such situations is covered by waiting line, or queuing, theory.

A number of considerations enter into the development of waiting line models – the arrival pattern of items or people at the service facility; the queue discipline and structure; the number of channels at the service facility; the characteristics of the servicing time. The ratio of the service time to the time interval between arrivals for servicing is clearly of basic concern. Even if arrivals and service times are constant, if this ratio exceeds unity, an ever-increasing queue will develop. Where arrivals and service times are randomly variable, a queue will build up at values of the ratio well below unity. In practical situations, information is required on the possible queue length, or the appropriate arrival rate to match the characteristics of a given service facility. In certain cases, where the interval between arrivals and the service time distributions conform to the exponential distribution, analytical models for the queue characteristics are possible. For example, if a is the mean arrival rate, and s the mean servicing rate at a single channel facility, it can be shown that*:

1. $\dfrac{a}{s-a}$ is the average number of units in the system (queue + service facility)

2. $\dfrac{1}{s-a}$ is the average time an arrival spends in the system

3. $\dfrac{a}{s(s-a)}$ is the average waiting time of an arrival

While these expressions can be extended to cover multiple channel servicing facilities, and modifications of the arrival and service time distributions, the complexity of the analysis makes this approach infeasible for many problem situations. Monte Carlo type simulation is the alternative, and most queuing problems can be tackled by a combination of simulation and analytical methods.

Essentially, waiting line models are descriptive, rather than optimizing, models. As such they are primarily of use in the design phase of a production process. They provide both insights and measures of performance, and provide means of experimenting with alternatives.

Conclusion

The paper has touched on the more significant categories of models finding current application in a variety of production fields. Their generality of application is such that they cannot be considered as being confined to production applications; the essential interrelationships of production with marketing and finance means that they can rarely, if ever, be used by production management in isolation. To an increasing extent, they are becoming a means of communicating and reflecting the characteristics of production functions into the corporate planning and control process.

---

* Full treatments can be found in several texts:
  e.g., Morse, P.M., *Queues, Inventories, and Maintenance,* Wiley, New York, 1958;
  Lee, A., *Applied Queuing Theory,* Macmillan, London, 1966.

10. FINANCIAL MODELS

C. G. EDGE

CONTENTS

I. Introduction

I believe it was Professor Ackoff who said that "Managers are superb at controlling systems they do not understand and relatively poor at controlling the ones they do—on the other hand, scientists are superb at controlling systems they do understand, but poor at controlling the ones they do not"

The purpose of this paper is to see how we can get a better blend of management skills with those of the scientists in the financial field.

I have chosen to take a broad definition of financial models since the senior financial officer in a company usually has a dual role.

1. Participating in corporate strategy—the allocation of limited resources, for selected projects, in proper dimensions of time, for the furtherance of specified projects.

The task being carried out in the climate of an "uncertain future economic environment".

Obviously one of the resources being allocated is money.

2. The financing function, financial planning, financial policy, dividend policy, etc.

Financial management and financial planning are a mixture of judgement and analysis. Formal quantitative analysis has increased significantly in recent times and is likely to continue this trend. Developments in financial theory and information processing technology have been major factors, and computer oriented models are likely to come progressively into vogue in the selection and implementation of corporate strategies and financial planning.

Undoubtedly effective application of analytical techniques to financial problems requires an underlying understanding of the management science techniques involved but this by itself is not enough. It requires an appreciation of the company, an understanding of accounting and financial concepts and policies, but above all, a "feel" for the full perspective of factors managers take into account in choosing between alternative courses of action.

These criteria also point to another important aspect—namely the ability to design models which are effective in solving problems yet are simple enough for the practical purpose required, and in addition the cost of getting the information is reasonable in relation to the benefit anticipated. It is not unusual for large sophisticated models to accurately reflect the problem but to be too costly or too unwieldly for all practical purposes.

By their inherent nature, models are merely abstractions or representations of a problem. They rarely represent all of the factors which management must evaluate in arriving at a decision. Yet, some analysts fall too easily into the trap of regarding the model as the real life problem itself.

The advantages in using financial models derives from what Professor Whisler would call a "manager-machine interface". Managers are superb at perceiving problems, defining them, at evaluating results and making decisions based on incomplete information—but are poor calculators. The computer, on the other hand, is a magnificent calculator but a moron in terms of its ability to perceive, define, evaluate and communicate. The manager-machine interface enables us to use the managers' strengths with those of the computer in an effective team. It enables:—

1. A far wider range of alternatives to be examined—and an alternative to be selected closer to the optimum—compared with manual methods.

2. Many, many alternatives to be evaluated in a short space of time.

3. The risk likely to be incurred to be measured more effectively.

Financial models can be used for a number of purposes and I have chosen to classify them as:—

Manipulative
Perceptive
Predictive
Complexity
Uncertainty

A few words of amplification follow, with each class of model being examined more thoroughly later.

Manipulative models

Accounting formed the earliest model of a company in terms of its profit and loss statement and balance sheet. These models have been further refined and manipulated using computers for preparing budgets, plans, and for determining growth and profitability objectives.

Perceptive models

These tend to be more in the form of mathematical equations and assist management in perceiving relationships—an awareness of which may have a major impact on corporate strategy. Examples would include:—

Formulae linking future and present values.

Effect of dividend policy on growth.

Relationship of rate of inflation to real return on equity.

Predictive models

These are used for forecasting purposes. Short run forecasting as in inventory control and scheduling, and in the construction of momentum indexes for stock prices. It generally uses exponential smoothing—a system of weighted averages. Longer term forecasting is often based on regression analysis.

Complexity models

These would include the optimization of a company's operations using linear programming, or the use of the critical path method to reduce construction time on large complex projects.

Uncertainty models

These recognize that virtually all data about the future are uncertain. Using simulation methods the risk in major investment decisions can be gauged, and decision trees can be used to select an optimum strategy from a range of alternatives.

Scientific method and techniques

The approach to using financial models is analogous to the use of scientific methods. It consists of: −

1. Constructing a model.

2. Defining the decision criteria.

3. Obtaining estimates of the parameters or variables in the model.

4. Carrying out mathematical computations.

5. Determining the sensitivity of results.

For corporate strategic planning, three types of models would generally be used.

1. An environmental model—which provides data in the climate in which the company will be operating including price demands and cost of contracts, labor, etc.

2. A decision model—which optimizes the activity for the company concerned

3. A financial model—which produces income statements and balance sheets reflecting the results.

Before attempting a synthesis of the various aspects of a typical problem using a financial model—some insight will be given into the various techniques applicable to each type of model or financial problem.

II. Manipulative models

Manipulative models are essentially designed to take the "dreariness" out of grinding out financial statements and, more importantly, to permit a wider range of alternatives to be examined and permit changes to plans to be processed more readily. Most managers are only too well aware of major changed circumstances at the time they are finalizing their plans and which they would like incorporated in them—only to be told that it is too late and affects too many other schedules to permit the changes to be made.

Fortunately accountants perceived the benefits of the computer and were early pioneers in the business application for the recording of transactions and the preparation of financial statements. Progress had proceeded so far that a company as large as Westinghouse could proclaim that its profit and loss statements and balance sheets were produced "untouched by human hands".

The computer program became in fact a model. The cost and time taken to produce a computer program does involve a commitment to a common code of accounts and to a stable system for preparing the financial statements.

Since the essence of control is comparison of actual with budget, accountants have wisely ensured that the budget is prepared on the same accounting system as the actual accounts are processed. There has, therefore, been a growing tendency to "program" the budget, thus reducing details required from managers. Sub-programs will often convert annual totals to monthly totals, calculate values by multiplying prices and volumes, calculate subtotals and totals, etc.

The accountant's preoccupation with accounts and budgets has made him slower to devise planning models. These are often much simpler than a fully fledged budget and have the prime purpose of examining a wide range of alternatives. (It is, in my opinion, more important to select the right plan than effectively control the wrong one). The growing use of time sharing computer terminals and simple computer languages such as BASIC have greatly facilitated the planner's ability to program his own model and then test out various inputs into the model.

Models may comprise such aspects as consolidating divisional results into consolidated profit and loss statements, cash flow statements and balance sheets and then calculate standard financial ratios such as return on assets, return on equity, earnings per share, etc. More sophisticated models may start from detailed sales forecasts into optimized plans, using linear programming, then be linked with a production scheduling and inventory system which provides the input into the financial plan itself.

In this age of "conglomerates" mergers and acquisitions, and diversifications, simple models using time sharing terminals are extremely convenient for examining the implication of putting two or more profit and loss statements and balance sheets together on varying terms for merging or acquiring companies and examining the impact on earnings per share and potential dilution, etc.

In our company we are using a time sharing terminal linked to Trans Canada Computer Utility to manipulate a model programmed in BASIC to examine growth and profitability goals for the company. The model enables various assumptions to be made on the growth of earnings per share and calculates the return on investment needed in new projects to attain this goal. It takes into account:−

1. The future earnings profile of existing businesses.

2. Dividend policy.

3. Debt raising ability (but not equity).

4. Reinvestment of free cash in projects, with lagged earnings in relation to th
outlays.

5. Allowance for working capital requirements and special types of capital
expenditures such as maintenance of business and cost projects.

The model is relatively simple and does not fully cope with such factors as
changes in the provision for future taxes. It does, however, indicate the trade-off
between having a simple model which can be easily manipulated and is suitable fo
the practical purposes required, and having a more sophisticated but unwieldy
model in relation to the purposes required.

III. Perceptive models

Models may take many forms such as computer programs, matrices for linear
programs, and arrow diagrams for critical path networks. However, some fundamental financial and financing relationships can be expressed by some simple
mathematical equations. These will be developed in this section and cover the
relationships between present and future values, inflation, growth, debt-equity
effect on growth, dividend policies, effect of experience on costs curves and
implications for pricing strategy, competitive strategy and corporate strategy. In
this section I would like to acknowledge my debt to the Boston Consulting Grou
and in particular their two books *Perspectives on Experience* and *Perspectives
on Corporate Strategy*.

1. *Present and future values*

Considering first present and future values, these are linked by compound
interest formulae. For example, assuming earnings each year are the same and
i is the interest rate and n the number of years

$$\text{Present Value (Price)} = \text{Earnings}\left[\frac{1}{1+i} + \frac{1}{(1+i)^2} + \frac{1}{(1+i)^3} \cdots \frac{1}{(1+i)^n}\right]$$

If earnings continue indefinitely

$$\text{Present Value (Price)} = \text{Earnings}\left(\frac{1}{i}\right)$$

Therefore
$$\frac{\text{Price}}{\text{Earnings}} = \frac{1}{i}$$

For example, if the return on equity is say 10% then the price/earnings ratio
would be $\frac{1}{\cdot 1} = 10$

2. *Inflation*

If earnings are eroded each year by a factor of n, then

$$\text{Present Value (Price)} = \text{Earnings} \left[\frac{1}{(1+i)(1+n)} + \frac{1}{(1+i)^2(1+n)^2} + \frac{1}{(1+i)^3(1+n)^3} \right]$$

If earnings continue indefinitely

$$\text{Present Value (Price)} = \text{Earnings} \frac{1}{(i+n)}$$

For example, if the return on equity is 10% but earnings are being eroded by 4% then the price/earnings ratio would be reduced to $\dfrac{1}{\cdot 10 + \cdot 04} = 7\%$

As an approximate guide, inflation reduces the return on equity by the rate of inflation.

3. *Growth*

Suppose, for example, that earnings grow each year by a factor of x, then

$$\text{Present Value (Price)} = \text{Earnings} \left[\frac{1+x}{1+i} + \frac{(1+x)^2}{(1+i)^2} + \frac{(1+x)^3}{(1+i)^3} + \text{etc.} \right]$$

If this trend continues indefinitely

$$\text{Present Value (Price)} = \text{Earnings} \frac{1}{(i-x)}$$

Therefore, if one expected a Price/Earnings Ratio of 10 if earnings were to continue at the same rate each year, then if the same initial earnings were to grow at 5% a year one would expect a price earnings ratio of $\dfrac{1}{\cdot 10 - \cdot 05}$ or 20.

Of course, if earnings grew at more than 10% a year forever the present value would be infinite—but nothing grows at this rate indefinitely.

4. *Growth rate and reinvestment of retained earnings*

It is assumed that

1. Assets = Equity (No debt financing)

2. Return on new assets equals the return on present assets.

Then	Year 1	Year 2	Year 3
Assets on Equity	$100	$110	$112
Return on Assets or Equity	10%	10%	10%
Profit	$10·00	$11·00	$12·10
Retained Earnings reinvested	$10·00	$11·00	$12·10

Therefore, *the growth rate in earnings equals the return on equity* (provided there is no debt and all earnings are reinvested).

5. *Use of debt and effect on return on equity and growth rate*
   (all earnings are reinvested)

The only change in the preceding data is the substitution of debt for 50% of the equity. It is assumed that the after tax cost of interest is 4%.

	Year 1	Year 2	Year 3
Total Assets	$100·00	$116·00	$134·56
Equity	50·00	58·00	67·28
Debt	50·00	58·00	67·28
Return (before interest) on assets	10%	10%	10%
Profit before interest	$ 10·00	$ 11·60	$ 13·46
Interest	2·00	2·32	2·69
Profit after Interest	8·00	9·28	10·77
Return on Equity	16%	16%	16%
Equity Reinvestment	$ 8·00	$ 9·28	$ 10·77
New Debt	8·00	9·28	10·77
Total New Investment	16·00	18·56	21·54
Growth of Equity	16%	16%	16%

The *use of debt* therefore

1. Enables the *return on equity to be levered up* from 10% to 16%.

2. Enables the *growth in equity to be levered up* from 10% to 16%.

It also enables business risks to be balanced against financing risks. For example, by varying the proportion of debt to equity, depending on the business risk, it should be possible:

1. To accept a lower return on assets criteria for low business risk, highly levered projects.

2. Set a higher return on asset criteria for high business risk, lowly levered projects.

6. *Effect of dividend payout or growth rate in equity*

It is assumed that the dividend payout is 50%—all other data being the same as in the previous example.

	Year 1	*Year 2*	*Year 3*
Total Assets	$100·00	$108·00	$116·64
Equity	50·00	54·00	58·32
Debt	50·00	54·00	58·32
Return (before interest) on assets	10%	10%	10%
Profit before interest	$ 10·00	$ 10·80	$ 11·66
Interest	2·00	2·16	2·33
Profit after interest	8·00	8·64	9·33
Return on Equity	16%	16%	16%
Dividends	$ 4·00	$ 4·32	$ 4·66
Dividend Payout	50%	50%	50%
Equity Reinvestment	$ 4·00	$ 4·32	$ 4·66
New Debt	4·00	4·32	4·66
Total new investment	8·00	8·64	9·32
Growth in Equity	8%	8%	8%

Therefore, *a dividend payout of 50% cuts the growth rate in equity by one half* (from 16% in the previous example to 8%).

From this one could draw the inference that high growth companies should have low dividend payout policies and low growth companies should have high dividend payout policies.

There is also a direct trade-off between present and future dividends. For example, consider the following situations:

	Company A	Company B
Equity	$50	$50
Return on Equity	16%	16%
Dividend Payout	20%	80%
Growth in Equity	12·8%	3·2%
Initial Dividend	$ 1·60	$ 6·40
Dividend in 15th year	$10·00	$10·00

Beyond the 15th year the absolute dividend payout for Company A, which has the low dividend payout policy, will exceed that for Company B which has the high dividend payout policy.

7. *Deviation of formula for interrelation of growth, debt, dividend payout, etc.*

Let G = Rate of Growth in Equity

D = Debt

E = Equity

A = Assets

R = Return (before interest) on Assets

i = Interest rate on debt

P = Proportion of earnings retained and reinvested

Then

Profit $= R.A - i.D$

Profit $= R(D+E) - i.D$

$$\frac{\text{Profit}}{\text{Equity}} = \frac{R.D}{E} + R - i\frac{D}{E}$$

$$= \frac{D}{E}(R - i) + R$$

Assuming no dividends are paid

$$G = \frac{D}{E}(R - i) + R$$

If proportion of earnings retained and reinvested is P, then

$$G = \frac{D}{E}(R - i)P + RP$$

Using the data in section 6 above

$$G = \frac{1}{1}(0.10 - 0.04)\ 0.5 + (0.10 \times 0.05)$$

$$= (.06 \times 0.5) + (0.10 \times 0.05)$$

$$= \quad .03 \quad + \quad .05$$

$$= \quad .08 \quad \text{or} \quad 8\%$$

8. *Dilution if earnings are paid out in dividends and new equity capital is raised to finance growth*

There is minor dilution in earnings per share if dividends are paid out and new equity is raised. This minor dilution could be offset by the shareholder investing his dividends in other companies at rates of return at least equal to the present company.

A comparison of the two payout policies follows overleaf.

	100% earnings reinvested		100% earnings paid out as dividends	
	Year 1	*Year 2*	*Year 1*	*Year 2*
Total Equity	$1 000	$1 200	$1 000	$1 200
Return on Equity	20%	20%	20%	20%
Profit	$ 200	$ 240	$ 200	$ 240
Shares outstanding	100	100	100	105
Earnings per share	$ 2·00	$ 2·40	$ 2·00	$ 2·29
Stock Price (20 x EPS)	$40·00	$48·00	$40·00	$45·80
Price Earnings Ratio	20:1	20:1	20:1	20:1
Dividends			$200	$240
New Equity required			$200	
Number of shares sold			5	
New Investment	$200	$240	$200	$240

In other words, the earnings per share in the second year on full dividend pay-out is only $2·29 compared with $2·40 on full dividend payout.

9. *Sensitivity of factors affecting growth*

Using the basic data in section 6 the sensitivity to a 10% change in each factor can be determined.

Return (before interest) on Assets	Growth rate	% Change in growth rate for 10% change in factor
10·0%	8·00	
11·0%	9·00	12·5%
Interest Rate		
4·0%	8·00	
4·4%	7·80	2·5%

Debt/Equity Ratio	Growth rate	% Change in growth rate for 10% change in factor
1:1	8·00	
1·1:1	8·30	3·75%
Dividend Payout		
50%	8·00	
55%	8·80	10·0%

It could be expected that the intrinsic return on assets of the business would be the largest single factor affecting growth. It is perhaps more surprising that dividend payment policies are the second largest influence on growth rates.

10. Cost curves and experience

The Boston Consulting Group have enumerated the proposition that:—

"Costs appear to go down on value added (in constant dollars) at about 20 to 30% every time total product experience doubles for the industry as a whole, as well as for individual producers".

This trend has been well tested out on a wide range of products and has been verified in our own group of companies.

The implications of such a proposition are profound and can only briefly be touched on here. The implications relate to growth rates, market share, pricing and competitive strategy and the reader is referred to *Perspectives on Experience* published by the Boston Consulting Group.

First let us examine the implications of growth on accumulated experience and hence costs:—

(see overleaf)

RELATION OF EXPERIENCE TO COST

Year	Level Annual Production				10% Growth in Annual Production			
	Production	Accumulated experience	% Increase in experience	Cost trend	Production	Accumulated experience	% Increase in experience	Cost trend
1	1	1	–	100	1	1·00	–	100
2	1	2	100%	75	1·10	2·10	110·1	74
3	1	3	50	66	1·21	3·31	57·6	63
4	1	4	33⅓	60	1·33	4·64	40·2	56
5	1	5	25	56	1·46	6·11	31·5	50
6	1	6	20	52	1·61	7·81	26·4	46
7	1	7	16⅔	49	1·77	9·58	22·7	44
8	1	8	14	47	1·95	11·53	20·4	42
9	1	9	12½	46	2·14	13·67	18·6	40
10	1	10	11	44	2·35	16·02	17·2	38
11	1	11	10	43	2·59	18·61	16·2	36
12	1	12	9	42	2·85	21·46	15·3	34
13	1	13	8⅓	41	3·14	24·60	14·6	32
14	1	14	7	41	3·45	28·05	14·0	31
15	1	15	6⅔	40	3·80	31·85	13·5	30

From this general thesis, the following conclusions can be drawn, although they are not argued in this article.

1. It pays to invest in market share because costs fall faster because experience is accumulated more quickly.

2. If prices are above the cost trend then either:

(a) inefficiency is being tolerated among the smaller producers,

(b) there is an invitation for another supplier to enter the market,

(c) the market is unstable.

3. The economies of scale are reinforced by economies arising from the "experience" cost curves. Therefore, anti-combines legislation designed to protect the inefficient small producer may be doing a disservice to the country at large.

4. Either one should attempt to dominate the market—as a segment of the market or phase-out.

5. Once a dominant share of the market has been obtained, prices should be reduced in line with industry cost trends.

6. Security and holding a dominant market share of a growth business will yield outstanding profits—but during the period of rapid growth injections of cash may exceed cash generated.

IV. Predictive models

Management is almost entirely concerned with the future and a future dominated by uncertainty. The ability to predict the future is therefore a valuable management aid. Short-run predictions are useful for operating management control. For example, short-run forecasts of up to three months ahead for each of several hundred small products may be a boon to production scheduling and inventory control. A computerized technique such as exponential smoothing combined with the seasonal index is often used for this. Likewise, for strategic planning, larger range forecasts are needed, input-output models and regression equations are often used for this purpose.

1. Short range forecasting

Season factors preferably require up to four or five years' history and can be calculated through a standard computer technique called "Shiskin" analysis. These seasonal indices can then be combined with an exponential smoothing method of forecasting.

This method is essentially a system of moving averages. The weights given to the previous months' actual results are directly related to the proximity of those months; the closer months being weighted more heavily than earlier months. The weighting factor is known as α. The lower the value of α, say $0 \cdot 1$, means that closer months are given slightly higher weights than earlier months, whereas an α factor of say $0 \cdot 3$ would mean that recent experience is given several times the weight of the actual results a year ago.

Computer simulation models are available to test out the earlier history of a product and determine which factor will give better predictions for that product

The benefit from the exponential smoothing method is that it can be easily computerized with all the historic data stored in the computer. All that it requires for say a new three months' forecast by months adjusted for seasonal factors, is the actual results for the current month. Since the actual results are often generated on the computer, the output tape can be used to provide the input for generating the forecast. Several hundred forecasts can be made routinely at a few cents each.

Lest the above commentary makes the process sound too easy, let us hasten to add that it requires top flight systems work to overcome the practical problems of introducing a new product, giving it a new code, and determining how to treat a new product without previous history. These are typical of the problems that the system should take care of. Furthermore, the product managers using the forecasts should not apply the results blindly without taking account of special factors not included in the computerized forecast such as strikes at customers' plants and other unusual features. Nevertheless, there is an opportunity for developing a low cost computerized forecasting system which ca contribute to more effective production schedules and inventory controls compared with manual methods.

2. *Long range forecasting*

When Professor Wassily Leontief pioneered the development of input-output analysis thirty-five years ago, he probably did not envisage it would become a fashionable forecasting device in 1969.

An input-output model is basically a matrix which shows how much each of the producing segments in the economy purchase from each of the same segment the final demand being equal to the Gross National Product. The condensed table for the U.S. economy shown on the following page illustrates an input-output table.

The main power of the input-output method is, however, derived from the inverse coefficient matrix. It shows the total requirements imposed on a column sector per dollar delivery to final demand. It therefore shows the *interdependencies* between the various sectors of the economy. For example, if the mining

INPUT-OUTPUT TRANSACTIONS TABLE OF THE U.S. ECONOMY

Producing sectors	Purchasing sectors Agri.	Mining	Mfg.	Others	Intermediate demand	Final demand	Total output
Agriculture	17	–	38	3	58	1	59
Mining	–	2	20	3	25	-2	23
Manufacturing	8	2	228	52	290	290	580
Other	9	4	78	141	232 $605	375	607
Value added	25	15	216	408		$664	
Total input	59	23	580	607			$1269

industry's output increases by 5% it shows what effect this will have on the chemical industry. An example of an inverse coefficient follows:—

INVERSE COEFFICIENT TABLE

| Producing sectors | Purchasing sectors | | | |
	Agriculture	Mining	Manufacturing	Others
Agriculture	1·44	·02	·16	·03
Mining	·02	1·09	·07	·02
Manufacturing	·38	·22	1·75	·20
Other	·36	·31	·35	1·35

Input-output methods are still in their infancy as far as business forecasting is concerned, but individual companies are beginning to construct their own models. Earlier models were static, they reflected the situation in a given year only. Now methods of chaining together a series of years and incorporating shifts in technology have been developed. For example, Arthur D. Little are just completing a multi-client study which will contain an input-output analysis of the U.S. economy up to 1980.

An overview of development in the input-output field is contained in the July 1969 edition of the *EDP Analyser.*

V. Complexity models

The computer is a valuable tool for solving complex problems because of its power to handle many thousands of computations at fantastic speed and at low cost. The human brain is comparatively poor at this problem. However, the combination of the manager defining the problem, the computer calculating optimum combinations from a range of alternatives, and the manager evaluating the results and adapting them to the actual situation, is a powerful team.

One application is touched on briefly, namely, the "Critical Path Method". Another, probably the most powerful analytical tool at management's command, linear programming, is discussed at greater length.

1. *Critical path method*

Control over the physical phase of the construction of new facilities was often carried out by using Gannt charts which showed when individual parts of the project were planned to start and finish and how actual events compared with plan. They did not bring out adequately the inter-relationship between the individual parts of a project, or provide enough data on leads and lags or cost control.

A powerful new management tool for doing this, which avoids the pitfalls of oversimplification as well as excessive details, is now available in the form of "Network Analyses" (see diagram on the opposite page). Network Analysis simulates the project and allows quantitative evaluation of alternatives prior to committal of funds. Network Analysis makes use of the critical path principle, which states that in each major project, whether building an entire pulp mill or expanding existing facilities, about 10% to 20% of the jobs determines the time for the entire project. Consequently, management's attention is focused on the key elements of a project, which is particularly essential in those cases where a multitude of interrelated activities with their various time, cost, and reliability aspects exist.

Although originally created as a means of planning and controlling the physical and cost control of the construction of a plant or production facilities, its use has been extended beyond this to provide a means of planning a variety of activities, sometimes starting with the research phase and ending when the product is in full scale manufacture and the market is fully developed.

The two basic methods of Network Analysis are Program Evaluation and Review Techniques (PERT) and Critical Path Method (CPM). Both methods have received considerable attention since about 1958. Recent versions are PERT II,

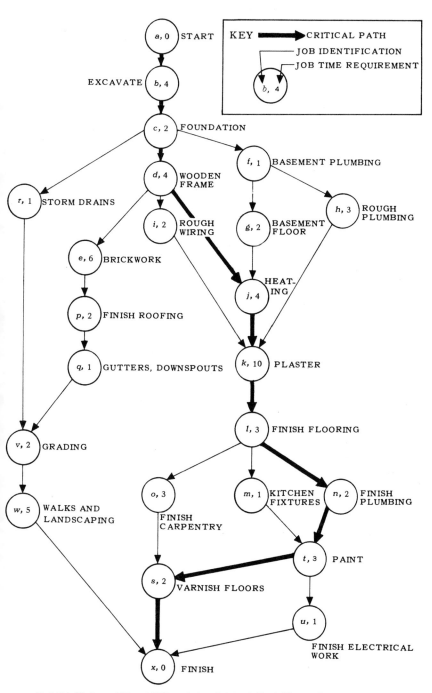

Exhibit II from "The ABC's of the Critical Path Method" by Ferdinand K. Levy, Gerald L. Thompson, and Jerome D. Wiest, *Harvard Business Review*, September–October 1963, p. 101.

PERT III, PEP, PEPCO, and super-PERT, etc. In addition, there are combinations of PERT and CPM. The special feature of PERT is the use of a three-way time estimate: optimistic, most likely, pessimistic, and the statistical evaluation of the degree of certainty of meeting an event schedule.

Both basic methods involve the construction of a project model by listing either events or activities in logical sequence with normal and crash time and costs. The critical path is that path in the network from the starting event (activity) to the objective event (activity) that takes the greatest amount of time to traverse. All other paths include slack, i.e. time an event or activity may be delayed withou affecting the overall projection completion.

Depending on the size and complexity of the network, complete programs are available to determine critical paths, slack areas, expected completion time, expected project direct costs by skill, work, and department. With the help of computers alternatives can be evaluated prior to decision making. Once a capital expenditure project has been approved the network can be used to monitor progress and to indicate when management action might be required and also what the alternatives are in meeting a specific deadline.

These techniques are not yet fully developed, but there can be little doubt of their acceptance. The trend of the times is that some leading companies are demanding that CPM or PERT network diagrams accompany all project proposals. They are an indication to top management that the construction and implementation phase of a project has been adequately planned.

Source:—*A Practical Manual on the Appraisal of Capital Expenditures.* Special Study No. 1 published by the Society of Industrial Accountants, Hamilton, Ontario.

Standard computer programs are available from most computer manufacturers and an example of a print-out from such a program is attached as Appendix A.

The use of the method has been extended from control of the physical construction of a capital project to a wide range of other complex planning activities. For example:

> Maintenance shutdown.

> Month-end accounting routines.

> Total development phase of a project including market research, piloting and commercialization.

2. *Linear programming*

Management's task has been described as the allocation of scarce resources among competing ends so as to maximize profits. Likewise, linear programming can be described as the allocation of scarce resources (they are subject to constraints) so as to optimize the economic benefit. Both goals are, therefore, virtually synonymous and this is why linear programming is such a powerful management tool. Its potential has, however, not yet been realized.

A linear program consists of two types of equations:–

1. An economic function such as profit which is maximized subject to

2. a series of constraint equations. These equations are usual where the left hand side is either equal to or less than the right hand side or equal to or greater than the right hand side.

In a manufacturing and marketing optimization the economic function consists of product prices and production costs, and the constraint equations represent process capacities (in a multi-process operation) and the market size for each product.

While undoubtedly great benefit is obtained from being able to optimize complex equations (sometimes several hundred variables and several hundred constraint equations) and find the best combination, considerable value can be obtained from by-product information. A linear program derives the marginal economic value from changing each of the constraints or changing the value of each of the items in the economic function (product prices and process costs, for example). While a management responsibility may be to find the best combination from a given set of alternatives, a more important problem may be changing or easing the constraints (such as debottlenecking a process or enlarging the market for a product) so as to enable profit to be increased. The marginal values of each constraint are significant indicators of the most effective points on which to spend management talent.

A brief description of linear programming and its various applications is contained in Appendix B.

From a financial point of view linear programming has two aspects. First, ensuring the most favourable plan of operations has been formulated, and secondly, and this application has hardly been developed at this time, for capital budgeting purposes–allocating funds among competing projects for those funds.

1. *Operating plans*

The advantages of using linear programming for operating plans are:–

a) it provides a much sharper tool than normal cost accounting methods for optimizing profits. (The results of the LP may need retranslating in standard financial formats for ease of understanding).

b) it integrates views which may be oriented towards individual segments. For example, a woods manager is preoccupied with species, logging terrain and logging costs; a sawmill manager with size and diameter, species, grades of lumber and current lumber selling prices; whereas a pulp mill manager thinks of mill processing costs, capacity of digesters, dryers, etc. A linear programme designed to optimize the whole forest operation will synthesize all these individual viewpoint and may shed new light on operating conditions in each of the individual areas based on the optimization of the whole. The marginal values will not only shed light on wood availability from any area and pulp and sawmill process capacity but also on socio-economic constraints such as the obligation to provide work for logging communities in remote areas.

c) It is an objective way of setting transfer prices between one process and another and one division and another. It is, therefore, a way of reducing the emotion in these decisions which often accompanies traditional ways of resolving these problems.

2. *Capital budgeting*

A capital budgeting problem is essentially the allocation of available cash over a series of years in order to optimize the benefit from the project.

The greatest single difficulty is that for many individual projects, economic costs and benefits are not known with any reasonable degree of accuracy even for a few months ahead, let alone for projects which may not be initiated for three or four years. Moreover, if a project has to be deferred for a year, the pattern of its economic benefits may shift as the market and market share may be different if it is delayed a year.

Reorganizing these limitations, a capital budgeting model can be constructed along the following lines:

1. The economic function is the "net present value" for each project. This has the benefit of being additive for a number of projects whereas the D.C.F. (discount cash flow) return is not.

2. Each potential project is offered in the matrix over three consecutive years (It may not be physically feasible to start a project for two years, it would then be offered in years 3, 4 and 5). Projects which have to be undertaken can be *forced* into the solution.

3. The cash available each year is indicated. Any unused cash can be invested at interest and rolled over to the next year.

4. Additional debt financing can be included where it is related to increases in assets allowable for debt purposes.

5. Some minimum growth in profit or earnings per share may be stipulated as a constraint. This may be needed to keep a balance between short run earnings and long term net present value and also to preserve the right sort of growth climate for additional financing in the short term.

Some general observations

Lest the above comments imply the effective use of linear programming is too easy, let me enumerate some key factors essential to success. They are:—

1. The leadership and support of a senior executive who has the authority to act on the results from the operation as a whole. Often linear programs, which cut across divisional boundaries, give rise to political repercussions or power plays.

2. A thorough understanding of the operation by the analyst concerned.

3. The ability to generate the essential information for incorporation in the model. This may be more refined than standard cost accounting data and may be difficult and costly to obtain. Moreover, it should have the blessing of the line manager concerned before it is used. (This endorsement is, in my opinion, essential before the LP is optimized so that if the results are unexpected—as they sometimes are—it cannot be blamed on faulty input-information).

4. A capable model designer. There is much expertise in designing matrices which reflect the actual situation realistically and practically, and which are solved efficiently inside the computer.

5. The ability to interpret the computer print-outs and highlight the significant findings in a format easily understandable by management, and in a way which facilitates action on the results.

6. The ability to use the marginal economic data so as to formulate additional questions which should be examined.

7. Finally, a mathematical model will never fully reflect all aspects of a real life situation. A manager will therefore often have to modify the results of the linear program to reflect additional factors from a management viewpoint.

VI. Uncertainty models

Management is primarily concerned with the future, the future is uncertain, and uncertainty problems require the application of probability concepts. Yet accountants are traditionally raised on single point (deterministic) estimates of the future. The use of probability is, therefore, one of the greatest needs of the financial function.

Probabilities are either *objective*—determined by logic or experience and independent of the person concerned, or *subjective*, which depend on the wisdom and experience of the manager concerned. Objective probabilities are more useful but are rarely available for several types of management problems, whereas, although *subjective* probabilities are often less reliable, they may be very useful for certain classes of management problems.

Two types of uncertainty models are considered. First is the use of "pay-offs" based on probabilities and which are used in "decision trees" for strategic planning; and secondly is a simulation of the spread for risk in making an investment decision on a specific project.

Probability

The two essential aspects of probability are first that the sum of the probabilities always equals one. For example:—

Probability	Outcome
·1	10
·3	20
·6	30

Total	1·0

Secondly, the expected value is the weighted average of the individual probabilities. For example, using the distribution above:

$$·1 \times 10 \ = \ 1·0$$

$$·3 \times 20 \ = \ 6·0$$

$$·6 \times 30 \ = \ 18·0$$

Weighted average	25·0

The *weighted average* or *expected value* of each of several distributions can be added together and the sum of the expected value of the individual distribution will be the expected value of the combined distribution.

A delightful book giving insights into the use of pay-off matrices is *The Compleat Strategyst* by J. D. Williams.

Decision Trees

Decision trees are used in strategic planning. They represent a quantification of the effect of four factors:—

1. An external environmental factor (which a scientist would call "a state of nature") such as a market of a given size.

2. A probability of the external factor occurring.

3. A management action in relation to the external environmental factor.

4. The pay-off from the management action.

For example:—

1. Market size of   5 MM lb
                or   10 MM lb
                or   15 MM lb

2. Probabilities of such market sizes occurring are:

      P ·2   of   5 MM lb
      P ·5   of   10 MM lb
      P ·3   of   15 MM lb

3. Management Action

      Build a large plant.
      Build a small plant (and expand later if warranted).
      Do not build a plant but buy for resale.

4. A pay-off matrix as follows:

Management action	Market size (MM lb)		
	5	10	15
Build large plant	$0MM	$5MM	$15MM
Build small plant	$5MM	$6MM	$ 6MM
Do not build plant	$1MM	$2MM	$ 3MM

Pay-off

The weighted averages can now be calculated for each management action as follows:

Build large plant   ·2 x 0 + ·5 x 5 + ·3 x 15
               =   0 + 2·5 +   4·5   = 7·0

Build small plant   ·2 x 5 + ·5 x 6 + ·3 x 6
               =   1·0 + 3·0 +   1·8   = 5·8

Do not build plant   ·2 x 1 + ·5 x 2 + ·3 x 3
               =   0·2 + 1·0 +   0·9   = 2·1

Based on this information above, the decision would be to build a large plant.

This technique can also be used to judge the value of obtaining better information. For example, if a more detailed market survey revealed that the market probabilities are as follows:

$$10 \text{ MM lb} \qquad P \quad \cdot 3$$
$$15 \text{ MM lb} \qquad P \quad \cdot 7$$

the pay-off for building the large plant would be

$$\cdot 3 \times 5 + \cdot 7 \times 15$$
$$= \quad 1\cdot 5 \quad + \quad 10\cdot 5 \quad = \underline{12\cdot 0}$$

A gain of $12\cdot 0 - 7\cdot 0$ or $5\cdot 0$ MM. It is just possible that the initial pay-off of $7 MM might not justify the investment in a large plant, whereas a pay-off of $12 MM might be more than adequate to justify it. This would give some clue as to the amount which could be spent on market research for better information to reduce uncertainty.

Simulation of risk in investment decision

Most investment decisions because of their complexity and uncertainty in relation to the future are based partly on quantified analysis and partly on subjective judgment. The aim being to bring out in quantified analysis all that is reasonably practical to do.

Many companies prepare single point estimates of the future return on investment expected over a project life and then compare this work at a minimum cut-off point, such as cost of capital. The return on investment over the project life is supported by single point estimates of cash flow or profits each year. Since most large projects require Board of Director approval information on the project is usually conveyed in written form up the hierarchy of the organization until the final approval level is reached. It has been my experience that these single point estimates and the accompanying "story" of the reason for the project give top management an inadequate appreciation of the degree of risk in undertaking a project.

It is true that some companies support their project with what is called "a Sensitivity Analysis". This analysis shows, for example, how much the return on investment would change if a single factor, such as capital cost of the equipment, market volume, market price efficiency etc. were changed by 10%. It does not in any way give a clue to the *likelihood* or *probability* of such a change taking place. This is because all the wisdom and experience of managers down the line on the degree of risk involved has been "squeezed out" of the estimates by using "single point" forecasts each year.

One way of overcoming this is to use a simulation model for evaluating the risk in the project as a whole. The project is first considered in its isolated points such as:

Capital Expenditure Estimate
Product Lines   Manufacturing Cost
  Market Size   Raw Material Price
  Market Share   Labor Rates
  Price   Efficiencies

For each of these estimates a probability profile is constructed of risk of the estimate being different from the most likely value. For example:

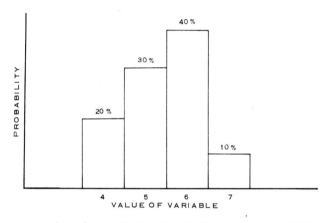

There are a number of ways that "subjective" estimates of individual managers can be recorded such as in a histogram. One method is described in Appendix C.

When each of the probability profiles has been recorded, the problem is to determine the probability profile for the return on investment for the project as a whole. This is done by taking a large number of samples, each sample takes a random estimate for each of the factors and then calculates the return on investment. After say 200 or 1 000 samples have been taken a frequency distribution or histogram can be drawn for the return on investment profile as follows:

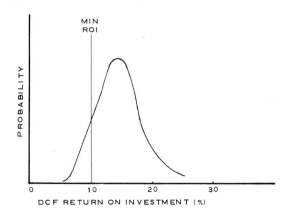

A cumulative frequency distribution

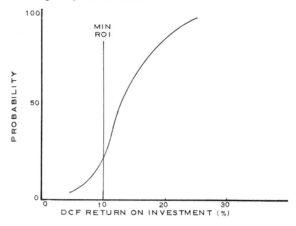

shows the probability of the return on investment falling below a certain minimum standard.

An example of the way the sample is selected will be demonstrated in the simulation exercise to follow. The random selection can be carried out very quickly at low cost on the computer, which then calculates the discounted cash flow (DCF) return on investment and will even print out the probability profile of the return on investment. There are a number of computer programs that will do this. One developed by Chemcell and widely used in Canada is available from Trans Canada Computer Utility Ltd.

The pioneer article on Risk Analysis appeared in the January/February 1964 issue of the *Harvard Business Review* and was authored by David B. Hertz of Mckinsey fame. It is well worth reading for a fuller understanding of the subject.

Undoubtedly "Risk Analysis" of investment decisions will grow in favour because the penalty of being wrong as plants increase in size with new technology can be catastrophic for a company.

As a sequel to the article mentioned earlier, David Hertz published another article in the January/February 1968 issue of the *Harvard Business Review* on "Investment Policies that Pay-Off". In this he shows the growing trend towards indicating minimum return on investment criteria with an acceptable spread of risk at that rate of return. The spread for risk being higher as the expected rate of return increases.

David Hertz then by a series of simulations compared over a period of time the effect on the earnings per share of a company of using various criteria and standards for evaluating investment projects such as:

Pay back   Return on investment
Discounted cash flow   Net present value methods

The simulation clearly demonstrated the gain from using time adjusted return on investment methods such as DCF or NPV techniques. It also showed the impact of different degrees of risk policies using the same DCF yardstick. More conservative policies as far as risk is concerned showed a slower rate of growth in earnings per share than higher risk policies. However, although the spread in earnings per share was higher than for low risk policies, the expected value was so much greater, it appeared to give a more beneficial result as a whole. However, the degree of risk which is appropriate to the present situation in any company is a matter of policy for that company alone.

VII. Summary

The above review has been based on describing financial models of different types. Many management problems do not fall neatly into one category or another but need a combination of approaches tailored to the specific situation concerned.

However, using a scientific method approach aided by models can shed valuable light on desirable courses of management action and reduce the amount of uncertainty in many management problems concerned with the future.

The desirable steps would generally include:

1. Definition of the problem (preferably in writing).

2. Identifying all the alternatives.

3. Constructing a model.

4. Defining a criterion for evaluating the model.

5. Obtaining estimates of the parameters or variables in the model.

6. Making the mathematical computations.

7. Testing the results for sensitivity and risk.

Often the use of models for strategic problems falls into three phases:—

1. A computer model for generating alternatives in:—

    a) external economic environment,
    b) market size and growth,
    c) market share and trend,
    d) price trends,
    e) raw material prices and labor costs.

2. An optimization method such as linear programming to determine the most attractive alternatives.

3. A risk analysis of the most attractive alternatives to facilitate the selection of the course of action which appears most beneficial to the company.

The results of the analysis may not be precise and scientifically elegant but they may give management more confidence in making firm decisions generating strategic courses of action.

APPENDIX A

GE–PERT 600

FAIRWEATHER MISSILE CORP ***** TEST DECK FOR GE–PERT/600 ***** JPR

SYSTEM IDENTIFICATION TS DECK
USER IDENTIFICATION TEST 1
MOST CRITICAL SLACK – 48·4

NETWORK START DATE 01 JAN 65
REPORT DATE 08 MAR 65
NETWORK COMPLETION DATE 01 JAN 66

18 HRS. 10 MIN. 08/25/69
REPORT 001 PAGE 1
ACTIVITY REPORT
RUN NUMBER 01

29 EVENTS   SORTED BY SUCCESSOR, PREDECESSOR   47 ACTIVITIES

Predecessor event	Successor event	Activity code	Activity description	Expected Time	Expected Date	Latest Time	Latest Date	Activity Time	Slack	Sched date	
34-210-001	34-210-002	ENGR	Release spec for maintenance equip.	30·6	05 Aug 65	27·5	15 Jul 65	3·1	3·1		*N
34-210-001	34-210-003	ENGR	Design transportation vehicle	34·3	04 Oct 65	0·1	31 Dec 64	6·8	34·4		*N
34-210-001	34-210-004	ENGR	Release spec for missile fab							A 16 Jul 65	N
34-210-001	34-210-005	ENGR	Release spec for erection equip.							A 20 Jul 65	N
34-210-001	34-210-006	MTC	Let sub-contract for emplace equip.							A 22 Jul 65	N
34-210-001	34-210-007	ATC	Prepare maint personnel requirement							A 18 Jul 65	N
34-210-001	34-210-008	MTC	Let sub-contract for site construct	31·5	15 Sep 65	19·4	18 May 65	4·0	12·1		*N
34-210-001	34-210-009	AGE	Release spec for ground equip fab	27·7	16 Jul 65	4·2	02 Dec 64	0·2	31·9		*N
34-210-001	34-210-010	TEST	Release spec for instl & c/o equip.	27·7	16 Jul 65	2·0	16 Jan 65	0·2	25·7		*N
34-210-001	34-210-011	ATC	Prepare oper personnel requirements	31·5	15 Sep 65	5·2	25 Nov 64	4·0	36·7		*N
134-210-007	34-210-011	ATC	Develop training criteria							A 23 Jul 65	N
34-210-004	34-210-012	MFG	Fabricate missile	57·8	18 Mar 66	9·4	09 Mar 65	30·1	48·4		*N
34-210-012	34-210-013	MFG	Release missile for test	43·8	10 Dec 65	9·4	09 Mar 65	0·2	34·4		N
34-210-013	34-210-014	MFG	Release erect equip for test	31·7	16 Sep 65	9·4	09 Mar 65	0·4	22·3		N
34-210-003	34-210-015	MFG	Fab missile transportation vehicle	43·6	08 Dec 65	9·2	08 Mar 65	9·3	34·4		N
34-210-005	34-210-016	TEST	Test missile	67·6	25 May 66	35·5	13 Oct 65	9·8	32·1		N
34-210-013	34-210-016	MFG	Fabricate missile erection equip.	31·3	13 Sep 65	9·0	06 Mar 65	3·1	22·3		*N
34-210-014	34-210-016	MFG	Release vehicle to trans. officer	43·8	10 Dec 65	35·7	14 Oct 65	0·2	8·1		N
34-210-016	34-210-017	MFG	Release missile to trans. officer	67·8	27 May 66	35·7	14 Oct 65	0·2	32·1		N
34-210-016	34-210-018	MFG	Release erect equip to trans. officer	31·5	15 Sep 65	35·7	14 Oct 65	0·2	4·2		N
34-210-016	34-210-018	TRANS	Transport missile to site	70·6	15 Jun 66	40·7	17 Nov 65	2·8	30·1		*N
34-210-017	34-210-018	DEBUG	Activity to debug nccunt % 21	72·8	01 Jul 66	40·7	18 Nov 65	5·0	32·1		N
34-210-016	34-210-018	SUPY	Release missile to installers	70·8	17 Jun 66	40·7	18 Nov 65	0·2	30·1		N
34-210-018	34-210-021	SUPY	Release empl equip to installers	63·2	25 Apr 66	40·7	18 Nov 65	0·4	22·5		N
34-210-017	34-210-019	SUPY	Assign maint pers to duty	29·0	23 Jul 65	40·7	18 Nov 65	0·2	11·7		*N
34-210-019	34-210-019	OPS	Release site to installers	52·8	11 Feb 66	40·7	18 Nov 65	0·2	12·1		N
34-210-018	34-210-020	SUB	Procure and deliver equip.	56·6	09 Mar 66	14·4	13 Apr 65	28·1	42·2		N
34-210-021	34-210-021	CONT	Activity to debug nccunt % 11	62·8	22 Apr 66	14·4	13 Apr 65	5·0	48·4		N
34-210-006	34-210-008	DEBUG	Training maint personnel	52·6	09 Feb 66	40·5	17 Nov 65	21·1	12·1		N
134-210-007	34-210-009	ATC	Construct site facilities							A 24 Jul 65	N
34-210-012	34-210-019	SUB	Procure and deliver ground equip.	46·5	29 Dec 65	14·6	14 Apr 65	18·8	31·9		N
34-210-008	34-210-023	CONT	Advise that equip is on dock	63·0	23 Apr 66	14·6	14 Apr 65	0·2	48·4		N
34-210-009	34-210-023	SUPY	Training maint personnel							A 26 Jul 65	N
34-210-019	34-210-023	ATC	Fabricate c/o equip	33·5	29 Sep 65	7·8	26 Feb 65	5·8	25·7		N
134-210-010	34-210-024	MFG	Training oper personnel	44·5	15 Dec 65	7·8	26 Feb 65	13·0	36·7		N
34-210-023	34-210-025	ATC	Test c/o equip.	51·3	31 Jan 66	14·6	14 Apr 65	6·8	36·7		N
134-210-011	34-210-011	TEST	Training operators	50·1	23 Jan 66	14·5	14 Apr 65	18·6	35·6		N
34-210-022	34-210-026	SUPY	Release gnd. equip to installers	63·2	25 Apr 66	14·8	16 Apr 65	0·2	48·4		N
34-210-024	34-210-026	SUPY	Release c/o equip to installers	51·5	02 Feb 66	14·8	16 Apr 65	0·2	36·7		N

APPENDIX B

LINEAR PROGRAMMING

The subject of estimating would not be complete without an introduction to one of the most important developments in the past decade. It is the optimization of profit using the method of linear programming. Its value in estimating the benefits from capital expenditures, is because it not only shows the optimum profit from existing operations, but it indicates the profit added if each process were expanded, and what the new optimum profit from the expanded facilities would be under a variety of assumptions.

One of the problems facing management is estimating the effect of changes on the business. Hitherto, the technique which has made the most important contribution is marginal or incremental economics. The discussion of estimating so far has been on this concept of change from an existing situation or the increment of sales, costs, and investment from the present situation. This concept is still valid, but may not be adequate for the complexity of modern business. Consider for example:

	Product A	Product B
Marginal profit $/lb.	4	5
Production rate		
Process X M lb/day	2	1
Process Y M lb/day	1	1·2

How much of each product should be produced to maximize profits? Furthermore, how does the profit increase when process X is expanded, or process Y, or a combination of both? The classical answer would be that one optimizes profit based on the scarce factor of production. For example, if process X were the limiting factor, it would be more important to sell Product A ($4 M profit per day) than Product B ($5 M profit per day). On the other hand, if process Y were limited, the profit would be $4 M per day for Product A, but $6 M for Product B. Marginal economics, by itself, is inadequate to answer the questions of optimizing the whole operation.

In practice, the problem is usually more complicated. Consider, for example, a company which has several manufacturing plants, a multi-product structure, multipurpose equipment, and opportunities to sell at first stage manufacture or up-grade to higher manufacture. What combinations of products, processes, and manufacturing plants will result in maximum or optimum profit? The answer can usually be found only by linear programming.

Linear programming is a branch of mathematics based on matrix algebra which enables equations of the type

$$5x+6y \leq 30$$
$$3x+2y \leq 12$$
$$x \geq 0$$
$$y \geq 0$$

to be solved.

In other words, the equations are of the form that something may not exceed a certain figure. The operation of a business is similar to this approach. The production capacity of each process is limited, yields or throughputs are limited, and the amount of product which can be sold in a given area is limited. If business equations can be formulated in this way, matrix algebra can be used to solve them. The second feature of linear programming is that, subject to the production and marketing constraints enumerated above, it optimizes an economic function—it either minimizes cost or maximizes profit.

A graphical representation of these two features of constraint or limitation equations and an economic function is illustrated on the following page. The optimum point is when the economic function is the furthest distance from the origin, but still within the capacity constraints.

In practice, many business problems can be represented in this mathematical form (for example, variable costs are a linear function of the volume produced). The number of equations in practice may be quite large, often several hundred and possibly several thousand. Solution of such problems did not become practical until the late 1940's and early 1950's due to two developments. The first was the simplex method of solving linear inequalities, pioneered by Dantzig, and secondly the development of high speed computers. Such complex problems are today routinely solved in a matter of minutes. They have wide application in the oil, chemical, textile, steel, forest, distributive and many other industries.

So far, only the problem of optimizing an existing situation has been discussed. However, a feature of the solution of such a problem, is that supplementary information is provided on the increase in profit if each of the production or marketing limitations were relaxed or increased. It therefore provides clues to the profitability of expansion. Assumptions can then be made of the most attractive routes for expansion (using shadow prices through the "dual" function).

A further feature of linear programming is the ability to examine alternative ways of expanding operations. For example, how does profit increase if process X is expanded by 20% or 50%, or process X by 20% and process Y by 50%? What is the effect on expansion if customer A's business can be secured, or if the price of certain products is increased? The computer will recalculate all the complex interaction of products and processes, and arrive at a new optimum profit (parametric programming).

It is these aspects which suggest that linear programming will be an important aid in evaluating various ways of expanding processes and markets. It may well be the most significant break-through in business economics since the introduction of the marginal or incremental approach.

This has been an introduction to the subject of linear programming and those interested are recommended to consult the reading list. The application of this method is restricted to linear relationships and more advanced methods of mathematical programming are available for non-linear functions.

PROFIT OPTIMIZATION

Graphic Solution of Linear Programming Problem

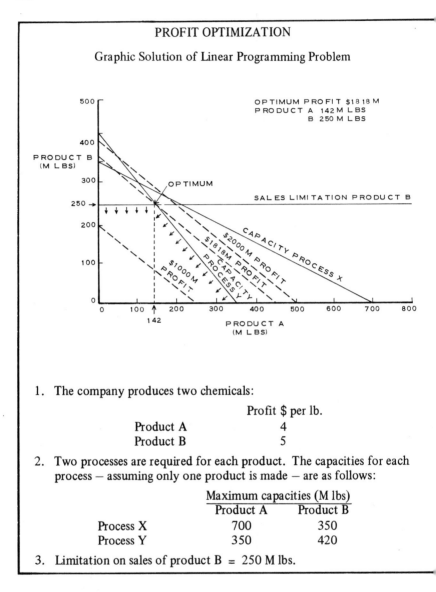

OPTIMUM PROFIT $18 18 M
PRODUCT A 142 M LBS
        B 250 M LBS

1. The company produces two chemicals:

	Profit $ per lb.
Product A	4
Product B	5

2. Two processes are required for each product. The capacities for each process – assuming only one product is made – are as follows:

| | Maximum capacities (M lbs) ||
	Product A	Product B
Process X	700	350
Process Y	350	420

3. Limitation on sales of product B = 250 M lbs.

Source: *A Practical Manual on the Appraisal of Capital Expenditures.* Special Study No. 1 published by the Society of Industrial Accountants, Hamilton, Ontario.

Linear programming is the most widely used of the operations research techniques. The word "programming" as used here refers to a deliberate choice of activities by the decision maker and does not refer to programming in the computer sense. The word "linear" is explained later. Linear programming is widely used partly because it is a powerful tool, partly because it can be applied in many practical situations, and partly because of the existence of excellent computer programming systems to carry out the analysis.

Linear programming is used in solving five general classes of problem:

1. *The diet mix, or blending problem.* In this case the goal is to find that mixture of ingredients of a mix or blend which will produce the greatest profit, at the same time respecting any required conditions or restraints on the amounts of each that may be used, as well as requirements of colour, taste, nutrition, etc. Examples are animal feeds, sausages, paints, etc.

2. *The production scheduling problem.* In this case the goal is to decide how much to make of a product in each time period to meet a given sales forecast, under known constraints with respect to production capacity, inventory, financial capability and so on.

3. *The product-mix problem.* In this case the object is to decide how much of each of several products to make when they compete for existing scarce resources such as manpower, machine time, raw materials, etc. The most profitable set of products and the amounts to make of each can be found by linear programming.

4. *The transportation problem.* This problem is a special case of linear programming that occurs with such frequency that special methods are available for solution. This is used where a single product can be made in any one of several plants up to the limit of their known capacities and can be shipped from any plant to any of a number of warehouses or consumers. The amount that is required by each "destination" is known as well as the transportation costs per unit of product between all pairs of origins and destinations. The solution by linear programming takes into account the transportation costs and any differential in the variable costs of production to yield the best production and shipping pattern. This technique is easy to learn, without specialized mathematical knowledge, and is feasible by hand calculation for problems up to four or five origins and ten to fifteen destinations, although "canned" computer programs are so generally available that they would normally be used for all but the very smallest problems.

5. *The assignment problem.* In this case the object is to assign people to jobs, jobs to machines, arriving aircraft to departing flights, etc., in such a way that the cost is minimized or the effectiveness maximized. Here again a special method is available for hand computation.

It is seen that each of the above seeks to find an optimum combination of the variables under the control of the decision-maker when certain constraints or conditions must also be satisfied.

The word "linear" in linear programming refers to the nature of the relationship between the variables. The method is only possible when there is a straight line relationship (not restricted to exact proportionality) between the decision variable and the desired objective. The relationships expressing the constraining condition must also be linear.

In spite of the restriction to "linear" situations, linear programming has found wide and very profitable use in the oil and chemical industry, the food industry, machine shops and many other places.

In non-linear situations, methods are also available, but these are much more complicated to apply and need much more computation. One of these areas is the problem of optimum portfolio selection for investors. A promising theory and method of solution due to Markowitz is under investigation by several research workers.

Source: *The Impact of Systems and Computers on Management and on the Accountant.* Special Study No. 6 published by the Society of Industrial Accountants, Hamilton, Ontario.

APPENDIX C

THE ANALYSIS OF RISK IN CAPITAL INVESTMENT PROPOSALS*

W. R. BLACKMORE
Chemcell Limited, Montreal†

Introduction

It is common practice today, in companies contemplating a major investment, to calculate expected rates of return as a guide to the desirability of proceeding with the project. These calculations are usually based on the best available estimates of markets, prices, and costs, and the ultimate accuracy of the results are inevitably dependent on how well these estimates reflect the actual conditions which will be encountered.

One method of estimating the degree of dependence of the results on the initial estimates is known as "sensitivity analysis." This consists of a series of calculations in which those factors which are considered to be most important to the project are allowed to vary by percentages judged appropriate by responsible executives. The effects of these variations on the return on total capital employed are then calculated. However, while this type of analysis provides a range of possible outcomes of the project, it does not include consideration of the likelihood of the variations considered ever taking place.

Methods of approach which provide an estimate of the risk associated with capital investments have been described in the recent literature.[1, 2, 3, 4.] In this type of analysis, a sales and profit statement is used as the basis of a mathematical model of the venture. Experienced executives are asked to estimate the ranges of variation and the probabilities of occurrence associated with key factors affecting the project. A Monte Carlo simulation is done using these subjective estimates to yield a probability distribution of the rates of return thought to be possible for the particular venture.

Application of the risk analysis method

Suppose a company is considering the expansion of a plant in an activity in which the executives have much experience. Suppose too, for the sake of this illustration, that the only factor affecting the project about which there is some uncertainty is the volume of sales to be expected each year in the future. It is a common practice that the marketing staff be asked to give their best estimate of the sales volumes to be expected each year. On the basis of this information,

*Received December 20, 1965
†From July 1, 1966 at School of Business, Queen's University, Kingston, Ontario

a discounted cash flow (*dcf*) rate of return on the project is normally calculated. If the volume of sales is considered to be a vital factor in this business, then a sensitivity analysis would also normally be done to show the effects on the return of having the volume drop by x per cent or rise by y per cent.

This procedure does not necessarily take advantage of all the capabilities and experience of the sales personnel, since a single estimate concerning the expected behaviour of the sales volume is all that has been requested. In the application of the risk analysis method, estimates of four factors affecting the sales volume are obtained:

First, a realistic market volume for each year in the life of the project. These need not be the same each year but may increase, decrease, remain constant, or move around in any way the marketing executives think is right.

Second, a lower limit on the market volume each year. These may differ too, in any way considered pertinent. This lower limit is the worst situation in which operating management might find itself if everything went badly.

Third, an upper limit each year. If everything went well, what might the upper limit be?

Fourth, the probability of the outcome being below the realistic estimate. The realistic market is the best estimate of what may happen, but the further into the future the calculations are extended, the less likely it is that the forecasts will be right. This fact is taken into account by asking the marketing staff to express their judgments about which way things might go if their realistic estimates were in fact, to prove inaccurate.

It should be pointed out that it is usually easy to obtain the kind of information required for the fourth parameter. When experienced executives are given time to reflect on the overall situation, a wealth of knowledge about the particular situation goes into their judgment of the outcome.

The estimates of the realistic market volume—lower limit and upper limit $(R, L,$ and $U)$—for each year may be used to construct a double triangular distribution such as is shown in Figure 1. The ratio of the areas of the triangles is selected as the ratio of the probabilities of the outcome being above or below the realistic outcome derived from the fourth parameter supplied by the marketing staff.

Market volumes (such as V_1 and V_2) are sampled from this distribution, and a distribution of the *dcf* rate of return on the investment is obtained, using a computer-based Monte Carlo technique. In practice, many other parameters, in addition to market volume, are treated in the same way and the resulting distribution indicates the effect of the simultaneous variation of all the parameters concerned in the calculation. A typical result is shown in Figure 2, in the cumulative form of the probability of achieving an indicated rate of return or less. The result

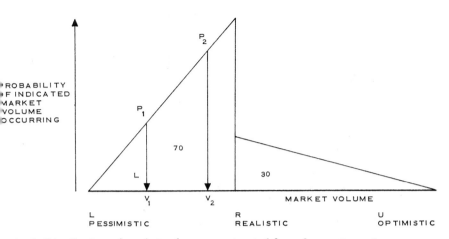

Fig. 1. Distribution of market volumes constructed from four estimated parameters.

can also be presented in the form of a probability density function, if this is more readily appreciated by the executives concerned.

The method can be applied equally well to other forms of distribution of the parameters entering the calculation. Also, the computer programme written to carry out the calculation can be constructed to take account of correlation between the variation of two or more parameters, and other constraints inherent in the judgment of those who provide the basic data, which are used as input for the calculations.

Advantages of the risk analysis method

Application of the risk analysis method has had the following advantages in practical use:

The judgments of experienced executives are explicitly obtained and used.

The experience of these executives is probed by requiring more information than a single best estimate on the parameters affecting the outcome.

The degree of financial risk associated with the project is explicitly shown: the chances of achieving different rates of return are clearly indicated.

The combined effect of the variation of several key factors on the distribution of possible outcomes can be calculated and illustrated.

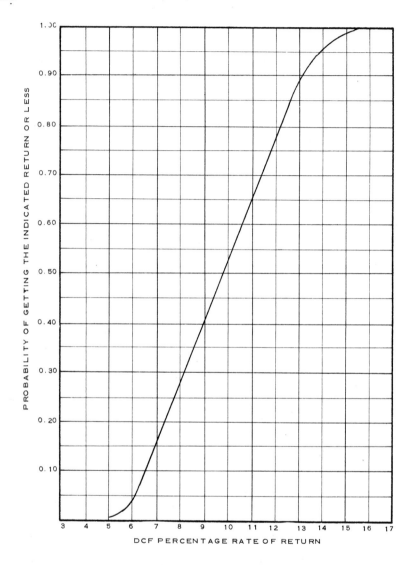

Fig. 2. Cumulative probability of achieving results.

ACKNOWLEDGMENTS

The author would like to acknowledge the help and assistance of all who have taken part in the studies on which this report is based. In particular, C. de Courv. and D. C. West of Canadian Industries Limited, and J. Roy of the Canadian Chemical Company have contributed significantly.

REFERENCES

1. H.M. Hawkins & O.E. Martin, "How to Evaluate Projects", Chemical Engineering Progress 60, No 12, December 1964.

2. D.B. Hertz, "Risk Analysis in Captial Investment", Harvard Business Review, Jan.–Feb., 1964.

3. S.W. Hess and H.A. Quigley, "Analysis of Risk in Investments using Monte Carlo Techniques", Chemical Engineering Symposium Series 42. Statistics and Numerical Methods in Chemical Engineering, New York: Am. Inst. Chem. Eng., 1963.

4. F.S. Hillier, "The Derivation of Probabilistic Information for the Evaluation of Risky investments", Management Science, April 1963, p. 443.

Source: *Canadian Operational Research Society Journal*, Volume 4, No. 2, July 1966.

BIBLIOGRAPHY

General

1. George W. Gershefski. Building a corporate financial model. *Harvard Business Review*, July–August 1969.

2. Robert H. Hayes. Qualitative insights from quantitative methods. *Harvard Business Review*, July–August 1969.

3. William Beranek. *Analysis for Financial Decisions.* Richard D. Irwin Inc. 1963.

Perceptive models

4. *Perspectives on Experience.* The Boston Consulting Group Inc., 100 Franklin Street, Boston, Mass.

5. *Perspectives on Corporate Strategy.* The Boston Consulting Group Inc., 100 Franklin Street, Boston, Mass.

Predictive models

6. Robert Goodell Brown. *Smoothing, Forecasting and Prediction of Discrete Time Series.* Prentice Hall 1963.

7. The Growing Use of Input-Output Models. *EDP Analyzer*, Vol. 7, No. 7, July 1969. Channing Publications Inc.

Complexity models

8. R. L. Martino. *Project Management and Control* (3 vols), American Management Association 1964–65.

9. E. Duckworth. *A guide to operational research.* Methuen & Company, London, 1962.

10. Arnold Kaufman. *Methods & Models of Operations Research,* Prentice Hall, 1963.

11. C. G. Edge. The Profit Contribution of Linear Programming to the Management of a Forest Industry Company. *CORS Journal,* July 1966.

12. C. G. Edge. Mathematical Programming. Greatest Advance since Marginal Economies. *The Business Quarterly,* University of Western Ontario, Fall 1964. Vol. 29, No. 3.

13. J. D. Williams. *The Compleat Strategyst.* McGraw Hill 1966.

14. John F. Magee. Decision Trees for Decision Making. *Harvard Business Review,* July–August 1964.

15. John F. Magee. How to Use Decision Trees in Capital Investment. *Harvard Business Review,* September–October 1964.

16. David B. Hertz. Risk Analysis in Capital Investment. *Harvard Business Review,* January–February 1964.

17. David B. Hertz. Investment Policies that Pay off. *Harvard Business Review,* January–February 1968.

18. "RISKAN". A risk analysis computer program available from Trans Canada Computer Utility Ltd., Montreal.

11. MODELS FOR PLANNING AND CONTROL

R. W. LINDER

CONTENTS

GENERAL INTRODUCTION

The time dimension in planning and control

In an earlier paper[1] the author developed a straightforward classification of airline planning and control systems in terms of the lead-times required for different levels of decision-making.

It was explained that, once corporate policy and objectives have been established appropriate strategic plans must be developed for attaining the long-term goals of the organisation. Such plans must consider the nature and magnitude of future demand for the products or services supplied by the organization, and the most profitable means of satisfying this demand. In a commercial airline strategic, or long-range planning decisions relate to the acquisition of such major resources as aircraft, airport terminal facilities and automatic reservations systems. Such decisions are also concerned with broad questions of deployment of these resources to both new and existing routes and services in the longer term.

The elapsed time between making a decision on such matters and the actual implementation of results is usually several years.

Once long-range plans have been developed for the organization as a whole, management must consider the details of their implementation in the light of current and immediate future conditions. It is here that tactical or short-range planning takes over the dominant rôle. In constructing any short-range plan the organization will be constrained by the many limitations of existing circumstances (including those created by previous planning decisions). Thus the range of opportunities in tactical planning is much more restricted than in the longer-term planning process. In a commercial airline most tactical plans relate to the detailed allocation of available resources for the immediate year or two ahead. The elapsed time between any tactical planning decision and the actual deployment of resources is therefore relatively short compared with the corresponding interval for strategic planning. This time span in fact coincides roughly with the delivery lead-time for the major resource of the Company—namely the modern commercial jet aircraft.

As the organization will generally be in a continuous state of operational activity, management must be able to monitor actual progress against the short-term goals established by the tactical planning processes. Feedback of information in the form of control decisions can then be used to adapt the operations to perceived changes in circumstances. Operational control decisions therefore have almost immediate effect, but only over a limited time-span. In an airline such as Air Canada most operating decisions are implemented within minutes or hours, and have an immediate but very short-term effect on the organization whose time-span can usually be measured in hours, days or weeks. The particular point here is that such decisions are usually based on analysis of existing conditions, rather than on forecasts of the situation which may exist in some future time period. This fact underlines a fundamental difference between planning and control systems, since in both strategic and tactical planning processes the decisions are based primarily on forecasts of future traffic volumes. Existing conditions are only useful for planning purposes to the extent that they indicate the direction of future events.

The foregoing distinctions between long-range planning, short-range planning and operational control served to introduce a useful classification scheme for the various planning and control models which have been developed in Air Canada. Since writing the earlier paper, however, the author has had time to reflect upon the relationships between the organization and its competitive and socio-economic environments. As a result it now seems worthwhile to reconsider these same planning and control models in relation to a second dimension—the dimension of space.

The space dimension in planning and control

The typical commercial airline is only one of a great many organized systems which together interact with and are influenced by the whole socio-economic environment. However, this interaction has a considerable effect on any particular airline, both in terms of planning and in terms of effective control of its operations. Quite clearly the economic conditions in those parts of the world in which an airline operates will directly influence the level of demand for its services, as well as the prices it must pay for its various factors of production. Social and political pressures will frequently define the airline's objectives in terms of providing cheap, comfortable and frequent services rather than solely in terms of profit. The operations of all airlines are controlled by national laws, international regulations and intergovernmental agreements which limit their freedom to operate services and to determine fares. Many airports and terminal facilities are owned, designed, built and operated by other authorities, each of which has its own ideas of effective design and management. And finally the operations of all airlines are of course influenced by the weather, and by the dependence on the human throughput which is common to all transportation industries. This latter point is manifested in terms of the anxieties that people have about travel in general and about flying in particular.

One particular aspect of the total environment which deserves special consideration in its own right is that of competition. No organization can afford to ignore the effects of the competitive environment when engaged in planning or operational decision-making. Both the total demand for the products and services offered by any industry, and the share of market obtained by each member of that industry will be significantly influenced by the combined decisions of all member organizations as well as by the overall condition of the larger socio-economic environment. In the commercial airline industry competition is a very real and important part of the environment of any particular airline, although a good deal of freedom to manoeuvre is given up through membership in industry associations and through commercial agreements between airlines. When fares and frequencies are limited by statutory bodies and international agreement, then aircraft type, quality of service and sales promotional activities are often the only variables left for manipulation. The 'selling' of destinations and all-inclusive tours rather than merely the means of transportation is one noticeable attempt to overcome these problems through diversification. The precise identification of the competitive environment of any airline will depend upon the geographical location and characteristics of its route structure, but clearly it need not always be confined to parallel air transportation services alone. Other modes of transportation will often have a measurable effect on some part of the operations of an airline.

The internal environment of a typical airline is geared primarily to the process of transporting passengers and cargo from departure points to arrival points. The mainstream of an airline's continuing operations therefore begins with the reception of passenger and cargo traffic, continues with ground handling functions at departure points, includes the flying operations which transport the traffic and the ground operations at arrival points, and concludes with the delivery of passengers and cargo at final destinations. Ancillary operations to this mainline process include passenger reservations facilities, maintenance functions and other supporting services. In all parts of the internal production process the main concern is with the effective use of resources, and the emphasis is on controlling the costs of labour and capital inputs in relation to the level of production and the quality of services offered.

Viewing the functions and operations of a commercial airline in the space dimension brings out more clearly certain requirements of planning and control models which may not be apparent solely in the context of time-spans for decision-making. It also suggests a second important classification scheme for such models which focuses on the relationships within the organization, and between the organization and its environment. At least three levels of relationship can be identified as follows:

1. *Across industries (the socio-economic environment).* Here most variables are outside the control of any individual organization. Relatively few models have been developed, except macro-econometric models for national planning. The exogenous nature of most variables implies a great deal of uncertainty for the individual organization. In Air Canada models for forecasting long-range passenge and cargo traffic using relationships with socio-economic, competitive and policy variables fall into this category.

2. *Within an industry (the competitive environment).* Here also many variables are outside the control of any individual organization. Some explanatory models have been developed, and these are concerned with marketing and revenue estimation (of necessity most organizations have at least developed purely descriptive revenue forecasting models in this category). At this level also there is still a good deal of uncertainty for the individual organization. In Air Canada descriptive short-range forecasting models, as well as schedule generation and evaluation models for short-range and long-range planning fall into this category. The emphasis is on market share and revenue estimation.

3. *Within the organization (the internal environment).* Here most variables are at least partially controllable by the organization. Many explanatory models have been developed, and these are typically concerned with the production function. The emphasis is on cost and/or quality control through the efficient utilization of resources. At this level there is much less uncertainty, and many planning and control models can usefully be developed as deterministic representations of reality. In Air Canada models for manpower and facilities budgeting for controlling day-to-day flight operations, reservations and inventory functions, and for monitoring the quality of services offered all fall into this category.

The above discussion of airline planning and control models in relation to the space dimension should not be construed as presenting an alternative to the earlier classification over time. Rather these two views complement one another in a very interesting way. Before passing on to the next part of this paper it is therefore instructive to arrange the various airline models already referred to in the two-dimensional tableau or matrix on the opposite page.

TIME

	Operational	Short-range	Long-range
Internal	Flight planning reservations control Inventory control Quality control	Manpower and facilities budgeting	
Competitive		Traffic forecasting Schedule evaluation	Traffic forecasting Schedule generation and evaluation
Socioeconomic			Market forecasting

SPACE

A careful consideration of these two dimensions of time and space, and their effect on both decision-makers and model-builders may help to explain why both the latter have tended to concentrate much of their attention on problems internal to any organization in the past. It may also help the reader to see how important it is becoming to develop models which show the interaction of the organization with its environments. Certainly a consideration of the space dimension brings out more clearly and in context the much greater degree of uncertainty which exists in the environment, and helps to focus our attention on the problems of dealing with this uncertainty in our model-building activities. It also helps to explain why the fundamental objective of so many organisations in the past has been the survival of the enterprise over the long term rather than profitability *per se*.

The problem of uncertainty in the environment is so important that a brief discussion of deterministic and probabilistic model-building seems worthwhile before proceeding to a discussion of some Air Canada planning models in this same context.

UNCERTAINTY AND THE SPACE DIMENSION

Deterministic models

In the literature of Operational Research the concept of a model is frequently presented as a functional relationship between some appropriate measure of effectiveness or utility on the one hand, and a set of controllable and uncontrollable variables on the other. Ackoff and Sasieni,[2] for example, characterize a typical model in the following form:

$$U = f(X_i, Y_j)$$

where U is the measure of value or utility for the system under study, X_i the set of controllable or policy variables, Y_j the set of uncontrollable variables, and where f signifies the functional relationship.

Solving such a model involves optimizing U or its expected value for a given se of estimated values of the Y_j. Such optimization may or may not be carried out subject to constraints on the possible values which the X_i may take. In either cas the solution expresses the X_i as a function of the estimated values of the Y_j, viz:

$$X_i = g(Y_j)$$

If these latter equations can be obtained in a closed analytical form they are frequently referred to as decision rules for fairly obvious reasons (the X_i are polic or decision variables). Ackoff and Sasieni sum up the solution approach as follows:

"Whatever procedure is used, an optimal or near-optimal solution is sought. An optimal solution is one that minimizes or maximizes (as appropriate) the performance measure in a model, subject to the conditions and constraints represented in that model."

In a different context Borch[3] presents the classical theory of the firm in the form of the following deterministic model:

$$P = qf(x_1, \ldots, x_n) - \sum_{i=1}^{n} P_i x_i$$

where: P = profit
q = unit price of output
y = $f(x_1, \ldots, x_n)$ is the production function which determines the output y from the amounts $x_1, \ldots, x_n$ of inputs (factors of production)
p_i = unit price of ith input

The solution which maximizes profit is the input vector $(x_1, \ldots, x_n)$ given by

$$q \frac{\partial f}{\partial x_i} = p_i \quad (i = 1, 2, \ldots, n)$$

Clearly these last equations represent decision rules in the sense used above since q and the x_i variables are the controllable or decision variables (the price of output and the levels of input), while the p_i are the uncontrollable prices of inputs. In fact this result confirms that profit is indeed maximized when marginal revenue equals marginal cost in this idealized situation.

The above model is a gross simplification of reality and has rarely found practical confirmation. Economists have tended to explain away its inadequacies by noting that organizations seldom have the sole objective of profit maximization. Borch, however, puts forward a different point of view when he states that:

". . . we ought to study the environment in which the decisions are made rather than the objectives behind the decisions. The environment will usually be made up of other decision-makers, and their decisions will create the situation in which our particular firm has to make its decision. This inevitably leads to a game-theoretical situation, and if mixed strategies enter, there will be uncertainty about the outcome."

The introduction of uncertainty through the uncontrollable variables implies that only in the most straightforward models of the internal environment can a completely deterministic approach be taken. Only in these situations can optimization in the mathematical sense be seriously entertained. This is not to say that deterministic models of the relationships between any organization and its environment cannot be built and solutions (decision rules) obtained through optimization techniques. However, in all such situations the model-builder is taking the potentially dangerous step of ignoring the uncertainty in the uncontrollable factors.

Probabilistic models

Once the presence of uncertainty is admitted the uncontrollable variables should be recognized and treated as stochastic (probabilistic) variables, each with a probability distribution over its possible outcomes. It then follows that the measure of effectiveness of the system under study will itself be a stochastic variable with a distribution of possible outcomes. In such situations Borch argues that it makes no sense to talk about optimizing the effectiveness of the system. The objective must rather be to select a set of values for the controllable or decision variables which will produce the "best" probability distribution for the effectiveness measure. The decision-maker (ideally the organization as a whole) must therefore have a preference ordering over the set of attainable distributions of effectiveness. Such a preference ordering can, for example, be generated in the following form (using the Bernoulli Principle):

$$U\{f\} = \sum_E u(E).f(E)$$

where $f(E)$ is an attainable probability distribution of the effectiveness E, and $u(E)$ is a utility function, unique up to a positive linear transformation.

So far this argument has considered only the uncertainty of the space dimension, i.e. that uncertainty which exists in the external environment of the organization. If the time dimension is also considered, and if for example profit is used as the measure of effectiveness, then there will be a stream of profits over time to be considered for any set of values of the decision variables (e.g. an initial investment, or choice of action). Furthermore this stream of profits will itself be a stochastic stream, since its magnitude in any time interval can only be represented in terms of a probability distribution.

A typical planning decision will generally lead to a sequence of cash flows. There will usually be some uncertainty about the outcomes, and therefore the resulting sequence will be a stochastic sequence. The problem of selecting a set of values for the decision variables therefore requires that the organization has a *preference ordering over a set of attainable stochastic sequences*. If such an ordering can be represented by a utility function of sufficient generality the problem is solved. But, as Borch explains, sufficiently general utility functions are not available (for example, simple discounting at any constant rate cannot allow for time preferences), and it is "therefore not surprising that businessmen have difficulties when they try to spell out the objectives of their firms."

It is precisely in this kind of uncertain environment that many of the models for planning and control in Air Canada have been built. Consciously or otherwise these models have been built to evaluate alternative courses of action, rather than to optimize any particular measure of effectiveness. It is with this dominant thought in mind that this paper now turns to a review of some airline planning models.

REVIEW OF SOME AIRLINE PLANNING MODELS

General remarks

In the earlier paper[1] on this same subject the author explained that comprehensive sets of models for each time span of decision-making had been developed, or were presently under development in Air Canada. Such is not the case to the same extent when one considers models of the relationships between the airline and its competitive and socio-economic environment. However, many of the existing planning models are used to bridge these gaps, and it is instructive to examine their strengths and their weaknesses from this point of view. It turns out that many of the problems discussed in the final part of the earlier paper are related to limitations of the existing models in the space dimension.

Consequently, the remainder of this paper will review, in some detail, four planning models selected from those which have been developed in Air Canada over the past few years. These four models are presented here in the same logical order in which they would be used in the planning processes (i.e. long-term models before short-term models, and models of the external environment before models of the internal operations of the airline). They are:

1. A Market Forecasting Model
   (Long-range/socio-economic environment)

2. A Traffic Forecasting Model
   (Short-range/competitive environment)

3. A Schedule Evaluation Model
   (Short-range/competitive environment)

4. A Manpower Budgeting Model
   (Short-range/internal environment)

These models, like most in Air Canada, were not originally conceived with any overall plan in mind. Rather they were developed as independent projects to answer specific and separate needs of the organization. It is only over time that the inter-relationship between these models has been consciously recognized, and a more sophisticated overall planning process developed through the integration of the component models. In essence each of these models serves as a processor function in a larger information system for planning decision-making, and in each case these systems are automated on electronic computers.

Several dichotomies will be referred to in this review. By far the most pertinent distinction is between deterministic and probabilistic models, but other distinctions are those made between analytical and simulation models, and between descriptive and explanatory models.

Finally, repeated reference will be made to the airline flight schedule as the manifestation of our future plans. Such plans are produced on a six-month basis (summer and winter periods), and cover several years into the future at varying levels of detail and finalization.

The econometric model for marketing[4]

Long-range forecasts of passenger traffic volumes are required in Air Canada in order to plan resource acquisitions and broad plans of operation up to ten or more years into the future. When forecasting only a short time into the future it is frequently only necessary to project recent past performance because the levels of the major factors affecting passenger volumes will likely remain in the same general relationship to one another. However, going further into the future, significant deviations from past relationships may begin to appear (e.g. economic recessions or booms, changes in competition, major fare, frequency or equipment changes, etc.). It then becomes desirable to predict these longer-term changes, and utilize this knowledge through forecasting models which depict the relationships between the airline and its external environment.

In Air Canada, therefore, a number of long-range forecasting models have been developed which relate passenger traffic to socio-economic and policy variables.

All the models so far developed are single-equation models and the coefficients are estimated from past data by multiple linear regression analysis. Several model structures were originally considered including additive, multiplicative (which can be made linear by a logarithmic transformation), and various non-linear forms. Few, if any, formal statistical techniques are available for identifying an optimal model structure, and our final choice of model type was based at least as much o judgement as on any objective analysis. The multiplicative model was eventually selected, since other experience with forecasting models had indicated that traffic reacted more directly to percentage changes than to absolute changes in external conditions. In addition most of the more "realistic" non-linear models that were suggested were nearer in form to the multiplicative model than to the additive model.

A typical model is therefore of the form:

$$T = C X_1^{a_1} X_2^{a_2} \ldots \ldots Y_1^{b_1} Y_2^{b_2} \ldots \ldots$$

where T = Traffic volume (total air market, or Air Canada share)
X_i = The ith policy variable
Y_j = The jth socio-economic or competitive variable
C is a scaling constant, and the a's and b's are the elasticities of T with respect to the various independent variables.

The dependent variable, T, is taken as total market size whenever this data is readily available; otherwise the regression is performed on Air Canada traffic data only. By putting forecast values of the socio-economic and policy variables into the model forecasts of future traffic volumes can be obtained. The models are up-dated annually and both the re-estimation and the forecasting are carried out by a series of computer programmes working with a data bank of all the relevant time series. Since the effects of individual months are not of too much interest in long-range forecasting, the historical monthly traffic and socio-economic time series are deseasonalised prior to carrying out the regression analysis. The results therefore appear as monthly trend forecasts which can be brought together to form annual totals or Summer and Winter 6-month totals to fit in with the airline's planning periods.

The regression equation is a statement of a cause-effect relationship and as such it should be logical. Some of the variables used relate to a population mass, e.g. disposable income, while others refer to a single individual, e.g. retail price index and airline fares. To improve the logical structure all variables are therefore put on a *per-capita* basis, and the models typically relate traffic per head (of population) to fares, income per head, production per head, etc.

In addition to the basic (or expected) rate of increase of the socio-economic variables in any model four additional rates are evaluated by adding an annual 1% and 2% to and from the basic rate. Thus five rates of increase are used to give five forecasts of the socio-economic variables, which in turn produce five different predictions of future traffic per head. These latter predictions are multiplied by the appropriate population forecasts (made externally to the system) to obtain the final traffic forecasts. Finally, the airline planners who use this forecasting system can themselves adjust the various policy variables and also alter the forecasts of the economy, and can rapidly see the results of these manipulations in terms of revised forecasts of future traffic volumes.

In constructing any model many of the so-called independent variables are found to be highly correlated with each other (multicollinearity). This frequently leads to illogical results until the number of socio-economic variables is significantly reduced (usually down to one or two). Inspection of the correlation matrix also may indicate high correlation between socio-economic and policy variables. Since any reduction in the number of policy variables destroys part of the usefulness of a model (i.e. its ability to evaluate alternative policies) the system allows the user to fix certain regression coefficients during the analysis.

The analysis of forecasting errors includes the estimation of the first-order auto correlation coefficient ρ_1. If this is found to be significantly different from zero each variable is transformed by $x_t - \rho_1 x_{t-1}$ (where t denotes time) before entering the regression analysis for a second time. This is as far as we go in allowing for autocorrelation, but it does give more efficient estimates of the coefficients of a model. An important additional benefit is that it also seems to reduce the multicollinearity problem quite significantly.

Recognizing that the interaction between changes in the economic environment and resulting volumes of passenger traffic will be distributed over time the dependent variable for a particular month is related to each socio-economic variable moving averaged over a 12-month period up to and including that month. This is a simple and straightforward way of imposing a six-month lag in the model, and no further allowances are made for any lagged relationships.

Clearly the econometric model for marketing makes a conscious effort to represent the relationship between the airline and its environment. Equally clearly it is much more a deterministic model than a probabilistic one, although some attempt is made to recognize the uncertainty in the uncontrollable (exogenous) variables. This is done in the traditional manner by estimating the standard error about the regression equation, and also by projecting the socio-economic variables at five different levels (in a way a kind of sensitivity analysis). Its potential as a policy evaluation tool is at least as great as its use as an "optimal" predictor, and this is consistent with the concepts already discussed in this paper in relation to environmental models. Finally it is an explanatory rather than a purely descriptive model (hence its evaluative abilities), and it is clearly an analytical rather than a simulation model.

The trend-projection forecasting model[5]

Short-range forecasts (up to two years ahead) are required for both passenger and cargo traffic at least twice a year in Air Canada. They are used as basic inputs in the development of detailed flight schedules for future summer and winter seasons. Forecasting errors in this area can therefore have serious consequences in terms of poor scheduling of future operations and potential loss of revenue and customer goodwill. The achievement of precise short-range traffic forecasts is therefore worth a good deal of effort, falling into two distinct categories:

1. The forward projection of historical traffic volumes.

2. The evaluation and modification of these projections in the light of current and expected future levels of competition, socio-economic conditions, etc.

These forecasts are required monthly for traffic between every pair of points in the Air Canada network (more than 3 000 in all). Not all pairs of points are worth a detailed study, however. As might be expected, some 200 combinations provide 85 to 90 percent of the Company's passenger traffic.

The forward projection of historical data consists of a large amount of tedious mechanical work, and the present short-range forecasting model has succeeded in transferring these particular operations to an electronic computer. In this way the human analysts in the system are able to devote most of their time and effort to the essential, but more subjective tasks of evaluating and modifying the results

The technique of exponential smoothing is used in this particular forecasting model, and a typical series of monthly traffic volumes is assumed to be made up of four components: an average level in any month, a trend or growth component from month to month, a seasonal pattern which repeats itself every twelve months, and a random or irregular component.

The exact formulation of the mathematical model depends on whether the trend and seasonal components are assumed to be additive or multiplicative in character. Extensive tests on a wide variety of traffic series have confirmed that the fully multiplicative model is most representative of Air Canada's data. The trend component is therefore measured as a percentage change from month to month, and the seasonal pattern is measured as a series of ratios of actual traffic volumes to their corresponding average levels in each month of the year.

The model consists of three exponential smoothing equations which are used to estimate the current average traffic level, the current trend factor, and the current monthly seasonal factor. The corresponding smoothing constants are called alpha, beta and gamma respectively. A fourth equation multiplies these current estimates together in a logical manner to produce the required monthly projections of future traffic volumes.

Based upon many initial experiments, and also on several years of experience with these models, all the smoothing constants are held at a nominal value of 0·10 as long as external conditions remain unchanged, and the forecasting system remains "under control". In this sense the forecasting model is like a black box or processor into which are fed historical data, and out of which are produced traffic projections. As long as conditions do not change, the magnitude of the forecasting error is determined by the amount of unexplained random variation in the data. If the process does go out of control, its response to changing conditions can be altered by changing the values of alpha, beta and gamma.

Extensive analyses of forecasting errors for a one-month lead-time have shown that the random component is also multiplicative for most Air Canada traffic series. It is therefore measured by the ratio of actual to forecast traffic, and is approximately normally distributed with a mean of unity (when the forecasting process is unbiased and under control), but with a variability which depends on the particular traffic series.

A straightforward control procedure compares the ratio error each month to appropriate control limits, and prints out warning signals on an exception basis. If a real cause can be found for the out-of-control condition, immediate action is taken by altering the smoothing constants according to a set of simple rules. If no cause can be identified, two successive warning signals must appear before any action is taken. The emphasis is on caution, and on the importance of retaining at least some of the past history contained in the current estimates of the trend and seasonal components.

This forecasting model has been in regular use since the beginning of 1963, and it adequately performs the task it was designed for. It is straightforward, economical on storage space and processing time in the computer, and fairly easy to adjust and control when changes have occurred or are expected. Its simplicity imposes a number of limitations on the results, but once these are clearly understood and accepted, the projections serve as an invaluable base from which to build up the final detailed forecasts required for schedules planning.

Clearly the Trend-Projection forecasting model is purely descriptive, and therefore cannot explain the short-term relationship between the airline and its competitive environment. Neither can it evaluate alternative short-term policies. Furthermore, in the manner in which it is used it is very much a deterministic rather than a probabilistic model. The uncertainty in the competitive environment is therefore completely ignored in the analytical projection process. In the face of such odds it may seem surprising that it can perform a useful forecasting job, until it is realized that over its effective time-span few significant changes occur. When such changes do occur the human being in the system can readily increase the adaptiveness of the model to the new circumstances, and also allow for them in his subsequent modifications of the computer projections. Nevertheless the limitations of a purely descriptive model for forecasting market shares (i.e. Air Canada traffic volumes) are quite significant, and this aspect will be taken up again in the concluding part of this paper.

The passenger allocation model[6]

A detailed flight schedule defines a network of paths over which passengers will flow from one point to another. Any point can usually be reached from any other by several different paths. The passenger preference for any alternative is influenced by the types of aircraft used, the number of en-route stops and connections, the frequency of service and the times of departure and arrival of the different flights.

In practice, any prospective passenger may be unable to travel on his preferred flight because it is already fully booked. He will then either choose some alternative flight, or some other means of transportation (e.g. a competing airline). The load-factors on the flights, and the schedules of competing carriers are therefore important influencing factors in this process.

Given a proposed flight schedule it therefore becomes important to evaluate it in terms of its ability to service the prospective passenger market in the most acceptable manner. The Passenger Allocation Model is a computer-based model which simulates the real-life processes by which passengers are allocated to Air Canada flights. In doing so it takes into account the above-mentioned factors in assigning the passenger traffic to the various flights available.

The primary inputs to this model are the complete set of point-to-point passenger forecasts obtained from the short-range forecasting model already described, and a coded version of the proposed flight schedule. The main outputs from the model are detailed and summary listings of expected passenger flows and resulting load-factors on all flights in the schedule. Three types of report are produced. The first summarizes the flow of passengers classified by their origin and destination points. It shows how each set of passengers distribute themselves among the alternative flights available. The second type of report concentrates on each flight throughout its entire routing, and shows the overall loads to be expected on each leg of the flight without regard to the mix of passengers. The final type of report examines the total flows of passengers over all flights operating between every pair of points in the network. These total leg flows as they are called, indicate the "importance" of each connecting arc in the whole system.

The model itself breaks down conveniently into three sub-processes as follows

1. The Attractive Path Generator which applies a series of decision rules to distinguish between the attractive and non-attractive paths between each pair of points in the network. The procedure selects, from all possible flight paths, a particular sub-set of paths which dominate all other possible paths (based primarily on their speed advantage). Each attractive flight defines a corresponding period of attraction about its departure time. These periods of attraction are mutually exclusive, and completely cover the effective travelling day.

2. The Traffic Distribution Estimator which breaks down the monthly passenger forecasts for every pair of points into traffic distributions by time-of-day, and by day-of-week. These detailed passenger breakdowns are accomplished using passenger behaviour information which is partly based on historical data and partly on the judgements of experienced airline personnel. Quite obviously

historical data alone is highly influenced by past schedules, and cannot be too heavily relied upon to predict the desired departure times of prospective passengers.

3. The Passenger Allocation Process which applies a further series of sequential decision rules to allocate passengers to particular flights. These rules take into account the times prior to flight departure at which passengers request space between the different pairs of points in the network. They also allow capacity constraints to come into play by removing fully-loaded attractive flights and introducing additional flights which were previously unattractive. Whenever this occurs, there is feedback to the first sub-process to redetermine the new periods of attraction of available flights. The allocation process terminates when all the traffic has been allocated between every pair of points in the system.

This model is presently being integrated into the tactical planning system in Air Canada. It will prove invaluable in identifying unforeseen bottlenecks in the flight schedule, and any under-utilized areas of capacity. It represents a powerful evaluation tool for the planning personnel in the Company.

The Passenger Allocation Model is a deterministic simulation of the real-life processes by which passengers select their flights. It is explanatory rather than descriptive, and hence it can be and is used primarily as an evaluation tool. In its present form it does not model the relationships between the airline and its competitive environment. However, there are no conceptual problems in extending it to include competitive schedules and services as well as those of Air Canada. If this were done the inputs or traffic forecasts would have to be on a total market basis, rather than merely Air Canada's traffic projections. At present it only models the internal environment, and hence does not need to consider the uncertainty in the competitive sphere. If it were extended in the above way it would have to recognize certain probabilistic elements (exogenous variables) more explicitly.

The aircrew scheduling model[7]

The manpower required to operate the flights specified by the detailed schedule or tactical plan must also be budgeted for and re-assessed whenever the schedule changes. This is a very important problem, and not the least because aircrews represent a very expensive resource. Not only are their basic salaries very high because of the tremendous responsibilities they undertake, but also the union agreements include a number of penalty clauses which can cost the airline a good deal of additional expense if the crews themselves are not scheduled or assigned to flights as efficiently as possible.

The crew scheduling model in Air Canada has been developed to solve the problem of crew allocation in such a way as to minimize the total variable or penalty costs incurred. It is recognized that some crew or other must fly every flight in the schedule on every day of operation, and therefore the basic crew costs

The first problem is to link up the individual flights in the schedule to form what are known as "pairings". A pairing is a sequence of flights of a particular aircraft type which will take a crew out of its home base in a circuit of paths which eventually return to that base. Many thousands of such pairings can be generated from a given flight schedule, but only a certain sub-set of these will be legal in the sense that they satisfy various regulatory and union constraints. Once the sub-set of legal pairings has been generated, they are arranged in a two-way table or matrix which identifies the particular flight-legs contained in each of the pairings. Each pairing also carries a certain cost which represents the magnitude of the penalty costs which would be incurred if that pairing were actually flown by an aircrew.

The second problem is to select a certain number of pairings from the table in such a way that each flight-leg is flown once and only once on each day, and the total variable cost of the complete schedule of pairings selected is minimized. This is a particular type of problem amenable to the techniques of linear programming. However, the solution must allocate integral or whole numbers of crews to the various pairings, and the particular methods of integer linear programming must be used in this situation. In fact only one crew may be assigned to a chosen pairing, so that the problem specializes to the particular case known as "zero-one" linear programming. Sophisticated algorithms have been developed for this particular case, but their reliability and efficiency leave a good deal to be desired.

The Air Canada crew scheduling model in fact adopts a more straightforward approach to the problem based on the idea of a guided trial and error or search technique. However, rather than enumerating all possible combinations of pairings, it takes advantage of any results already obtained to reduce the amount of searching at every stage. This implicit enumeration technique is popularly known as "branch and bound" because it branches out and searches through the set of pairings, but bounds the amount of searching that actually has to be performed. Even so the amount of computation is very great and the volume of data to be stored for any practical problem is enormous. Consequently the procedure has been programmed for a large computer in the Company, and the inputs and outputs which make up the total system have also been completely automated.

The model in this final example is a very simple analytical linear cost model which is completely deterministic, and entirely concerned with relationships internal to the organization. It is explanatory rather than merely descriptive, and because of the absence of any uncontrollable variables it is natural that the objective should be to optimize the appropriate measure of effectiveness (in this case total penalty costs). But what is fine in theory may not always be achievable in practice. The problem here is one of solving the model (in the sense of optimization) in terms of integral numbers of pairings, and as such it presents severe technical difficulties. Further technical problems are created by the sheer magnitude of many of the practical applications, and it is perhaps not too surprising that "good" crew schedules are more likely to be obtained than "optimal" results. In this situation also evaluation may play as important a rôle as optimization even though there is no uncertainty present in the model.

GENERAL CONCLUSIONS

The internal production function

It is often foolhardy to generalize—the danger of course being one of over-simplification. However, if generalization can provide a better "framework" for discussion, analysis and understanding then the risk is worth taking. In this present paper an initial framework has been extended in a second dimension to provide additional insights into the problems of model-building for business decision-making. Some existing planning models in Air Canada have been reviewed in relation to this framework, and new strengths and weaknesses of these models have been uncovered. Some conclusions and generalizations now seem in order.

We can begin to recognize that models of the internal environment of an organization can only be concerned with the production function. Most of the variables will be controllable, and hence deterministic models can often be contemplated even if the structural relationships are complex in form. This leads naturally to the objective of solving such models through optimization of the measure of effectiveness. What may be desirable and logical in theory, however, may be very difficult of attainment in practice. Analytical and/or computational problems of optimization may be prohibitive as in the case of Air Canada's crew scheduling model.

Having identified the internal production function as being mainly controllable with optimal solution as a reasonable, if not always attainable objective, it must also be recognized that uncertainty will frequently be present to some limited extent. In many production and inventory control situations item demand and/or supplier lead-times are stochastic variables, and the more realistic models reflect this fact (although they still tend to minimize total long-run average costs). In queueing or congestion situations at airports and in telephone reservations offices, both workload and processing times are usually stochastic variables (although the objective is still to minimize costs, subject to constraints on levels of service). In these situations the models are not completely deterministic, but contain certain probabilistic elements.

As Drucker has said "there are no revenues within the organization—only costs", and this comment contains the essence of the present argument. Whether the decisions are long-term, short-term or operational, if they are solely concerned with the internal production function they are only concerned with costs, and the appropriate models will invariably reflect this fact.

The external marketing function

It must be clear that the short-range traffic forecasting model in Air Canada does not produce results which are independent of any proposed plan of action. This results in an iterative process of market planning, where successive modifications are introduced to both plans and forecasts until the final result is both internally consistent and acceptable to management. The various automated models described in this and the earlier paper greatly reduce the time required for evaluation, making it feasible to consider more alternatives and modifications to any original proposal.

It is equally obvious that the present models confuse the sequential tasks of total market forecasting and market share determination. In fact the short-range planning models do not model the relationships between the airline and its competitive and socio-economic environments. What is needed is a short-range forecasting model which will predict total market size, and a series of explanatory evaluation models which will produce as outputs the very same traffic forecasts which now form the inputs to the existing set of models (i.e. which will produce as outputs market shares, and hence revenue estimates). These improved models would still be evaluative in character, and the planning process would still be an iterative one in terms of the marketing function. Ideally the models would recognize the uncertainty in the environment and produce probabilistic rather than deterministic outputs.

Whether this line of development can be carried to the extreme of predicting demand or potential market levels which are independent of any proposed plan or flight schedule now becomes a secondary consideration. Of more immediate importance is the problem of generating plans (flight schedules) for rapid evaluation by the battery of models available now and in the future. This is a complex problem, and up to now it has not been amenable (except in part) to any mathematical model-building approach. The long-term objective would be to develop flight schedules subject to obvious constraints on available resources, and then rapidly evaluate their marketability using the kinds of marketing models already described.

We can begin to see that models of the external environment are primarily concerned with the marketing function. Many of the variables are uncontrollable, and ideally such models should be probabilistic in nature. The presence of uncertainty implies the need to use such models as evaluative tools, rather than attempting to optimize over a series of expected values of the probabilistic variables. In the long-term such models should provide the decision-maker with probability distributions of sales and revenues for each alternative plan (course of action) to be considered.

Concluding remarks

One remaining type of model has not been discussed in relation to the space dimension, and that is the financial model. Ultimately the results of the internal cost models and the external revenue models must be brought together for the important "balancing act" which will determine the short and long-term financial implications of any proposed plan. Since at least one of the two major types of inputs will be subject to uncertainty, and since a stream of future fund flows must usually be considered, the problem of choice will, in theory, be extremely difficult. In practice, of course, the problem is usually avoided by working entirely with expected values, ignoring the uncertainty, and discounting where necessary to allow for the time value of money. More recently the techniques of risk analysis have been combined with discounted cash flow procedures to overcome some of these limitations, but the fundamental need to identify sufficiently generalized preference orderings still remains.

In conclusion it may be said that a reappraisal of planning and control models in terms of a two-dimensional framework over time and space has been fruitful. It has not been possible to review all the models which have been developed in Air Canada to aid in the decision-making processes. However, by concentrating on four specific planning models greater insight has perhaps been made possible. A great deal has already been accomplished in the Company using the scientific principles of model-building, but as much of this present paper indicates a great deal more remains to be done in the future.

REFERENCES

1. R. W. Linder (1968). Model-building for Airline Planning and Control Systems, *Proceedings of 2nd International Symposium on Model-Building in Business and Economics*, London, June, 1968 (Paper No. 2 in this volume).

2. R. L. Ackoff & M. Sasieni (1968). *Fundamentals of Operations Research*, J. W. Wiley, N.Y.

3. K. H. Borch (1968). *The Economics of Uncertainty*, Princeton University Press, N.J.

4. I. Elce (1965). The Econometric Model for Marketing, *Proceedings of 5th AGIFORS Symposium*, Chicago, 1965.

5. H. J. G. Whitton & R. W. Linder (1962). Computer Forecasting of Passenger Flows, *Proceedings of 2nd AGIFORS Symposium*, Rome, 1962.

6. J. G. Gagnon (1967). A Model for Flowing Passengers over Airline Networks, *Proceedings of 7th AGIFORS Symposium*, Noordwijk, 1967.

7. J. Fearnley (1966). Crew Scheduling Development in Air Canada, *Proceedings of 6th AGIFORS Symposium*, Killarney, 1966.

12. MODELS FOR FORECASTING GROSS NATIONAL PRODUCT

JOHN A. SAWYER

1. Purpose of Forecasting Gross National Product

(A) *By Business Firms*

Forecasts of gross national product (GNP), its major components, and related economic statistics such as the unemployment rate, may be required by firms in order that they can make their sales, production, and capital budgeting plans consistent with the forecast of general economic conditions. An intermediate step may be to develop a model which forecasts the outlook for a particular industry in relation to the general economic outlook. The individual firm may then develop sales forecasting models for various products in which industry variables and/or economy-wide variables appear.

(B) *By Governments*

Governments forecast GNP and other target variables (such as the rate of price change and the unemployment rate) in order to select values of instrument variables (such as tax rates and levels of bank cash). Conditional forecasts of GNP are made for various combinations of instrument variables in order to select that combination of instruments which produces the set of values for the target variables which maximizes the government's preference function. That is, governments forecast in order to *control* the economy by smoothing out short-run fluctuations about a growth path based on the achievement of potential output.

Business firms should be aware, therefore, that a forecast of GNP made on the assumption that present government policy will continue is likely to be in error because government may take action to change the forecast value of GNP if the forecast value is not in line with the target value.

2. Methods of Forecasting GNP

Three types of forecasting models can be distinguished: (a) statistical models which do not attempt to explain the behaviour of the economy but which rely entirely on observed statistical regularities in past behaviour, (b) surveys of business or consumer intentions, (c) econometric models which use economic theory to explain the behaviour of the economy and data on the history of the economic system to estimate the values of the parameters in the model.

(A) *Statistical Models*

  i) autoregressive

$$y_t = f(y_{t-1}, y_{t-2}, \ldots) + u_t$$

where y_t is GNP in period t

      f is a function which relates the current value of y to previous values, e.g., a weighted average in which recent values receive larger weights than earlier values.

      u_t is a random variable (a stochastic error or disturbance term).

  ii) leading indicators

$$y_t = g(x_{t-j}, z_{t-k}, \ldots) + v_t$$

where y_t is GNP in period t

      g is a function which relates the current value of y to the value of some variable x, j periods ago, to the value of some variable z, k periods ago, and so forth

      v_t is a random variable (a stochastic error or disturbance term).

(B) *Anticipations Data*

Surveys of consumers or businessmen may be used to make estimates of intended expenditures on consumer or producers' durables. Other methods may be used to estimate the remaining components of GNP. Anticipations data may also be incorporated into econometric equations.

(C) *Econometric Models*

The methods based on statistical regularities or survey data have two major disadvantages. They cannot handle changes in structure (e.g., a change in imports resulting from technical change in an industry or from discovery of natural resources) nor can they handle changes in policy instrument variables (e.g., a change in the personal income tax rates).

An econometric model usually consists of a number of simultaneous equations. A stochastic behavioural equation of an econometric model has the following form

$$y_{1t} = f(y_{2t}, y_{3t}, y_{3,t-1}, y_{1,t-1}, z_{1t}, z_{2t}) + u_{1t}$$

where the y_{it} ($i = 1, 2, 3$) are endogenous variables, some of which may be targets,

      z_{jt} ($j = 1, 2$) are exogenous variables, some of which may be instruments,

      f is a function explaining the systematic part of the behaviour of the endogenous variable y_1 in terms of current and past values of various endogenous and exogenous variables,

u_{1t} is a random variable (a stochastic disturbance) with expected value zero. (Various conditions are also imposed on its variance and covariance.)

There will be one equation of this form or a definitional equation for each endogenous variable of the model. Economic theory will be used to specify the variables entering as arguments of the function f and the mathematical form of the function. The specification will be constrained by the need to satisfy identification criteria and to avoid extreme multicollinearity. All systematic variation in y_{1t} should be explained by f so that the difference between y_{1t} and $\hat{y}_{1t}$, $t = 1, 2, \ldots, T$, (where $\hat{y}_{1t}$ is the value of y_{1t} calculated from the function f) behaves randomly. Thus, the task of the economist is to explain all the variation of y_{1t} except the residual unexplained behaviour, u_{1t}, which should be random.

Econometric theory is concerned with developing methods of estimating the parameters of the function f in such a way that the residuals $y_{1t} - \hat{y}_{1t}$ are random variables and the parameter estimates are unbiased (although this property may only be achieved for very large samples) and have minimum variance. Many of the problems facing the econometrician arise from the presence of endogenous variables, including lagged endogenous variables, as arguments of f. In some cases it is possible to specify a recursive (or causal-chain) model rather than an interdependent model. In this case the problem caused by current values of endogenous variables appearing as arguments will not arise, providing certain conditions concerning the covariance of disturbances are satisfied. Serial correlation in economic variables and errors in variables are other sources of econometric problems.

Most macro-econometric models are highly overidentified. Hence it is not possible to proceed by estimating the parameters of the reduced form and then deriving the structural parameters. If the interest is in forecasting and control, why bother with the structural parameters? Why not use the reduced form which relates instruments directly to targets? There are two reasons for deriving estimates of the structural parameters. In the first place, adjustment for changes in structure need only be made to the relevant structural parameters and the solution of the system of equations then takes account of the effect of this change on all endogenous variables of the system. It would be impossible to know how to adjust directly all the parameters of the reduced form if the structural parameters were not known. Secondly, experiments have shown that better forecasts are obtained in the over-identified case if the structural parameters are estimated and then the system of equations solved than if forecasts are made using only estimates of the reduced-form parameters. Use of the reduced form in the over-identified case ignores, of course, valuable information on which variables are omitted from particular structural equations.

Econometric models are frequently nonlinear and are solved to obtain the values of the endogenous variables for given values of the exogenous variables using iterative methods on high speed automatic computers. Thus, in fact, reduced forms (or analytical solutions) are not available and the effect of changes in instruments on targets is investigated by comparing solution values of the target variables for different values of the instruments, holding all other exogenou variables constant.

3. An Overview of a Macroeconomic Model

An econometric model designed for forecasting and controlling GNP must be based on a macroeconomic model of the economy. The following simplified model indicates the nature of such a model. Since econometric model building and testing is still in a developmental stage, the variables entering into each equation and the form of the equation will vary depending on the hypothesis being tested by the investigator and the nature of the particular economy to which the model applies.

The model is not the static equilibrium model of introductory economic textbooks but a dynamic disequilibrium model. Variables dated at different points of time appear so that once the initial conditions and values of exogenous variables are given the model will generate values of endogenous variables for future periods of time. For expositional purposes, only one domestic price index is used. This is a gross oversimplification.

The construction of a macroeconomic model involves aggregation of both transactions and transactors. The model groups transactors into four groups: the personal sector which includes households and private noncommercial institutions, the business sector which includes business firms and government business enterprises, the government sector which includes all government departments and other public institutions, and the rest of the world. Markets are aggregated into an aggregate commodity (goods and services market), an aggregate money market, a labour market, and a foreign exchange market. A production function is added to summarize the technology of the system.

(A) *Definition of Variables*

A lower case letter indicates a quantity in constant dollars or in physical units (except for f which is used as the general symbol for a function). Upper case letters denote a quantity in current dollars, a price index, or a percentage. As a superscript F means foreign and S means quantity supplied. The subscript t indicates the time period to which the value refers. Flows are measured over the length of the period. Stocks are measured at the beginning of the period. Greek letters refer to rates which may vary over time.

A	Government surplus
B	Index of import prices
c	Personal expenditure on consumer goods and services
D	Personal disposable income
e	Employment in man-hours per period

e^S Labour force in man-hours per period

G, g Government expenditure on goods and services

H Foreign exchange reserves

i Business gross fixed capital formation

J Index of world prices of exports

k Stock of producers capital goods (including housing) at the beginning of the period.

L Net capital inflow

M Stock of money in the middle of the period

n Imports of goods and services

P Implicit price index of gross national product (GNP)

q Population

R Rate of interest

R^F Rate of interest in the rest of the world

t Time

U Unemployment rate

v Value of the physical change in inventories

W, w Wage rate

x Exports of goods and services

Y, y Gross national product (GNP) at market prices

y^F An index of GNP in the rest of the world

y^O Potential GNP

Z Utilization rate (a proxy for productive capacity)

δ Rate of capital consumption

τ Rate of taxation

Endogenous variables are shown on the left-hand side of the twenty-two equations which comprise the model.

Exogenous variables or parameters are: $B, J, q, R^F, y^F, t, \delta$. Instrument variables are: G, M, τ.

(B) Aggregate Demand for Commodities

  (1) Personal expenditure on consumer goods and services

$$c_t = f(D_t/P_t, R_t, c_{t-1})$$

  (2) Government expenditure on goods and services

$$g_t = G_t/P_t$$

(3) Business gross fixed capital formation

$$i_t = f(y_t, R_t, k_t, i_{t-1})$$

(4) Value of the physical change in inventories

$$v_t = f(y_t - y_{t-1})$$

(5) Exports of goods and services

$$x_t = f(y_t^F, P_t/J_t)$$

(6) Imports of goods and services

$$n_t = f(y_t, Z_t, P_t/B_t)$$

(7) Gross national product at market prices (constant dollars)

$$y_t = c_t + g_t + i_t + v_t + x_t - n_t$$

(8) Gross national product at market prices (current dollars)

$$Y_t = P_t \, y_t$$

(C) *Potential Output and the Utilization Rate*

(9) Stock of business fixed capital

$$k_{t+1} = i_t + (1 - \delta) k_t$$

(10) Potential gross national product

$$y_t^0 = f(k_t, e_t^S, t)$$

(11) Utilization rate

$$Z_t = (y_t/y_t^0)$$

Growth in the stock of capital is provided for by equation (9). A production function, equation (10), is used to determine potential output of the economy while actual output is determined by aggregate demand in this model. Actual output is not independent of potential output (i.e., of supply constraints), however, since the utilization rate, which is a proxy for productive capacity, enters into the import equation and could also enter the capital formation and export equations.

(D) *Price and Wage Determination*

(12) Price index of gross national product

$$P_t = f[(W_t \, e_t)/y_t, B_t, Z_t]$$

(13) Wage rate (nominal)

$$W_t = W_{t-1} + f(P_t - P_{t-1}, U_t)$$

(14) Wage rate (real)

$$w_t = W_t/P_t$$

The price level is a function of unit labour costs, foreign prices, and the utilization rate. It is not assumed that the prices and wage rates which are established clear the commodity and labour markets since only partial adjustment to equilibrium levels is assumed in the price and wage determination equations. Thus disequilibrium exists and unplanned changes in inventories occur and unemployment exists. The specification of the business fixed capital formation and consumer expenditure equations should imply incomplete adjustment of actual stocks of consumer and producers' durables to desired levels.

(E) *Labour Market and Income Determination*

(15) Supply of labour

$$e_t^S = f(q_t, w_t)$$

(16) Employment

$$e_t = f(y_t, k_t, t, w_t)$$

(17) Unemployment rate

$$U = [(e_t^S - e_t)/e_t^S]$$

(18) Personal disposable income

$$D_t = (1 - \tau)Y_t$$

The determination of personal income has been overly simplified for this demonstration model since retained earnings by corporations and capital consumption allowances have been ignored.

(F) *Money Market and Foreign Exchange Market*

(19) Rate of interest

$$R_t = f(P_t, y_t, M_t^S)$$

(20) Inflow of capital (net)

$$L_t = f(R_t/R_t^F, y_t/y_t^F)$$

(21) Foreign exchange reserves

$$H_t = H_{t-1} + P_t x_t - B_t n_t + L_t$$

The model assumes exchange rates are fixed.

(G) *Government Account*

(22) Government surplus

$$A_t = \tau Y_t - G_t$$

A simplification of the model is that the only government revenue is tax revenue from personal direct taxes.

Another of the oversimplifications of this model is the omission of any feedback effects from changes in foreign exchange reserves or the government account on the money supply and interest rates.

To each of the structural equations 1, 3, 4, 5, 6, 10, 12, 13, 15, 16, 19 and 20 is added a stochastic disturbance term.

The actual path of the system cannot be established until the parameters of the various behavioural equations are estimated by econometric methods. Since an analytical solution is not possible for most large non-linear models, simulations will have to be made using a computer to see whether the time path of GNP is cyclical.

4. Econometric Models of Canada

Four econometric models of Canada exist in a form which makes them currently usable for forecasting GNP: (a) Model RDX1, a quarterly model, constructed for the Bank of Canada by J.F. Helliwell, L.H. Officer, H.T. Shapiro, I.A. Stewart (b) an annual model by H. Tsurumi and M.F.J. Prachowny of Queen's University; (c) an annual model by N.K. Choudhry, Y. Kotowitz, J.A. Sawyer and J.W.L. Winder of the University of Toronto (known as the TRACE model); and (d) an annual model originally constructed in the Department of Trade and Commerce by T.M. Brown and S.J. May and now in the Department of Finance. (References to the publications on these models appear at the end of the paper).

The specification of these models varies somewhat and the model outlined in the previous section comes closer to a description of the University of Toronto TRACE model than to the other models.

5. Forecasting Using an Econometric Model

Errors in forecasting using an econometric model arise from various sources.

a) Errors in specification of the model, i.e., errors in the economic theory of the behaviour of the economy.

b) The disturbance term not taking on its expected value.

c) Sampling errors, i.e., the parameter estimates differ from their actual values because only a small number of observations are available to estimate the parameters.

d) Estimation errors, i.e.; the parameters are estimated by methods which do not have the statistical property of consistency. If the sample is small, bias may still exist even if consistent estimators are used.

e) Errors in data (including lack of conformity between the variable measured and the variable specified by economic theory).

f) Computational errors.

g) Errors in forecasting the values of the policy instrument variables.

h) Errors in forecasting the values of the other exogenous variables.

i) The cumulative effect of errors in forecasting lagged endogenous variables when the forecast is for more than one period into the future.

The presence of lagged effects has implications for the choice of time periods in models. The cumulative effect of errors in forecasting lagged endogenous variables means that, in their present state of development, most models seem to be able to forecast only 4 to 8 periods into the future before going seriously off the track. Hence if a medium-term forecast (2-5 years) is required, an annual, rather than a quarterly, model seems to be necessary. On the other hand, lags which are shorter than one year are lost in these models; thus, they are not as well suited for exploring the dynamics of short-run economic fluctuations.

The long-run effect of a change in an exogenous variable can be obtained from these models by summing the effects over a number of periods. This assumes, however, that there is enough of an effect in each time period that the relevant parameters are estimated to be non-zero. In principle, therefore, the same model can be used to examine short-run, medium-run, and long-run effects. In practice, however, the difficulty of estimating parameters whose values are small when the time period is as short as a quarter of a year, coupled with the cumulative effects of errors in forecasting lagged variables, makes it necessary to have different models for different periods of analysis. Moreover, the longer the run the greater is the possibility of substitution of capital for labour. Hence, the production function will be different. Fixed proportions may be appropriate for the very short run while a Cobb-Douglas function is appropriate for a longer run.

The task of forecasting GNP is complicated by the uncertainty as to what one is actually forecasting. National Accounts revisions and the long time lag before final figures are available means that one is trying to hit a moving target. Does the model try to forecast the preliminary or the final GNP figure? The parameters are estimated using (more or less) final figures for previous years but attention is usually focussed on forecasting preliminary values for the forthcoming year as these are the ones used for stabilization policy decisions and managerial decisions.

SOME BOOKS ON FORECASTING AND RELATED TOPICS

1. C. Almon, Jr., *The American Economy to 1975: An Interindustry Forecast* (New York: Harper & Row, 1967).

2. A. Battersby, *Sales Forecasting* (London: Cassel, 1968).

3. G.E.P. Box and G.M. Jenkins, *Time Series Analysis, Forecasting, and Control* (San Francisco, Holden-Day, 1969).

4. W.F. Butler and R.A. Kavesh, *How Business Economists Forecast* (Englewood Cliffs: Prentice-Hall, 1966).

5. C.F. Christ, *Econometric Models and Methods* (New York: Wiley, 1966).

6. G.A. Coutie, *et. al.,* *Short-term Forecasting* (Edinburgh: Oliver & Boyd for Imperial Chemical Industries, 1964).

7. M.K. Evans, *Macroeconomic Activity: Theory, Forecasting and Control* (New York: Harper & Row, 1969).

8. M.K. Evans and L.R. Klein, *The Wharton Econometric Forecasting Model* (Philadelphia: University of Pennsylvania, 1967).

9. K.A. Fox, *Intermediate Economic Statistics* (New York: Wiley, 1968).

10. R.A. Gordon and L.R. Klein (ed.), *Readings in Business Cycles* (Homewood: Irwin, 1967).

11. H.S. Houthakker and L.D. Taylor, *Consumer Demand in the United States, 1929-1970: Analyses and Projections* (Cambridge: Harvard University Press, 1966).

12. L.R. Klein, *Introduction to Econometrics* (Englewood Cliffs: Prentice-Hall 1962).

13. C.E.V. Leser, *Econometric Techniques and Problems* (London: Griffin, 1966).

14. *Mathematical Model Building in Economics and Industry* (London: Griffin, 1968).

15. *Models of Income Determination,* Proceedings of a conference on Research in Income and Wealth, National Bureau of Economic Research, Studies in Income and Wealth, Vol. 28 (Princeton: Princeton University Press, 1964).

16. H. Theil, *Applied Economic Forecasting* (Chicago: Rand McNally, 1966).

17. A.A. Walters, *Introduction to Econometrics* (London: Macmillan, 1968).

18. P. Whittle, *Prediction and Regulation by Linear Least Squares Methods* (London: English Universities Press, 1963).

19. H.O.A. Wold, *Econometric Model Building* (Amsterdam: North-Holland, 1967).

20. A. Zellner, *Readings in Economic Statistics and Econometrics* (Boston: Little, Brown, 1968).

REFERENCES ON CANADIAN FORECASTING MODELS

21. T.M. Brown, "A Forecast Determination of National Product, Employment and the Price Level in Canada from an Econometric Model," (in reference 15).

22. N.K. Choudhry, Y. Kotowitz, J.A. Sawyer, and J.W.L. Winder, "TRACE 1969: An Annual Econometric Model of the Canadian Economy." Working Paper 6908, Institute for the Quantitative Analysis of Social and Economic Policy, University of Toronto, October, 1969.

23. J.F. Helliwell, L.H. Officer, H.T. Shapiro, and I.A. Stewart, *The Structure of RDX1* (Ottawa: Bank of Canada, 1969).

24. S.J. May, "Dynamic Multipliers and Their Use in Fiscal Decision-Making" in *Conference on Stabilization Policies* (Ottawa: Queen's Printer for the Economic Council of Canada, 1966, pp. 155-187).

25. J.A. Sawyer, "Policy-Oriented Econometric Models of the Canadian Economy," *Canadian Operational Research Society Journal,* VII (Nov., 1969), pp. 177-192.

26. H. Tsurumi and M.J.F. Prachowny, "A Four-Sector Growth Model of the Canadian Economy." Paper presented to the Evanston meetings of the Econometric Society, December, 1968.

13. MODEL BUILDING IN A CANADIAN MANAGEMENT CONTEXT

P. C. BRIANT

I am directing my remarks primarily to the General Managers in the audience. More particularly, I should like to raise on their behalf the questions which, it appears to me, the users of models would like to ask the technical experts who build them. In this way, I hope to provide a link between Dr. Kendall's three lectures and the addresses we are to hear over the next two days.

I also hope to forge a link between the model builders and the model users. Providing such a link recognizes a problem which exists in Canadian organizations today. My own forays into industry and government have revealed to me that a wide gulf exists in Canada between the information technologists (who have great technical competence in their disciplines but do not necessarily have business or managerial experience and awareness) and the decision makers (who may have abundant experience but only a limited understanding of the work of the technicians).

Earlier this year, for example, I attended a company seminar at which operational researchers and division managers were present. It became clear during the discussions that the two groups were not communicating effectively. The division managers asked why they had not been told of the availability of certain models to help them in their work. Sad though it is to relate, the researchers answered, in effect, that they had not been asked.

In other cases, there still seem to be managers who take the view that since the first syllable of 'management' is 'man', most of the important managerial problems must involve human beings and cannot, therefore, be dealt with by the methods of quantitative analysis. One finds, in such instances, that the model builders are restricted to working out problems involving machines and flows of goods and materials only.

The program for this conference shows, however, the generality of the model building process and must, inevitably, give rise to questions in the minds of line managers.

In his opening lectures, Dr. Kendall addressed himself, *inter alia*, to two

241

questions:— What is model building? How is it done? I propose to proceed from
this point and raise four more questions, for the art of management has been said
to be the art of asking the right questions. The questions which seem to me to be
relevant at this stage in our deliberations are the following:—

1. Is the concept of a model something relatively new in the management of an
organized system or is it, rather, that the concept of models developed by Dr.
Kendall, and with which we shall be concerned during the rest of this conference,
differs in some substantive way from other aspects of the term?

2. How can models, in the sense in which we are using the term here, help a
general manager in improving the efficiency and effectiveness of his total
operation?

3. Where can a manager go wrong in using the output of a model builder?
Where must he be on guard, or, to put the question in another form, what are the
responsibilities, if any, of the manager in the model building process?

4. Are there any aspects of the Canadian managerial environment which serve
as constraints on the development and use of models?

Before suggesting some answers to these questions, I should mention, paren-
thetically, that my observations can only be suggestive. Other views will doubtless
be provided by the speakers to follow. My observations are based on my own
experience through working with managers and watching managers at work.

Different aspects of models

Turning now to the first question, are Canadian managers familiar with the
concept of models, the answer is probably 'yes' and 'no'.

The answer is 'yes' in the sense that Canadian managers, in keeping with
managers in any other country, have long used descriptive and analogue models
in their work:—

(i) It may be said, for example, that, as individual human beings, we live by
models, that we have to abstract from, or simplify, reality. Psychologists and
semanticists have shown us that human behaviour, in a short time-span, is a
product of the internal state of an individual in interaction with the environment.
Since the brain cannot process all that the eye can perceive, some selection is
inevitable. In effect, then, in living our normal lives, we create models of reality
which are derived from our previous learning, our values and our goals.

In human communication, it is said, difficulties arise in the encoding and
decoding processes because the parties communicating have conflicting models
in their respective minds. These differences lead to such practices as the use of
different words to mean the same thing and the use of the same word to impart
different meanings.

(ii)   To consider another illustration, any manager who has reviewed an organization chart, an architect's plans, a blueprint or a painting has been exposed to descriptive models which represent only some parts of reality.

(iii)   For a third case, consider the financial statements which are the major output of a financial accounting system. These are surely models, or abstractions from reality. They are based on definitions, assumptions and axioms and are mute and static evidence of the ability of human beings to reduce and classify data and to simplify a complex reality.

(iv)   As a final illustration, I invite you to consider the fundamental identity of the organization behaviourists. These people state that the effectiveness of a human group is a function of the internal social system in interaction with environment.

We can apply such a model, unsophisticated though it may be, to the effectiveness of ourselves as a group of conferees. Assuming that we had some precise, quantified measure of effectiveness, we could appraise our actual performance against the predetermined standard. If our performance were below standard, we could attempt to identify the critical variables in the internal social system and the environment (states of Nature and Competitive Strategies, or Human Interactions in this case) and distinguish between the controllable and non-controllable variables. This room, for example, is a given variable, in the short run; so, probably, is the furniture and the composition of the group. But we could vary the seating arrangements, the temperature in the room and the volume of the P.A. system.

Thus we could develop a model and test out alternative courses of action to assess the performance of the system under varying assumptions.

Models of a human group come closer to the concept that Dr. Kendall has reviewed with us. They express functional relationships between variables (they do not merely describe reality), they tell us something about how the system works and they are oriented towards decisions.

Yet, they are not quite the same.

What, then is different about the models with which we are now concerned? Why can we say that Canadian managers may be, and yet, may not be, experienced in the use of models?

The differences are not numerous but are of crucial importance:—

(i)   Our models are symbolic, that is to say, they express functional relationships between variables in symbolic terms.

(ii)   They are easily manipulable.

(iii)   They can be quantified.

(iv)   They allow us to assess alternative courses of action against a measure of effectiveness expressed in quantitative terms.

(v)   They are, or can be, built to be dynamic.

Managerial uses of models

The notion of manipulable, symbolic models leads naturally into the second question: How can iconic models help the manager to improve his operations? It is clear that we do not need to ask whether or not such models can help managers in their work. The positive evidence is clear. But we do need to review eight ways in which the model building process aids and influences managerial styles and attitudes:—

(i)   In the first place, it seems to be apparent that the process of building a model requires a manager to take a much harder look at reality than would otherwise be the case and to give most careful consideration to identifying the critical controllable and non-controllable variables in a situation.

I am reminded here of a company which, not too long ago, decided to develop more sophisticated financial models for making its multi-period resource allocation decisions. Some executives were sceptical of the value of the new approach. Their company had been profitable and had grown rapidly in a period of monetary ease and a fast rate of general economic growth. They thought that the existing information systems merely needed some minor modifications and amplifications. Once the process of model building started, however, they soon saw that many factors which were critical to successful performance under current conditions (such as overall market size and rate of growth of the market) were entirely ignored in their past decision processes.

(ii)   Implicit in the case just cited is a second benefit of model building; the process causes managers to look at their organizations as a system. A model built for one part of a system seems to give insights into, and certainly creates an awareness of, how the total system works and what the critical interactions are.

Companies with transfer pricing problems find, for example, that a model of one division casts new light on transfer prices and may lead to a combined model encompassing two or more divisions and the elimination of transfer pricing procedures.

In other cases, an inventory model can lead to a review of production scheduling, short-term financing, credit policy, customer selection and so on.

(iii)   Symbolic, manipulable models also allow us, as we already know, to test the consequences of alternative courses of action in terms of some performance criteria. In other words, we can test policy alternatives. This very process causes managers to think more precisely and more imaginatively about the alternatives open to them.

(iv) Models, as we also know, can be deterministic or probabilistic. When an allowance for risk is built explicitly into a model, the manager is provided with a means to evaluate the alternatives in terms of his own and his organization's risk preferences. It is a healthy thing for a manager to have to decide whether he is a risk taker or risk averter. He has to dig deeply into his own soul and into his own value set.

While it is always hoped that managers are conscious of the influence of values on decisions, it is doubtful that an explicit assessment is mandatory in the absence of probabilistic models. Too much of the decision is left, otherwise, to intuition, hunch, feel or other indefensible rationales.

(v) Many models represent a programmable decision process. Where this is so, the decision maker is relieved of routine concerns and is free to deal with the non-programmable, the unique, the ethical, the long-term commitment, the precedent decision. These latter decisions are a legitimate part of the manager's work and are a major justification for his salary differential over those below managerial rank.

This seems to me to be a most important benefit of models, yet it is an aspect that gives rise to concern among more than a few men. An executive who has risen through the ranks is usually familiar with operating problems and variables. He is at home in the operating milieu. Consequently, he is tempted to resist the programming of these phases of his work and often needs retraining to learn to think creatively and imaginatively in order to deal with the non-programmable and to think holistically.

The last three points are sufficiently self-evident that they may be stated without elaboration or illustration.

(vi) Symbolic decision models assist us in orienting ourselves attitudinally to the future and to forecast in quantitative terms.

(vii) They help us to be scientific in our approach and to eliminate bias in our analysis.

(viii) Managers have a number of rôles to play, including information processors and resource allocators. Models provide an orderly way for organizing data and generating information, and improve the quality of tactical and strategic resource allocation decisions.

Managerial responsibilities

The third question posed at the beginning of this paper had to do with the possibility of misusing models and the responsibilities of managers in the model building process. There are almost as many issues to be considered here as there were in answer to the second question.

(i)   Most important of all dangers, perhaps, is the possibility of a manager abdicating his responsibilities to the model builder. It seems to be terribly easy to adopt the view, which I have heard expressed by some of my colleagues in academic life, that the model builders, or the information technocrats to use the popular term, will make the decisions. Proponents of this view argue that the world is too complex for the non-expert to understand and that the experts will feed the decision maker the information he needs to have in order to make the 'right decisions'. They will, in other words, bound the scope within which the decision maker may exercise freedom of choice.

.   While there are undoubtedly instances of experts exercising power in this way, such a lamentable state of affairs should never be allowed to develop. Models provide a vehicle for integrating the results of research with the knowledge and judgement of the manager. Models created without a constructive interaction between researcher and user stand a greater chance than otherwise of being irrelevant to the decision to be made. As Dr. Kendall pointed out, the object of a model is to enable a decision to be made. Thus, the test of admission or omission is relevance to the decision, and the manager cannot deny his responsibility for the decision.

(ii)   In any event, strategic and tactical models cannot generate all the information that may be relevant to a decision. Models in most human organizations are appropriate only to a particular time and place. They take time to build the relative importance of environmental factors may change, the controllable variables may vary over time and may not be precisely measurable. Furthermore, relevant information may come from a number of sources not available to the model builder. Telephone calls, luncheon conversations, news reports and directors' meetings are all information sources which may bear importantly on tactical or strategic decisions.

(iii)   It follows from the foregoing that the process of decision making involve more than just a model. Apart from *ad hoc* information, there are such factors as the ability to perceive the need for a decision, the collection and organization of the data input, the specification of the format of the information output and the decision itself.

In all of these areas, the model user has responsibilities to discharge. Quit clearly, it is the manager's job to perceive when and where a decision is to be made and, conversely, when and where a decision is not required. It is also his duty to ensure that the data from which the model may be derived and the data fed into the model are reliable. Some may argue that this is a task for an expert; others assert that, at the very least, the manager must be held responsible for satisfying himself as to the competence of his staff.

There can be little argument that the decision maker or model user has a duty to be available to the model builders, to provide them with an opportunity to acquire a feel for the organization and assess the relative importance of variables, and the desirability of including variables which can be measured relative to preferred variables which cannot be measured.

The really critical phase of the decision process and, in my view, the one that poses the greatest challenge to the manager, is that of specifying the output format. It is not so much, perhaps, the format that creates difficulties, but the specification of the decision criteria and the decision rules. Unless the manager acquires competence in these areas, he finds that models do not lighten but, in fact, add to his burdens, for he is unable to delegate or specify his information needs and is, instead, flooded with paper or overwhelmed by the choices he is asked to make.

(iv)   Up to this point it has been assumed that relevant models are always built. This is not always the case. In addition to ensuring that models are built right, managers must, therefore, assure themselves that the right models are being built.

There is no point, for example, in constructing a sophisticated financial model for a new plant or a new acquisition if the expansion or acquisition is not in accord with the philosophy of a company or with its purposes and policies.

Similarly, an inventory model to determine economic order quantities is of limited utility if the company has not first resolved the prior marketing-financial question of what products to carry in inventory.

In the same vein, scheduling models for the maintenance of, let us say, rolling stock are of dubious value unless the organization has first determined the optimal economic life of the equipment and the optimal amount of maintenance to be performed.

(v)   The experts in our midst will, I suspect, concur with the next point. It is a human problem.

There are numerous instances of executives failing to communicate to the model builders when decisions contrary to those recommended are made. To a large extent, this difficulty arises when the executives are privy to information which influences the decision but which cannot be incorporated into the model.

A case in point concerns a detailed study and evaluation of the feasibility of continuing to operate a plant which had been constructed only five years before. A model was constructed, numerous alternative solutions were tested and all indicated the wisdom of closing the plant, selling the assets and investing the money elsewhere. The plant was, nevertheless, kept in operation because the Chairman of the company had originally approved the project and had no intention of conceding that an error had been made.

A similar instance involved a careful evaluation of possible plant location in a number of provinces. The ultimate choice was not even one of the alternative considered: the plant was built close to the President's summer home and provide him with a convenient 'pied-à-terre' during his vacation.

It is hard to believe that such transgressions can occur, but they do. They are, fortunately, rare, but where they occur they can be very discouraging to those with skills in model building and may inhibit them in their work.

(vi)   Models, even iconic models, are full of very human implications. For on thing, the building process is often performed by an interdisciplinary team including mathematicians, statisticians, econometricians and computer scientists. They are all skilled in quantifying variables. It seems, however, to be a wise polic to include a social psychologist in the group; particularly with planning and control models, it is essential to allow for the impact of control systems on individual controlled by the system. We know that individuals behave in such a way that they endeavour to satisfy the established performance standards. There is a subtle interaction here between the model and human beings, an interaction that psychologists, by education and predeliction, are equipped to help resolve.

The Canadian case

We turn now to consider certain aspects of the Canadian managerial environment which may constrain, or pose, particular problems to model builders and users.

(i)   Canada, in its primary and secondary industries, is largely a nation of branch plants and subsidiaries of foreign parents. The picture has been portrayed in detail in the report of the Gordon Task Force.

The preponderance of foreign ownership created and maintained an engineering or production orientation in Canadian operations long after the foreign owners, particularly American owners, had shifted to a finance and marketing orientation. There are signs, now, of a shift in emphasis to finance and marketing to, in other words, an output, instead of an input, orientation. Instances of strategic planning models are, however, relatively rare; for strategy is determined by the foreign owners.

It could be that the particular nature of the ownership of large sectors of Canadian industry has restricted the application of the model process to operational problems. There is no evidence to support or refute the hypothesis. Perhaps the operational emphasis is largely a reflection of the state of the art.

(ii)   In addition to being predominantly foreign-owned, Canadian industry mainly comprises relatively small enterprises. There are a few giants in the top five hundred companies, but there are many more with sales from $20 million to $150 million annually.

Companies in this range are intuitively conscious of the fact that the cost of a solution is a function of the size of the problem; the benefits a function of the size of the organization. Consequently, many of the problems of relatively small companies remain unsolved. They recognize that information has a price and that the benefits of improved information must exceed the costs of obtaining it.

(iii)   Model building in Canada has, therefore, been most actively pursued in the federal government and its branches, the universities, very large manufacturing companies and regulated industries. In the case of the latter, regulation tends to mitigate a great deal of the uncertainty that is normally associated with the environment. A natural monopoly does not need to allow for competitive strategies!

For manufacturing and resource industry companies, whose environment is usually fraught with uncertainty, it is fair to say that effort and expertise has been focused chiefly on the development of production models. Many companies in these sections have not yet accumulated experience in incorporating uncertainty into their models.

The Canadian economy shows some signs of becoming more price competitive; however, witness the legislation in banking and the pharmaceutical industry. If it is true that the quality of management is a function of the intensity of price competition, we may be on the verge of a more widespread application of financial and marketing models and intensified demands to recognize uncertainty explicitly.

(iv)   An increase in the application of comprehensive models for tactical and strategic planning and control will probably take some time. These models require the integration of parts of the systems into the greater whole. This process can be quite difficult for a subsidiary company, especially when, as is sometimes the fact, the managers of the subsidiary are not sure of the measures or standards used to assess the effectiveness of their operation. In addition, the executives of many of these subsidiaries have to overcome the production orientation which was once expected of them, before they can perceive the value of comprehensive models for planning and control.

(v)   Professor Sawyer will probably refer to the openness of the Canadian economy, its dependence on foreign trade. In 1968, for example, exports were $16·7 billion when Gross National Product at market prices totalled $67·4 billion. Exports were equal to 39% of consumer expenditures of $40·9 billion and amounted to almost 30% more than Gross Fixed Capital Formation.

The precise impact of foreign trade on the focus of attention of model builders in industry is hard to assess, but to the extent that the uncertainty in foreign markets is greater than the uncertainty in domestic markets, an emphasis on production models would be understandable.

This concludes the questions and related observations that I wish to put before you this afternoon. Many other questions come to mind:—

How is a model tested?

How do we know whether we have a good model?

What are the main problems encountered by model builders?

I am sure that the answers to these and other questions will emerge during the remainder of this conference.

14. ECONOMIC AND STATISTICAL MARKETING MODELS

R. J. BALL

The purpose of this paper is to attempt some survey of developments in the application of economic and statistical model building and analysis to marketing problems. The literature is now increasingly voluminous and any complete survey would require a paper of inordinate length. The strategy followed here, therefore, is to select certain broad and important areas of development and to illustrate the nature of the work that has been done and is in progress.

A convenient starting point is some rough taxonomy of marketing models for analysis. This might be achieved by adopting some classification of types by technique of analysis, e.g. programming, probability models, regression models, etc., but from the point of view of the economist and the market decision maker, a classification by problem types seems more appropriate. The nature of any division is somewhat rough, and is not always precisely adhered to below. It is certainly not intended that what follows is an optimal classification, but an attempt has been made to structure the discussion around market decisions and decision making.

Marketing Decisions and Decision Making

The decisions of marketing executives range over a wide variety of problems whose solutions depend on information and analysis determined from economics, from quantitative methods, from finance and accounting and from organisational behaviour. Finance and accounting contribute to the control of marketing operations by contributing to the measurement of performance and the development of financial criteria for decision making. Organisational and behavioural models contribute to problems of organisational design in marketing and to one's understanding of the behaviour and motives of buyers. In this paper we shall not deal in any detail with either financial or organisational models but will focus on those aspects of marketing decision making which draw most heavily on economic and quantitative analysis. Moreover, a wide class of marketing decisions depend on market forecasts *per se*, which opens up the general problem of forecasting and forecasting techniques. A full treatment of forecasting problems as such would also demand more space than is readily available and so will be treated only peripherally as relevant.

The central focus of this paper is on market behaviour and decisions designed
to affect market behaviour. From an economic point of view this implies starting
from the concept of the revenue function of the firm which relates the value of
the firm's sales to a wide class of economic and organisational arguments. Clearly
total sales and the sales of individual products are related not simply to what
might be defined as economic variables, but also to the organisational design of
marketing operations which encompasses the organisational structure and
motivation of the sales force and the control and design of distribution. However, as specified, these fall outside the present terms of reference and as such
will in the main be taken as given. Taking these factors as given, the sales of a
product may be broadly assumed to depend on economic factors that are both
internal and external to the firm. External factors are defined to be those factors
which roughly speaking affect the firm but are not affected by the firm itself.
These will include elements in the external economic environment such as the
level and distribution of overall economic activity and the market behaviour of
competitors. Internal factors are those over which the firm in principle has
control. These will include prices set for individual products, product quality,
the extent of capacity affecting delivery dates and the allocation and size of
promotional and advertising resources.

In the remainder of this paper we shall discuss a number of approaches to
model building designed to generate information for decision making in these
areas. In addition, some attention will be paid to the link between model
building and decision making as manifested in the development of Bayesian
analysis.

The Nature of Model Building

It is as well to begin with some general comment on the nature of model
building, particularly as there are some material divisions of opinion on the
subject. The main points at issue have been well put by Ehrenberg [6]. Ehrenberg
classifies model building into three types: (a) what he calls the scientification
of non-knowledge, (b) the statistical search for significance, and (c) empirical
generalisation, laws and models.

Some rough distinctions between these three approaches can perhaps be
illustrated by reference to the following simple problem. Suppose that we are
concerned to examine the way in which changes in the incomes of a body of
consumers affect their total spending on consumption goods. To begin with
let us specify some hypothesis about how consumers behave in relation to income
changes and let this be derived from some further initial hypothesis about how
consumers maximise their utility in fixing the proportion of their incomes that
they wish to spend as opposed to saving. Then in advance of any known information about how consumers behaved this would fall into class (a) of the
Ehrenberg classification, the scientification of non-knowledge or what has also
been termed speculative model building. The natural procedure for this type
of model builder would then be to obtain some data on spending and income
and then consider in what sense his hypothesis was consistent with that data.

Roughly speaking the model builder in class (b) would not bother with any particular initial speculations about the nature of behaviour, but would jump directly to the second stage, obtain some data and then attempt, using various methods of multivariate analysis, to determine what weight should be accorded to the various input factors in accounting for the observed behaviour of spending, in the course of which he might be able to say something about the effect of income. The third type of model builder, however, would do neither of these things. He would be looking for some empirical constancy in the behaviour of consumers in relation to income which would result not just from one sample of data but which would apply to all bodies of comparable data. Thus for example the model builder in class (a) might put forward the hypothesis that consumer spending is proportional to income, and using data on a sample of consumers estimate that on average consumers in the sample spent 90% of their income. The model builder in class (b) might also, partly accidentally, reach the same conclusion. But this in itself would be of no interest to the generaliser in the Ehrenberg sense of class (c). For what he is looking for is in the context of a particular problem, a result which holds generally over all such bodies of data. Thus the fact that in this sample of data the spending ratio was 90% is of no particular interest unless it is also true for all bodies of like data. In that event we have, it is said, established an important fact, and our ultimate theory must be built up as a set of generalisations based upon such facts. If it turns out that in all samples of like data the ratio is 90% which might be consistent with the underlying hypothesis advanced by the model builder of class (a) this fact, according to Ehrenberg, is of no significance. For he says, " . . . it does not seem to add either to the basic validity or to the practical usefulness of a descriptive model of fact".

Now the distinctions drawn by Ehrenberg between the different types of models are important and valuable — however the appraisal is extremely one-sided. In the first place the terminology is in itself emotive and question begging — thus the model builder in class (a) is said to be speculative and to have no facts, while the empirical generalist deals only in facts and facts are *ipso facto* good. However, it may equally well be argued that the empirical generalist is at one level far more speculative, for he is simply collecting a mass of factual information in the hope that some empirical regularities are about to show themselves. He also speculates. Moreover, it is not generally true that the speculative model builder, in the Ehrenberg sense, is as devoid of empirical observation as Ehrenberg implies. Typically economic model builders often do attempt to provide a rationalisation for some observed constancy. But this, by the Ehrenberg standard, is a waste of time. Why not simply accept the fact? The answer to this must vary from case to case. Sometimes it is not worth going any further. But in other cases we seek to explain an observed fact, in the Ehrenberg sense, in order to guide us further into the implications of that fact within a wider system of behaviour. For example, a famous economic fact that was once much quoted was that the share of wages in the national income was relatively constant, an observation that held across economies. A number of attempts have been made to produce models of the behaviour of economies which attempt to explain this fact. These models of the generation of this fact are important to us insofar as they generate other predictions which may confirm or refute our hypothesis and which suggest under what conditions the constant might no longer be a constant but a variable, or which might explain what differences exist in that constant between countries. The general point perhaps is that with laws in the social sciences there is always the danger that the observed constancies do not possess the characteristics of the constancies that we observe in the physical sciences. A number of mistakes have occurred in economic analysis over the years from accepting certain economic facts or constancies which have a habit of breaking down.

A further point is that in practice constancies and regularities in economic and market data will generally be multivariate in character. In this case the extraction of information from a body of factual data without any guidance from speculation is in itself inefficient. Moreover, in many of these multivariate exercises we are seeking to make policy to change particular situations and therefore require to make explicit how the decision variables are related to the outcomes. Thus, for example, we may wish to build a model to help us to decide on the price for a particular type of product. Now, in Ehrenberg's sense, the interesting facts that research can throw up are facts such as for a particular class of product brands, the percentage of total sales of a brand in a given period, which is accounted for by repeat buyers, is monotonically related to the average number of units bought per buyer. Now facts of this type may be extremely valuable together with other facts of this nature in predicting the performance of the brand once some information about its initial performance is known. But to suppose that we are completely in the hands of such facts is to suppose further that we have no hope of changing the pattern of that development, by alternative pricing and promotional policies, for example.

The general conclusion to be drawn is for a variety of different purposes alternative model building approaches and treatments of 'fact' are useful. The kind of debate discussed above is not in the present author's view a particularly fruitful one. Speculative model building in the Ehrenberg sense has had as respectable a history in the physical sciences as in the social sciences and this will continue. At the same time the search for and use of particular kinds of behavioural constancy in the Ehrenberg sense will also go on and prove useful. The danger is that whosoever tries to pin down scientific method in any simple way will tie himself in a methodological box from which he cannot escape.

Market Demand Analysis

A major interest of the economist in the marketing field is the analysis of market demand. Typically we start from some general specification of the demand function for say the quantity of the *i-th* commodity, Q_i,

$$(1) \quad Q_i = f(X_{1i} \ldots X_{ni}; Z_1 \ldots Z_k)$$

where the X_{ji} are a set of economic variables controlled by the firm and the

Z_s are a set of uncontrolled or external factors. The problem for the economist is to consider alternative specification of (1) and then estimate the parameters of the resulting alternative models. This is part of the problem of speculative model building. Typically, included among the set of controlled variables, or instruments for the *i-th* product will be the price of the product, the delivery date (if appropriate), some index of quality, and advertising and promotional variables. The external factors will typically include measures of purchasing power that are external to the firm, such as the level of consumers' incomes in total, or the total incomes of corporate customers. They may also include where appropriate external tax and credit variables. In general the uncontrolled variables will include such measurements on the position of competitors as can be given, including their prices and some measure of their non-price competitive activity via promotion and the like.

The extent to which it is possible to assign weights to the complex of factors generally specified as entering into equation (1) does not lend itself to generalisation. In part success depends on the particular data that is available in a specific market. The nature of the data may affect study in two kinds of ways. The trivial first is, of course, that it may simply be incomplete or not in itself measure what you want. The second, however, is that despite possessing the required raw data on the basic set of variables included in (1) such data may still not be used for obtaining the desired set of weights. This may arise because, for example, the range of experience exhibited by the data is itself limited or because the various statistical series are too collinear to provide reliable estimates of the contribution of each factor.

To illustrate the nature of economic demand analysis we may take an example from a recent paper by Cowling and Rayner [5] dealing with the market for tractors in the United Kingdom. The object of the exercise was to attempt to assess the effects of changes in the prices of tractors by different manufacturers on their overall market shares, and on the shares of particular brands.

It is, of course, a basic tenet of standard market demand theory that other things being equal the share of a particular manufacturer in a certain market will in part depend on its or his price relative to competitors. But typically economic theory has paid little attention to the problem of quality differences between products. To compare prices over a series of brands we need, however, in effect to standardise each price for quality. Following other writers Cowling and Rayner tend to identify qualities here with certain objective characteristics of the product. In the case of tractors, for example, such qualities are identified as, having or not having a diesel engine, and the overall belt horse power. Thus a particular set of what may be differentiated products may be in some sense compared together as alternative bundles of these characteristics or qualities. The question of whether a particular brand price, or the average price of a manufacturer is high or low may be turned into a question about the extent to which the valuations put on these qualities by the manufacturer deviate from the implicit valuations that are put on in the market as a whole. Note that this analysis is strictly relative.

Cheapness or dearness is not here being considered in any absolute sense, but in the sense of one brand or manufacturer relative to another.

To illustrate the point in general consider a set of brands that are particular manifestations of a set of qualities or characteristics that are susceptible of either continuous measurement or which may be defined on a zero-one basis, (e.g. brands may be with or without a particular feature). Let us define these qualities on the set $C_1 \ldots C_N$. The procedure suggested by Cowling and Rayner is to start by considering the price of the i-th brand as depending on the levels of the different qualities. Thus for the i-th brand we have

$$(2) \quad P_i = f(C_{1i} \ldots C_{Ni} : U_i)$$

where P_i = price of i-th brand and U_i = random disturbance. Now if we have information on all brand prices and the quality measurements over all brands we may estimate (2) by regression analysis and so obtain estimates of the average market weights applied to the particular qualities which are used to explain the variations in price between brands. The equation to be estimated may be put in the form,

$$(3) \quad P_i = \sum_j w_j C_{ij} + U_i$$

where U is a random error, and the w_j constitute a set of weights to be estimated. It follows from this that the observed error for the i-th brand measures in some degree the extent to which the price of the i-th brand deviates from the price that would be set on the basis of an average market weighting of the values of the set of qualities for that brand. Thus a brand with a positive error will be in a relative sense expensive, and that with a negative error relatively cheap.

In the case of tractors, the conclusion reached by Cowling and Rayner was that only two qualities are required to explain a major part of the variation in tractor prices, namely the presence or absence of a diesel engine, and the horsepower. Other qualities were also identified but were held for the most part to be correlated with these two, which might, therefore, be called principal qualities. As an example of an equation for the year 1953, we have,

$$(4) \quad P_i = 223 \cdot 5 + 8 \cdot 1020 \, hp_i + 85 \cdot 5 \, D_i + U_i \qquad\qquad R^2 = 0 \cdot 83$$

P_i = basic price of model i, hp = belt-horsepower, D_i = 1, for diesel engine, 0 others, U_i = residual for model i and where R^2 is the proportion of the variation in observed prices accounted for. Applying this kind of analysis led to a time series of errors or deviations from the average for both brands and for manufacturers. The sample data included some twenty or so brands over the period studied from 1948 to 1965, and covered the six major manufacturers in the field.

The next step in the analysis is to specify the particular factors determining brand shares and manufacturers' shares. It is convenient to take as dependent variables the relevant shares, since if the actual brand, for example, is taken as the dependent variable, one has to include as specific variables those factors which are determining the general level of the market. On the assumption that these external factors, such as changes in rate of use of tractors in general in agriculture, affect all brands and manufacturers more or less equally, by taking the market shares, brand performance is in some sense standardised and what are left are the competitive factors that are determining brand share and manufacturers' share. The Cowling — Rayner hypothesis is that the share of a particular brand is in part determined by the relative price of the brand, as measured by the deviation of the brand price from the quality adjusted price, the latter being obtained by weighting up the qualities for the specific brand using the weights from equation (4).

Of course this is not the end of the story. The share of a specific brand will not only depend on the price differential, but also on other factors. Other forms of non-price competition, such as the level of advertising, may also enter in. Moreover, the share of a specific brand at a point of time is likely to depend in part on how long that brand has been on the market. Other brands will enter in as competition and brands will in general have some typical form of life cycle. Furthermore, the factors that have been referred to may be best interpreted as determining in a sense the equilibrium share of the brand, for typically lagged behaviour will be the rule rather than the exception and the effects of price changes will be distributed over time. Thus Cowling and Rayner suggest a dynamic response function of the form,

$$(5) \quad S_i(t) = \lambda\,(S_i^*(t) - S_i(t-1))$$

where S_i^* is the equilibrium share of the brand as determined by factors, such as those referred to, and λ is a constant coefficient reflecting the speed of adjustment.

The results of their enquiry into brand and manufacturers' shares are summarised in the attached Tables I and II, for which a guide sheet is attached.

In Table I we see that the price variable U_{it} is statistically significant in all the least-squares regressions. From equation 7 we see that the price variable, the level of advertising and the lagged share account for 88% of the variation in the log of the manufacturers' share. In Table II the linear forms seem to do best, with over 90% of the variation in brand share accounted for in equation 6. The price variable is always significant. The other factor that always seems important is the length of time since the brand was introduced. This reflects the obsolescence of particular brands. Thus the Cowling–Rayner approach goes a long way toward explaining the behaviour of both manufactures' and brand shares.

A further immediate result of the Cowling—Rayner calculations is that we may directly estimate the own price elasticity of demand for each manufacturer, holding the prices of the others constant. These are given by principal manufacturers in Table III. The short run elasticities give a measure of the impact effect of price changes, and the long run elasticities the effect on market share after the dynamic process as specified in (5) has worked itself out. It may be noted that all demands are elastic.

Taking these calculations at their face value it is possible for particular manufac
turers to assess not only their general price competitiveness but also their competitiveness with respect to particular brands. It is often said that a particular
product put on the market was a good product, but the price was not 'right'.
The kind of exercise discussed here is part of an attempt to derive a more objective assessment of such statements.

The purpose of the illustration is not to offer any sort of general model for
examining such problems, but to illustrate the nature of speculative economic
building in the field. In some cases it may not be possible to define the qualities
of products in such a simple way, although this may be got round by using
factor analysis to define composite qualities which might be used. Moreover
in some cases this particular approach may be upset by the introduction of new
products. However, the extent to which this upsetting goes will in part depend on
the extent to which the introduction of a new product introduces new qualities
into the game, rather than being a different value collection of the same set of
qualities.

The study discussed is, however, typical in its form of the economic approach
to market analysis. The general problem derives, as indicated earlier, from the
specification and estimation of functions of the general form of (1). Typically
economists have confined themselves to analysis at the industry or total market
level, since this is where their specific interests have led them. The example
discussed concerns itself with brand shares and gives some indication of the
nature of extensions of this type of work to particular brands.

Markov Processes in Consumer Demand Models

All statistical models are by definition probabilistic, and this is true of the
regression models discussed in the last section. The essential characteristic of
such econometric models is that they are probabilistic and do not assume that
economic relationships are in any sense exact. In the analysis of consumer
behaviour, however, some use has been made more directly of certain results
from the theory of probability and stochastic processes. This appears to have
originated from the theory and application of Markov chains.

Those who have studied and drawn conclusions from consumer panel data
about the preference patterns of consumers, have sometimes been troubled
by the apparent inconsistency of individual consumers to particular questions
about such preferences. The conclusion has sometimes been drawn that the
consumer is essentially fickle and unreliable and little weight can be placed on
what he or she says. Observed deviations, however, from one time to another
are perfectly consistent with the view that the responses of the individual consumer to market situations can be looked at as the results of random drawings
from a probability distribution of such responses. That is to say, the behaviour
of the individual consumer, like that of the elements in statistical mechanics,
can be thought of as generated by such a probability distribution.

TABLE I MANUFACTURERS' SHARE RESULTS

Equation	Dependent variable	Constant	$\hat{U}_{it}$	$\dfrac{\hat{U}_{it}}{\bar{P}_t}$	$\Delta\hat{U}_{it}$	A_{it}	$\log S_{it-1}$	R^2	V/N ratio
1	S_{it}	25·0202	−0·1920 (−6·41)					0·334	1·98
2	S_{ivt}	25·1106	−0·1830 (−6·08)					0·311	1·96
3	$\log S_{it}$	1·2338	−0·0060 (−8·20)					0·450	2·02
4	$\log S_{it}$	0·4019	−0·0019 (−4·17)				0·6944 (15·64)	0·863	1·77
5	$\log S_{it}$	1·1783		−1·7927 (−3·27)			0·5975 (13·81)	0·842	1·39
6	$\log S_{it}$	0·3132	−0·0013 (−2·43)		−0·0015 (−2·37)		0·7566 (14·98)	0·872	1·72
7	$\log S_{it}$	0·9406	−0·0050 (−4·75)			0·0256 (4·00)	0·4873 (11·29)	0·882	1·71

N.B. Figures in parentheses are the t-values of the associated parameter estimates.

TABLE II MODEL MARKET SHARE RESULTS (ALL MANUFACTURERS)

Equation	Dependent variable	Constant	$\hat{U}_{it}$	t_i	N_i	$\dfrac{\hat{U}_{it}}{\bar{P}_t}$	T	TL	$S_{it\text{-}1}$	$\log S_{it\text{-}1}$	$\bar{R}^2$	VN ratio
1	S_{it}	4·794	−0·0168 (−2·7996)	−0·9905 (−4·9748)	−2·2660 (−2·2064)			0·1262 (2·0998)	0·8314 (22·1706)		0·735	2·35
2	S_{ivt}	4·087	−0·1603 (−2·7590)	−0·9821 (−4·4040)	0·0266 (0·0220)			0·1478 (2·5537)	0·8491 (22·9870)		0·751	2·19
3	S_{it}	2·2878	−0·0079 (−2·17)	−0·4668 (−4·01)	−1·1833 (−1·92)			0·0425 (1·18)	0·9087* (41·75)		0·904	2·70
4	S_{it}	2·2490		−0·4641 (−3·9785)	−1·2192 (−1·97)	−3·6273 (−1·91)		0·0371 (1·03)	0·9108* (41·79)		0·903	2·70
5	$\log S_{it}$	1·5670	−0·0084 (−7·40)	−0·2001 (5·31)	−0·2012 (1·02)			0·0121 (1·07)		0·3962* (11·91)	0·566	1·88
6	S_{it}	3·1442	−0·0098 (−2·54)	−0·4294 (−3·62)	−1·1251 (−1·82)		−0·0927 (−1·45)	0·0781 (1·80)	0·8990* (39·60)		0·904	2·71
7	$\log S_{it}$	2·2914	−0·0099 (−8·69)	−0·1675 (−4·56)	−0·1667 (−0·89)		−0·0860 (−4·64)	0·0455 (3·49)		0·3780* (11·79)	0·603	2·08

* Adjusted where appropriate for replaced model.

N.B. Figures in parentheses are the t-values of the associated parameter estimates.

Guide to Tables I and II

Table I

S_{it} = Manufacturers' total share in t

$\hat{U}_{it}$ = Deviation from quality adjusted price by manufacturer in t

$\bar{P}_t$ = Market average price in t

A_{it} = Advertising

R = Multiple correlation coefficient

VN = Measurement of first order serial correlation

Table II

S_{it} = Share of brand i in t

S_{ivt} = Share of brand i by value in t

$\hat{U}_{it}$ = Deviation from adjusted prices by brand in t

t_i = Time since the i-th brand was introduced

N_i = Dummy $(0, 1)$ variable to allow for exceptional promotion at time of model launch

TL = Interaction variable between time and large tractors.

TABLE III MARKET SHARE ELASTICITIES FOR MANUFACTURERS
(derived from equations 4, 5, and 7 in Table I)

Firm (average over the period 1947-1965)	Equation 4		Equation 5		Equation 7	
	Short run	Long run	Short run	Long run	Short run	Long run
Massey-Ferguson	−1·03	−3·35	−1·65	−4·14	−2·48	−4·52
Ford	−1·08	−3·51	−1·75	−4·38	−2·60	−4·73
David Brown	−1·15	−3·76	−1·88	−4·69	−2·79	−5·07
International Harvester	−1·20	−3·91	−1·95	−4·88	−2·90	−5·27
Nuffield	−1·23	−4·03	−2·01	−5·03	−2·99	−5·43
Average (All Manufacturers)	−1·10	−3·59	−1·79	−4·48	−2·66	−4·84
1965						
Massey-Ferguson	−1·62	−5·29	−2·00	−5·01	−3·92	−7·12
Ford	−1·93	−6·30	−2·39	−5·97	−4·67	−8·48
David Brown	−1·48	−4·82	−1·83	−4·57	−3·57	−6·49
International Havester	−1·41	−4·60	−1·74	−4·36	−3·41	−6·1
Nuffield	−1·57	−5·13	−1·95	−4·48	−3·80	−6·91
Average (All Manufacturers)	−1·45	−4·73	−2·36	−5·90	−3·50	−6·37

The initial development of this idea seems to have come in the field of brand switching. The conceptual framework here starts from the basic proposition that given at a point of time a set of consumers and a set of brands of a good, there exists for each consumer a set of probabilities relating to his purchase behaviour in any particular period. That is to say if, for example, the time period is a month and there are three brands, A, B and C, we can assign to each individual a probability that he will purchase one of these brands. There are clearly a number of complicating factors surrounding the application and development of this basic theme, some of which have not yet been adequately treated in practice. There is no difficulty formally in allowing for the fact that some people buying the product may in fact buy none of the brands in a given period. This can be taken into account by including a dummy brand defined as the null brand. However, considerable difficulties stem from the fact that purchases in a given period may not be exclusive; that is to say more than one brand may be purchased by a given individual during a particular purchase period. Further the simple period analysis model is disturbed by cases in which the purchase time itself is irregular. For a variety of reasons decisions to buy or not to buy may not be made in each purchase period as arbitrarily defined, but the approach implicitly assumes that such decisions are made in each period. Finally, and perhaps most crucially, we are faced with the problem that variations in the transitional probabilities of the Markov schemes have to be taken into account. The remainder of this discussion will focus on this point.

The simple Markov model may be set out as follows. Let us suppose for the sake of argument that there are only two goods with a constant population of buyers, that there is no entry or exit. It is assumed also that all individuals behave in the same way, such that under a specified set of common conditions the probability of purchase of a given brand for all individuals in a given period is the same. In the simple Markov case the probabilities of purchase are represented as transition probabilities that are conditional only on the brand purchased in the previous period. Thus the difference between the probabilities of two individuals purchasing brand A in the next period will be determined solely by what brand each bought in the last period. Thus for all individuals who bought brand B in the last period the probability of buying A in this are the same. The simplest model further assumes that the brands can be expressed in comparable units and that each purchaser buys only one unit in the period. Thus the market share of a particular brand in this special case is given by the proportion of all buyers actually buying the given brand.

Formally we may represent this type of model by the set of equations

$$(6) \quad A(t) = P_{AA} A(t-1) + P_{AB} B(t-1)$$

$$B(t) = P_{BA} A(t-1) + P_{BB} B(t-1)$$

where A and B denote the volumes of sales (= no. of purchases) of each brand and the P's are the transitional probabilities. Thus P_{AA} denotes the probability that an individual purchasing brand A in period $(t-1)$ will purchase it in period

t. It follows by the closure of the system that $P_{AA} + P_{BA} = P_{AB} + P_{BB} = 1$.

Thus treating the probabilities as constants a Markov scheme of this kind can be depicted as a set of linear difference equations. Special interest focuses on particular solutions of the set, namely the equilibrium levels to which the system will converge, convergence guaranteed by the values of the parameters involved. In stationary equilibrium we have $A(t) = A(t-1)$ etc. so that the equilibrium values A^*, B^* will satisfy

$$(7) \quad \frac{A^*}{B^*} = \frac{P_{AB}}{1 - P_{AA}}$$

Defining the total market (constant) by $M = A + B$, the equilibrium share of A, S_A^*, will be

$$(8) \quad S_A^* = \frac{P_{AB}}{(1 - P_{AA}) + P_{AB}}$$

Thus suppose we have

$$P_{AA} = 0 \cdot 55 \qquad\qquad P_{BA} = 0 \cdot 45$$

$$P_{BB} = 0 \cdot 80 \qquad\qquad P_{AB} = 0 \cdot 20$$

then the equilibrium share for A will be about 30%. The equilibrium level of A cannot, of course, be determined solely from equations (6) which are homogenec However, a solution clearly exists once the total market is specified. This can be done directly from (8), but in view of the previous comment, it is worth noting the alternative route. Since M is assumed to be independent of t then $M = B(t-1) + A(t-1)$, and so

$$(9) \quad A(t) = (P_{AA} - P_{AB}) A(t-1) + P_{AB} M$$

obviously provided that $|P_{AA} - P_{AB}| < 1$ A will converge to a stationary solution

$$(10) \quad A^* = \frac{P_{AB}}{1 - P_{AA} + P_{AB}} \cdot M \qquad\qquad \centerdot$$

which is the same as (8).

All this, of course, holds on the assumption that the probabilities are constant. This model has not only been objected to on the ground that this is unrealistic, but also that it is not reversible, in the sense that backward extrapolation leads to an increasing variance in brand share. More realistically indeed it is obviously limited to treat the transitional probabilities as constant.

This is probably true even in the case of pure forecasting, but is by definition so in cases where the main problem is to examine the effects of price and promotional changes on brand shares in a given market. Here the transitional probabilities are taken to be variable and the problem is to identify and quantify the sources of variation.

There seem to be at least two non-mutually exclusive directions that development can now take. The first is to consider some adaptive scheme for revising the transitional probabilities which still depends only on the observed behaviour of brand shares and consumer purchases. Thus one suggestion (see Kuehn and Day [9]) is the introduction of a decision rule that revises up the probability of an individual purchasing brand A if it is purchased in a given period, and writes down the probability of purchasing it if A is not purchased in the given period. A formal expression of the suggested procedure is given by taking the probabilities in the system as states of the system, rather than the brand last purchased, and writing the two equations

$$(11) \quad P_{i,t\text{-}1} = P_{i,t\text{-}1} + g\,(U_i - P_{i,t\text{-}1})$$

$$(12) \quad P_{i,t} = P_{i,t\text{-}1} - h\,(P_{i,t\text{-}1} - L_i)$$

where g and h are parameters, U_i is the upper limit to the purchase probability for the brand, and L_i is the lower limit. Equation (11) will modify the probability of purchasing the brand for those who actually purchased the brand in the previous period, while (12) will modify the probability of purchase for those who bought another brand. For a given brand A, the procedure may be illustrated graphically as in Figure I. U_A and L_A are the upper and lower purchase limits respectively.

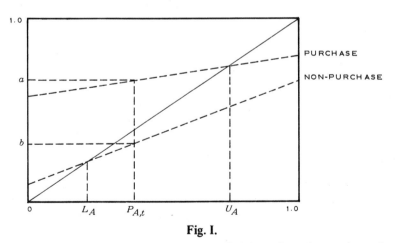

Fig. I.

Thus for a given consumer with a current probability of purchasing A equal to $P_{A,t}$ his probability of purchase in the next period will be either a or b depending whether he actually purchases A in period t or not. In the first case his probability will be raised and in the second lowered. Equations (11) and (12) can be finally combined to yield an expected purchase probability by weighting the first by $P_{i,t\text{-}1}$ and second by $(1 - P_{i,t\text{-}1})$. If g and h are constant for all brands, then in a closed market system with no entry or exit of brands we find that g and h will be equal and the final equation reduces to

$$(13) \quad P_{i,t} = P_{i,t-1} \; 1 - g(1 - U_i + L_i) + gL_i$$

This model has been used by Kuehn [10] as part of a more elaborate model used to distribute advertising expenditure by brands. This type of approach has been used to examine the effects of special promotions after first estimating the parameters of behaviour from recent panel data. The effects of 'deals' and promotions were then estimated by comparing the observed purchase frequencies with those predicted by the model.

It should be emphasized that this type of work is still at the experimental stage. There appears to be considerable scope for considering other adaptive forms along the same lines. The approach is suggestive although its value is still not proven, and there are those who remain strictly sceptical about the general method.

A second direction of approach starts from an initial formulation of the brand switching model in terms of a Markov process of the kind described earlier, but again, dropping the assumption of constancy in the transitional probabilities. However, instead of imposing some adaptive scheme to revise the probabilities, the probabilities are treated as variables which, as in the first section of this paper, are related to specific economic factors such as own price, competing prices and promotional and advertising elements. Following these lines an elaborate study was carried out by Telser [12] with the principal aim of estimating the effects of price changes on brand market shares, for four products in the United States, frozen orange juice, instant coffee, regular coffee, and margarine. In the event, an elaborate theoretical development is boiled down by Telser into a relatively simple regression equation relating brand share to the previous level of brand share and the difference between brand price and the market average. As would be clear from the previous section of this paper, the assumption of a Markov chain process with variable parameters is not the only way to derive this form of equation. However, the interpretation of the model coefficients will obviously not be the same. Using consumer panel data Telser estimated functions of this general type for these branded commodities. A sample of results for frozen orange juice concentrate and coffee are given as Table IV.

As may be seen the price variables are nearly all statistically significant. The interpretation of the model coefficients in a Markov sense also enables estimates to be made of the repeat market characteristics of the different commodities. It turned out that at mean prices the average probability of a repeat purchase was about 0•53 for orange juice, 0•43 for regular coffee, 0•65 for instant coffee and about 0•48 for margarine. In general over the brands concerned Telser obtained estimates of price elasticity well over unity. On a one month basis he estimated average elasticities for orange juice of 2•7, regular coffee 2•6 and 1•8 for instant coffee. These results certainly encourage the further application of this type of model where the appropriate panel data are available.

TABLE IV

—FROZEN ORANGE JUICE CONCENTRATE REGRESSIONS, APRIL 1954–MARCH 1957

Brand	Constant	Coefficients of $m_{i,t-1}$	Coefficients of $p_{it} = P_{it} - \bar{P}_{it}$	R [a]	p_s [b]	N [c]
A	•10754	•5247 (•1126) [d]	— •01755 (•004026)	•8107	•278	556
B	•03253	•7932 (•09568)	— •008946 (•003886)	•8627	•063	173
C	•04659	•4662 (•1254)	— •01009 (•002907)	•8540	•331	228
D	•02285	•4252 (•1472)	— •008890 (•003248)	•7585	— •041	166
E	•02785	•5337 (•1234)	— •01757 (•004664)	•7449	•175	146
F	•01353	•2343 (•1198)	— •008510 (•001482)	•8915	— •087	220

a Multiple correlation.

b Auto-correlation coefficient of residual.

c Raw counts of the number of distinct families who bought the indicated brand for the 13 week period, December, 1959 – February, 1960. This quarter is three years after the end of the sample period but should still give a fair approximation to the numbers in the relevant period. Since there does not appear to be much of a seasonal variation, the figures approximately apply for an entire year. To find the number of different families who purchase the product during a month, the quarterly figure should be multiplied about •67. Note that the lowest multiple R is E which has the smallest N. It is not true, however, that the largest R has the highest N.

d The numbers in parentheses are the standard errors of the regression coefficients.

—INSTANT COFFEE REGRESSIONS, APRIL 1954 – MARCH 1957

Brand	Constant	Coefficients of $m_{i,t-1}$	Coefficients of p_{it}	R	p_s	N [a]
A	•1806	•5642 (•100)	— •004809 (•00151)	•7955	•017	602
B	•0821	•7651 (•0928)	— •005812 (•00180)	•8733	•058	148
C	•0228	•3663 (•150)	— •001339 (•000554)	•5664	— •144	60
D	•0388	•7852 (•0916)	— •001690 (•000733)	•9228	— •212	128

a Estimated average number of panel families who bought the indicated brand per month of 1955. Note that the smallest R has the smallest N.

–REGULAR COFFEE REGRESSIONS, APRIL 1954 – MARCH 1957

Brand	Constant	Coefficients of		R	p_s	N^a
		$m_{i,t-1}$	p_{it}			
A	•1111	•2833 (•129)	− •004758 (•00106)	•6965	•345	583
B	•0349	•3204 (•101)	− •001976 (•000314)	•8956	•087	237
C	•0234	•8116 (•0981)	− •000542 (•000987)	•8256	− •040	520
D	•0709	•1674 (•143)	− •003135 (•000612)	•8057	•141	272
E	•0768	•4158 (•105)	− •001833 (•000371)	•9242	•022	358

a   Estimated average number of panel families who bought the indicated brand per month during 1955. This product class is the only exception to the rule that the smallest *R* has the smallest *N*.

Note. $m_{i,t-1}$ = market share of brand *i* in period $(t-1)$

p_{it} = deviation of the *i-th* brand price from the market average.

Further Probability Models of Buying Behaviour

As opposed to the econometric and Markov process-type models of buying behaviour, important developments in the stationary behaviour of non-durable brand purchases have been made by Ehrenberg (see [6] as an example).

The Ehrenberg approach has been to exercise the nature of regularities occurring in brand purchase behaviour and then to set up probability models that generalise to different sets of purchasing behaviour. Examples of such regularities presented in [6] are:

(a)   That the percentage of total sales of a brand in a given period which is accounted for by so-called repeat buyers is monotonically related to the average number of units *w* bought per buyer.

(b)   That this percentage of sales accounted for by repeat buyers is approximately the same as the percentage of sales accounted for by the buyers of more than one unit in the time period.

(c)   That the average number of units bought per new buyer is roughly constant at about 1•4.

Ehrenberg has shown that these findings hold for a wide variety of non-durable product fields. Formally, for example, the proportion of repeat-buyers from one period to the next may be approximated by

$$2(1 - w)/(1 - 2 \cdot 3w)$$

where w is the average number of units bought per buyer. In addition the average number of units bought per repeat buyer in each period is approximately

$$1 \cdot 23 \, w \qquad \text{for } w > 1 \cdot 5$$

so that under stationary conditions the repeat buyers' average purchase rate is about 20% above the average. A further conclusion is that the average purchase rate for a new buyer is about $1 \cdot 4$ and constant.

These results derive from the Logarithmic Series Distribution, or *LSD*, applied to stationary purchasing behaviour. Ehrenberg has also demonstrated the use of the Negative Binomial Distribution, or *NBD*, whose probability generating function takes the form

$$\left\{ 1 + a \sum_{i=1}^{t} T_i(1 - U_i) \right\}^{-k}$$

where $a = m/k$, the U_i are dummy variables and m is the average amount bought in some time period of 'unit' length. The *NBD* gives the distribution of people buying r_i units in the *i-th* period out of t periods of length T_i. More generally, as shown in (12), the *NBD/LSD* models of stationary purchasing behaviour can be derived from a compound Poisson formulation.

It must be emphasized that these are models of stationary behaviour. As such, of course, they provide important initial information in assessing the impact of policy changes on what has previously become a stationary situation. These analyses suggest a considerable regularity in purchasing behaviour in stationary markets. However, this is clearly a beginning of the story. There remains an extension to the problems of dynamic adjustment, particularly of new products.

Models of Advertising Performance

Approaches to market and brand analysis of the types discussed in the two previous sections have, of course, been extended to models which include some measure of advertising as an independent variable. Such extensions attempt to bring the level of advertising into some direct relationship with brand or market sales.

There is, of course, a vast and growing literature which might be put under the heading of advertising research. A great deal of it falls into the field of the behavioural sciences and as such is excluded by the terms of reference of this paper. It may, however, be observed here, that the bulk of this research has been micro, in the sense that it has concentrated on the behavioural responses of individuals to advertising, the ways in which advertising may be said to 'work' and the impact of particular advertisements. This would, of course, seem eminently sensible insofar as this kind of information is key in the creative process. At the creative stage one is concerned with criteria for assessing a particular advertisement, or in choosing between alternative advertisements. Generalising a little, one might say that the effectiveness of advertising on sales has both a quality and a scale dimension. Advertising research seems to have concentrated heavily on the quality aspects of the problem, attempting to derive criteria which allow quality to be assessed. However, little or no effort has been made generally to relate any such quality assessments to sales. Good or bad advertising is thought of in terms of what might be called intermediary rather than direct criteria which would be sales related. Whatever the reason for this, it is clear that no complete assessment in terms of sales is possible without taking the scale effect into account. Curiously enough, advertising researchers and marketing economists have on the whole tended to look at different aspects of the total problem. Advertising agencies, for example, research their own advertising in a sense attempting to measure quality while keeping the scale or quantity constant while marketing economists have tended to concentrate on building models about the scale effect of advertising while assuming something like average quality. The first is, of course, germane to the problem of advertising creation and the second to the question of advertising budgeting. No doubt in principle one might be prepared to argue that these things are inter-related — although what the nature of that relationship is has probably been inadequately explored. Indeed, the trade off between quality and quantity might well be perverse — if a particular advertisement is a 'bad' advertisement, this cannot be compensated for by showing it twice as much as in the normal case! Indeed quite the reverse. Thus the 'economist' type models have tended to exclude by assumption problem of quality variation and focus on the relationship between sales and advertising level and volume. The remainder of the discussion here will follow that line.

Knowledge of the relationship between advertising levels and sales performance has obvious implications both socially and individually. Economists have written a good deal about the 'effects' of advertising, out of all proportion to the attempt to measure such effects, where effects here are thought of as sales related directly. In certain cases one may be able to assess the effect of changes in advertising policy either in terms of approach or level, by considering the deviation of actual from what would have been thought of as expected performance from some model of behaviour derived from data before the change. This is a kind of an assessment by exception policy which may in certain short period cases be very valuable. The difficulty is that in the long period many things change together which both necessitates and makes difficult the application of various forms of multivariate analysis. Markov models of the type discussed in a earlier section have been used from time to time in making such short period assessments. A more sophisticated and general treatment of such models for brand advertising has been suggested by Kuehn [10].

Models have also been used which relate to the kind discussed in the first section of this paper. In building such models economists and operational research workers have tended in recent years to separate out a number of basic ideas with regard to the relationship between advertising level on sales, on the assumption of given quality. The first of these is the important idea that advertising expenditures must be looked at in a stock rather than a flow context. Advertising expenditures are not operating expenditures and by analogy come closest to investment in capital stock — the capital stock here being conceived of as a stock of goodwill that has been created. This is, of course, consistent with the view that advertising takes time to work, and its effect will be in general distributed over time. Thus the goodwill created by advertising needs to be sustained since it will depreciate if not serviced just like physical capital equipment. The formal implication of this for economic model building in the advertising field is that the current rate of advertising expenditure is related to the change in some form rather than the level of sales. It is the net stock of goodwill that is in fact related to sales level. These ideas have been explored by many — useful references are Vidale and Wolfe [13] and Arrow and Nerlove [2]. A second principal idea is that diminishing returns will set in governed by some sales level beyond which the marginal value of advertising will be zero.

These points may be illustrated by the use of the Vidale and Wolfe type model. In discrete terms the model may be expressed in the form

$$(14) \quad S(t) - S(t-1) = \alpha A(t)\left[\frac{M - S(t-1)}{M}\right] - \lambda S(t-1)$$

where α and λ are parameters, S = value of sales, A = advertising expenditures, M = market saturation level. In the case of $A(t) = 0$, the S will decline the proportion rate λ, which may be described as the decay constant. The term in the square bracket reflects the effect of the distance from the saturation level on the response to another pound of advertising. If we can ignore that term we may note the close affinity to a capital stock model of advertising effect. Let total sales be related to the stock of goodwill K, by

$$(15) \quad S(t) = \alpha + \beta K(t)$$

and

$$(16) \quad K(t) = K(t-1) + A(t) - \lambda K(t-1)$$

where λ is now interpreted as the depreciation rate on the stock of goodwill. It is easily seen that ignoring the saturation effect this is equivalent to the basic model.

Re-arranging (14) we have

$$(17) \quad S(t) = \alpha A(t) + \left[1 - \lambda - \frac{\alpha A(t)}{M}\right]S(t-1)$$

In the fixed rate of advertising case with A independent of t, (17) is simply a first order difference equation in S, with an equilibrium solution

$$(18) \quad S^* = \alpha A / \lambda + \frac{\alpha A}{M}$$

If it is possible to estimate the parameters of (18), we can then, of course, proce
to the next stage of selecting the optimal level of advertising expenditure to yield
given equilibrium level of sales. From (18) we also see that the elasticity of the
equilibrium sales level with respect to advertising, E_A, is given by

$$(19)\ E_A = \frac{dS^*}{dA}\frac{A}{S^*} = \frac{\alpha\,\lambda}{\dfrac{\alpha A}{(\lambda + M)^2}}$$

which implies that the elasticity will decline with the level of advertising which
seems highly plausible.

Results of the application of this kind of model have been reported in general
terms by Vidale and Wolfe [13], who recorded having applied it in analysing
performance for a large number of brands. A general adjustment model of this
type was recently applied by Ball and Agarwala [1] to the effect of generic
advertising on tea, using the stock concept of advertising as set out in (16). A
typical result explained that consumption *per capita* (four quarter moving average
from the Family Expenditure Survey, by the statistical equation

$$(20)\quad C(t) =\ \ 2{\cdot}62\ +\ 0{\cdot}057U(t) +\ 0{\cdot}014t\ -\ 0{\cdot}00054t^2\ +\ 0{\cdot}031K(t)$$
$$(0{\cdot}05)\ \ (0{\cdot}017)\qquad (0{\cdot}003)\quad\ (0{\cdot}00009)\qquad (0{\cdot}007)$$
$$R^2\ =\ 0{\cdot}87$$

where C = *per capita* tea consumption, oz per person per week, t = time trend,
K = stock of advertising with a depreciation rate of 10% per quarter, U = percentage unemployment rate. This equation was then used to consider the
implications of alternative advertising expenditure strategies.

Both Markov process-type and multivariate models of this kind are likely to
undergo further development and testing in this field. There is enormous scope
for consideration of the problems of attempting to derive more direct sales
linked type models in order to assess market and advertising performance.

Market Decision Making and Bayesian Analysis

The model making discussed in the previous sections has provided examples of
developments which are aimed at providing formal frameworks in which to
experiment with and assess the effects of pricing and promotional policies. The
modelling itself is only part, of course, of a total process, the parts of which are
in broad measure interdependent. For present purposes we may roughly divide
that process up into firstly the collection and organisation of raw data, secondly
the model building activity which seeks to establish the relationships between
the data, and finally the process of decision making itself.

In forecasting, pricing and setting promotional and advertising expenditures,
the marketing executive is typically taking decisions under uncertainty. As
pointed out earlier, equally typically the models constructed to account for

the relationships between the raw data are probability models of some form or other whose great advantage is that they provide a framework within which to assess the risks involved in any particular decision.

The recognition of decision making as a probabilistic activity has encouraged the development of Bayesian analysis in considering alternatives. More generally this has been part of the development of the subject of decision theory which considers the relationship between information inputs in probability terms and the making of decisions or the selection of strategies. The Bayesian approach has the advantage that in this process it provides a formal way of integrating the judgment and prior knowledge of executives with the results of research. It provides a formal approach to revising subjective probabilities about particular outcomes as new information becomes available. The subject will only be briefly developed here. For a more detailed account one may consult the standard works by Schlaifer [11], Chernoff and Moses [4] and the papers by Green [7], [8].

The Bayesian approach to decision making is based on Bayes' theorem. Firstly this simply states that

$$(21) \quad p(\theta|X) = \frac{p(X|\theta)\, p(\theta)}{p(X)}$$

where the p's are probabilities. Suppose that θ is a parameter that defines the responsiveness of a product to a price cut. The classical procedure is then to conduct some experiment with data, which, let us say, produces a specific outcome, X. Using the outcome an estimate of θ is then made, probably following a criterion such as the principle of maximum likelihood. Thus the estimate is arrived at by asking the question, what estimate maximises the likelihood of observing the particular experimental result obtained? Thus it may be seen from (21) that $p(\theta|X)$ is equal to the likelihood function $p(X|\theta)$ multiplied by $p(\theta)/p(X)$. The Bayesian approach modifies the likelihood function, weighting it by the prior probability of θ which may be purely subjective. Thus the Bayesian analysis starts with some view about the probability distribution of θ, and then asks how experiment may be used to alter and improve that assumption.

As a naive example consider the following. A marketing executive is deciding whether to cut the price of his product. Suppose that there are (unrealistically) two states of nature, θ_1 and θ_2; θ_1 says that the price elasticity of demand is $2 \cdot 0$ and θ_2 that it is a half, so that if θ_1 is the true state of nature, it pays to cut prices and if it is θ_2, it pays to leave them. Suppose further that the executive, on the basis of his experience, feels that he cannot choose between them − they are both equally likely. Thus the prior distribution of θ for his subjective estimate is $p(\theta_1) = 0 \cdot 5 = p(\theta_2)$.

Now suppose that an experiment is conducted among a representative set of consumers that simulates buying behaviour. The result is that the simulated volume of sales incomes increases let us say by 8% after a 5% price reduction.

We now need to modify the original subjective estimates $p(\theta_1)$ and $p(\theta_2)$ in the light of this information. To do this we must specify the likelihood function $p(X|\theta)$. In the absence of other information, in practice this is often assumed to be normal. In the present case we simplify by hypothesising that if θ_1 is the state of nature, 80% of the consumers will give a sales response at least as large as this, unlike if θ_2 is the case, only 20%. The experiment is treated as two-valued, either above or below 8%. Thus in the θ_1 case we want to know what is the probability of θ_1 being the state of nature given this experimental outcome X. Thus we have, writing (21) a little differently

$$(22) \quad p(\theta_1 \mid \geq 8\%) = \frac{p(\geq 8\% \mid \theta_1)\, p(\theta_1)}{p(\geq 18\% \mid \theta_1)\, {}^*p(\theta_1) + p(\geq 8\% \mid \theta_2)\, p(\theta_2)}$$

$$= \frac{0 \cdot 8 \times 0 \cdot 5}{(0 \cdot 8 \quad 0 \cdot 5) + (0 \cdot 2 \times 0 \cdot 5)} = \frac{4}{5} = 80\%$$

and

$$(23) \quad p(\theta_2 \mid \geq 8\%) = \frac{p(\geq 8\% \mid \theta_2)\, p(\theta_2)}{5} = \frac{1}{5} = 20\%$$

Thus the experimental evidence has caused us to revise our initial probabilities in favour of θ_1 and against θ_2.

This is simply the bare mechanism of calculation. In practice information costs money and the executive must in the beginning decide whether to undertake the trial or not.

If no trial is taken with consumers, and the executive uses a criterion of expected monetary value, then prices will be cut or not depending on whether the expected value is positive or negative. Let the pay off for a price cut if $\theta = \theta_1$ be £200,000 and for $\theta = \theta_2$, – £200,000. The price would not be cut since the expected value is

$$(24) \quad E = 0 \cdot 5(\pounds200{,}000 - \pounds220{,}000) = -\pounds10{,}000$$

But suppose he experiments. We will assume, for the sake of argument, that it costs him £10,000 to undertake the trial. The procedure may be illustrated by reference to Figure II. The initial choice is whether to experiment or not. If we do not experiment, the best we can get is an expected monetary value of zero. Now suppose we experiment. What is the expected value of the experiment? To find this we must consider two alternative routes, according to whether the experiment produces $X_1 (\geq 8\%)$ or $X_2 (< 8\%)$ and finally the implications of the cut/no-cut decisions. The gross expected value of the experiment will equal the pay-offs from the best courses of action along the two alternative branches X_1 and X_2, weighted by the probabilities of obtaining X_1 and X_2.

The best course of action if X_1 is the result, is clearly to cut prices. In this case the expected value of the price cut will be

$$(25) \quad E = (0 \cdot 8 \times \pounds200{,}000) - (0 \cdot 2 \times \pounds220{,}000) = \pounds116{,}000$$

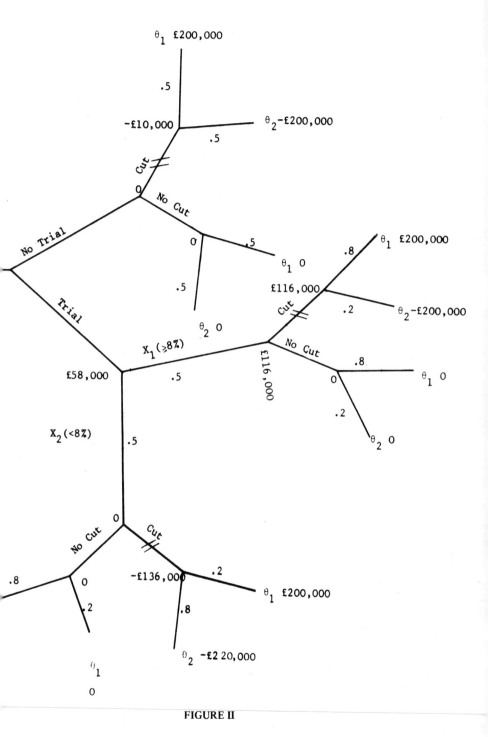

FIGURE II

the prior probabilities now being amended as the result of X_1 turning up in the trial. For the best course of action following a result X_2, the pay-off is zero. Thus the gross expected value of the trial is

$$(26) \quad E = (0 \cdot 5 \times \text{£}116{,}000) - (0 \cdot 5 \times 0) = \text{£}58{,}000$$

Since this clearly exceeds the cost of the trial (£10,000), the net expected value is positive. Thus the option of carrying it out is clearly better on this criterion than the no-trial best value which is zero.

This approach to decision making is, of course, essentially complementary in general terms to model building exercises. The construction of statistical market models helps to provide the inputs into statistical decision making processes of the Bayesian kind. There are obviously other than Bayesian criteria that may be applied to the inputs but the general development of decision theory encompasses them all.

Final Comments

The purpose of this paper has been to offer a limited survey of economic and statistical model building in the marketing field. It has been intended to offer only the flavour of these kinds of activity rather than any detailed and definitive treatment. Such a treatment would fill a volume.

Economic and statistical model building for marketing decisions is an activity designed to provide information where possible that will combine with the judgment of marketing executives. Models are no substitute for the final judgments that have to be made in making price, promotional and product decisions. As models they provide systematic approaches to reducing available information into patterns that suggest particular decisions and particular strategies. They do not provide formulas to substitute for individual judgment but information that will modify judgment. In many cases the techniques are still new in their applications, and it takes time and a great deal of empirical work before we can validate their usefulness. Work of the kind described in this paper is simply part of the ongoing process of research that is designed to narrow the region of ignorance in which the marketing executive operates.

REFERENCES

1. Agarwala and Ball, "An Econometric Analysis of the Effects of Generic Advertising in the Tea Market", *London Business School Discussion Paper,* 1969.

2. Arrow and Nerlove, "Optimal Advertising Policy under Dynamic Conditions", *Stanford University Discussion Paper,* 1961.

3. Chatfield, Ehrenberg and Goodhardt, "Progress on a simplified model of stationary purchasing behaviour", *Journal of the Royal Statistical Society,* Series A, 1966.

4. Chernoff and Moses, *Elementary Decision Theory,* Wiley 1959.

5. Cowling and Rayner, "Price, Quality and Market Share", *Warwick Economic Research Papers,* Number 7.

6. Ehrenberg, "Models of Fact : Examples from Marketing", in *Mathematical Model Building in Economics and Industry,* Griffin 1968.

7. Green, "Bayesian Decision Theory in Pricing Strategy", *Journal of Marketing*, January 1963.

8. Green, "Bayesian Decision Theory in Advertising", *Journal of Advertising Research*, December 1962.

9. Kuehn and Day, "Probabilistic Models of Consumer Buying Behaviour" *Journal of Marketing*, October 1964.

10. Kuehn, "A Model for Budgetary Advertising", in *Mathematical Models and Methods in Marketing*, Irwin 1961.

11. Schlaifer, *Introduction to Statistics for Business Decisions*, McGraw Hill 1959.

12. Telser, "The Demand for Branded Goods as Estimated from Consumer Panel Data", *Review of Economics and Statistics*, August 1962.

13. Vidale and Wolfe, "An Operations Research Study of Sales Response to Advertising", *Operations Research*, June 1967.